T. W. (Thomas Wallace) Wright

Text-Book of Mechanics

With numerous Examples

T. W. (Thomas Wallace) Wright

Text-Book of Mechanics

With numerous Examples

ISBN/EAN: 9783337119737

Printed in Europe, USA, Canada, Australia, Japan

Cover: Foto ©ninafisch / pixelio.de

More available books at **www.hansebooks.com**

OF

MECHANICS.

WITH NUMEROUS EXAMPLES.

BY

THOMAS WALLACE WRIGHT,
PROFESSOR IN UNION COLLEGE.

The concrete in which lies always the perennial.—CARLYLE.

NEW YORK:
D. VAN NOSTRAND COMPANY,
23 MURRAY AND 27 WARREN STREETS.
1890.

CONTENTS.

	PAGE
INTRODUCTION,	7
CHAP. I. MOTION,	9
II. FORCE AND MOTION,	30
III. DYNAMICS OF A PARTICLE,	44
IV. STATICS OF A RIGID BODY,	86
V. FRICTION,	129
VI. WORK AND ENERGY,	148
VII. KINETICS OF A RIGID BODY,	174
VIII. ELASTIC SOLIDS,	201
IX. STATICS OF FLUIDS,	212
X. KINETICS OF FLUIDS,	243

PREFACE.

The science of mechanics, as all other departments of physical science, has made great advances in recent years. In this book I have endeavored to unfold the principles of modern mechanics systematically, and also to call the attention of the student to the more useful applications of the subject. It has long seemed to me that the more practical parts might with advantage be presented to the beginner at least as fully as the more abstract, and that, too, without any sacrifice of scientific precision. The book is so arranged that the student, whether intending to make a specialty of engineering, physics, or astronomy, can branch out in his special direction without difficulty.

It has been the aim to make the examples as practical as possible. Thus while writing the Strong locomotive (No. 444) was brought out by the L. V. R. R. Co., and the Westinghouse air-brake tests (1887) were being made. Many problems founded on these and other mechanisms have been introduced.

It has been the aim also to make the examples typical. Instead of making them mere numerical illustrations of formulas, the idea has been to encourage independent thought. In many cases different methods of solution have been indicated to encourage the student to trust rather to an independent investigation than to an answer so called.

Considerable attention has been paid to the graphical method of solution, guarding, however, against making it a "complicated weapon with which one can attack all sorts of problems which are more easily solved in other ways."

In several applications of the subject approximate formulas are of the utmost importance, and many such formulas are here developed. In all cases the rigorous formula has been given first, and the approximate deduced from it. In this way the degree of approximation can be estimated.

As regards the nomenclature of mechanics, I have endeavored to be modern and at the same time conservative. One or two terms have been introduced, the better to illustrate the second law of motion and the appropriateness of the expression moment of inertia. The words *weight* and *pound* have been used in the double sense employed in ordinary life. No confusion need arise from this, as the context is always sufficient to show the sense intended. (See p. 40.)

Other departures from the traditional treatment will be noticed. Thus the usual chapter on the Mechanical Powers has been omitted, though the "Powers" themselves have been discussed in their proper places. All dynamical equations have been expressed in terms of the absolute units. By doing this it has been possible to ignore the expression $w = mg$, the source of so much confusion in dynamics.

The Calculus has been used in all cases where its use is attended with marked advantage. In the earlier chapters two parallel courses are given, one with and one without Calculus. This I think an advantage in that it shows the student the *oneness* of what are called elementary and analytical mechanics. If thought advisable, a course may easily be selected into which no Calculus enters.

A few historical notes have been interspersed as tending to add a living interest. The use of the symbol $/$ as the sign of division has added to the compact form of the book by preventing spacing about formulas.

I have to thank several friends for assistance rendered, particularly Prof. Klein of Lehigh, Pres. Staley of Case, and Prof. Ziwet of Michigan.

T. W. W.

Schenectady, N. Y., June, 1890.

MECHANICS.

INTRODUCTION.

1. If a body occupies a certain position at one time and another position at another time we say that the change of position must be due to the operation of some cause which we call *force*. If the form of the body has undergone a change, we say that the change of form is due to the action of force. The fundamental idea of force is derived from the use of our muscles, and to muscular effort or to any cause producing a like effect we give the name force. Muscular effort is exerted as a push or a pull or some combination of them. We will therefore for the present consider force in the sense of a *push* or a *pull* no matter by what exerted. The science which treats of the different effects of force on bodies is called **Mechanics.***

2. Bodies exist in various states which may roughly be classed under two general divisions, the solid and the fluid. Experiment shows that the result of the action of a force on a solid is very different from the result of the action on a liquid. Hence it will tend to clearness and simplicity if

---

* "Strictly speaking, the derivation of this word should have prevented the use of it as the designation of a pure science. It has been, however, employed for a long time in English speech in the identical sense that the French attach to *Mécanique pure* or the Germans to *reine Mechanik*. These terms are employed to denote what we should prefer to call *abstract dynamics*—the pure science which treats of the action of force upon matter, which is correctly the **science of matter and motion.**" (Tait.)

7

we study the Mechanics of Solids and the Mechanics of Fluids separately.

Experiment shows, too, that the effects of force are very different on different solids and on different fluids. Compare, for example, iron and putty, molasses and water. Hence still more minute subdivisions are necessary for purposes of study.

3. On account of the infinite variety of solids and fluids it becomes necessary as a first step to seize on some phase of the problem applicable to all, and then to discuss the special cases in detail. Now every substance in nature may be conceived to be composed of an indefinitely great number of minute portions or particles so small that any external force acting on such a particle will act equally on all its parts. By considering the action of forces on a single particle we may develop principles applicable to bodies in all forms considered as composed of particles.

Still further. Conceive a particle acted on by forces. It will in general move in a path of some kind, either straight or curved. The particle is so small that the path may be regarded as a geometrical line. If we leave the forces acting out of view and consider only the *positions* of the particle in this path at different times, the relations between these different positions will be in the nature of a geometrical problem. Hence, as every particle is endowed with at least some of the properties of the body which it goes to make up, we may conceive these properties abstracted from it, thus converting it as it were into a geometrical point, and consider the motion of this point only as it traces out its path during an assigned time and thus be able to study motion in its simplest form. To this idea of motion in which neither the nature of the particle moved nor of the force acting is considered the name **Kinematics** (= science of motion) is given. Kinematics is therefore motion in the abstract, and its principles are developed by an extension of the principles of geometry by the introduction of the idea of time.

4. From this bird's-eye view of the subject it is seen that the course to be followed is in general outline something of this kind: First geometrical motion, next the action of force on a single particle and on a system of two or more particles either independent or forming a body, and last the modifications in body motion resulting from the peculiar constitution of the various states of matter solid or fluid.

CHAPTER I.

MOTION.

5. THE elements of a motion which characterize it are change of position (*displacement*) with change of time. We know the position of a body only by noting its relations to other bodies in its neighborhood. Thus the position of a point P situated in the plane of the paper is defined with reference to a point O chosen as the point of reference, either by measuring the distance OP and the angle XOP made by OP with a known line OX (polar coördinates) or by measuring the distances PM, MO drawn parallel to two known lines OY, OX in the plane (Cartesian coördinates). Any displacement in the plane of the paper* would be measured by the changes in these coördinates.

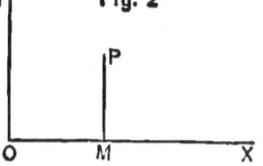

The motions of different points may therefore be compared by comparing the changes in their coördinates that

---

* If the displacement does not take place in one plane the point is similarly referred to three coördinate axes in space, but we shall not at present enter into a discussion of this.

take place in the same time. To render this possible, it is necessary to fix on units of angle, time, and distance.

The unit of angle is the **Degree**, or the ninetieth part of a right angle. The unit of time is the **Second**. The unit of distance is the **Foot** or **Meter**, according as we follow the British or the metric system. We shall give both systems, as it can be done without confusion, and both are in use in the application of mechanical principles. Thus the civil engineer uses the British system of the foot and its subdivisions, the physicist the metric system, and the electrical engineer both systems.

For convenience of statement distances measured in one direction along a line are considered positive, and distances measured in the opposite direction negative. The directions are arbitrary, but it is usual to take distances to the right $+$, to the left $-$; distance upwards $+$, downwards $-$.

6. The successive positions occupied by the point in its motion trace its **Path**. This path may be either a straight line or a curve of some kind. As most simple, we shall first of all consider motion in a straight line (rectilinear motion).

MOTION IN A STRAIGHT LINE.

Motion in a straight path may be uniform, or it may vary from time to time. Thus an engine on a straight track may run for a time with the same speed, or it may vary its speed.

7. Velocity.—The rate at which a moving point changes its position is called its velocity. If the rate of change is constant, that is, if equal distances are passed over in equal times, the velocity is said to be uniform or constant. Thus if the point moves uniformly over a distance s in a time t its velocity v is s/t. This may be abbreviated into

$$v = s/t.$$

If we place $s = 1$, $t = 1$, we find $v = 1$; or, the *unit of velocity* is the distance described in unit time. The measure of a velocity is therefore expressed as so many feet (meters) per second.

Clearing of fractions, we may write

$$s = vt,$$

or the number of units of distance is equal to the product of the number of units of velocity by the number of units of time.

As the point may move in the direction of positive distance or in the opposite direction, it is necessary to regard the sign of the velocity. It is agreed that the same rule of signs shall apply to velocity as to distance. The velocity is $+$ if the direction of motion is in the $+$ direction, and $-$ if in the opposite direction.

The term *speed* is sometimes used to denote the magnitude only of a velocity.

Ex. 1. A point moves uniformly with a velocity of 2 meters per second. In what time will it pass over a kilometer? *Ans.* 8 min. 20 sec.

2. A passenger sitting in a railroad car counts 44 telegraph poles (distant 100 ft.) passed in one minute: show that the train is running at 50 miles an hour.

3. A man a ft. in height walks along a level street at the rate of c miles an hour in a straight line from an electric light b ft. in height: find the velocity of the end of his shadow. *Ans.* $bc/(b-a)$ miles per hour.

4. The "limited" trains on the N. Y. C. & H. R. R. R. running on parallel tracks pass at a certain place in $6\frac{1}{4}$ seconds. If each train has the same velocity, and consists of 8 Pullman coaches of 52 ft. 9 in. length, find the rate per hour. *Ans.* 46 miles per hour.

5. Show that the velocity of a point on the equator arising from the earth's rotation on its axis is about 463 meters per second.

8. Curve of Velocity.—A velocity, being distance per second, may be appropriately represented by a straight line whose length will show the magnitude of the velocity on any assigned scale, and whose direction as indicated by an arrow will show the direction of the motion. We may hence give a geometrical representation of constant velocity. Along a straight line OX (Fig. 3) lay off equal distances OA, AB, . . . to any convenient scale (as 10 sec. = 1 in.) for as many seconds as the motion has continued. Let the velocities at the points O, A, B, . . . be represented by OY, Aa, . . . to any scale (as 10 ft. = 1 in.). Now since the velocity is constant, the lines OY, Aa, . . . are equal to one another, and the *curve of velocity* Yd is a straight line parallel to OX, the time line. Also

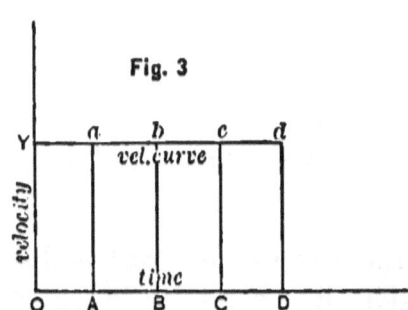

Fig. 3

$$\text{Dist. passed over} = OY \times OD$$
$$= \text{area } YD;$$

that is, the number of feet (meters) in the distance described would be represented by the number of square feet (square meters) in the area of the rectangle YD.

Ex. Plot a velocity of 60 miles an hour on a scale of 11 inches = 1 ft. per second, and also the distance passed over in one minute.

[For plotting it is convenient to use cross-section paper.]

9. If a point in motion does not move over equal distances in equal intervals of time, the motion is said to be *variable*. Variable motion is thus not uniform in every part of its path. The velocities Oy, Aa, Bb, . . . at the times 0, OA, OB, . . . if plotted and their extremities y, a, b . . . joined would form a line yab . . . not parallel to the time line OX, as in the case of uniform motion (Fig. 4). This line would be the velocity curve. The points $A, B, \ldots$ may be conceived to be taken so close together that the velocities between may be considered uniform and the figures $Oa, Ab \ldots$ formed to be rectangles. 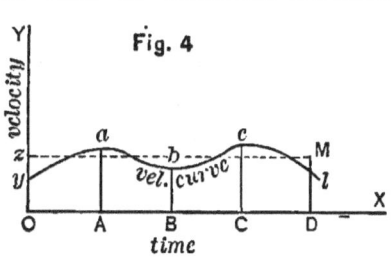 Each rectangle represents a distance passed over, and therefore the total distance would be represented by the sum of these rectangles, that is, by the area Ol.

Conceive now a point to start from O, and moving with uniform velocity Oz, to describe the same distance s in the time t as the point moving with the variable velocity. The distance would be represented by the rectangle OM. But with the variable velocities it is represented by the figure Ol. Hence the rectangle OM is equal to the figure Ol, which can happen only when Oz is the *average* (mean) of the values $Oy, Aa, Bb, \ldots$ Hence, if we can find the average velocity v, or the velocity of a point which, moving uniformly, passes over the same distance in the same time t as the point moving with variable velocity, we can find the distance s described, from the equation

$$s = vt.$$

10. A velocity curve may also be constructed by laying off $OA, OB, \ldots$ along the line OX to represent the *distances* passed over, and $Aa, Bb, \ldots$ at right angles to OX to represent the corresponding velocities. The line through the points $a, b, \ldots$ would represent the curve of velocities.

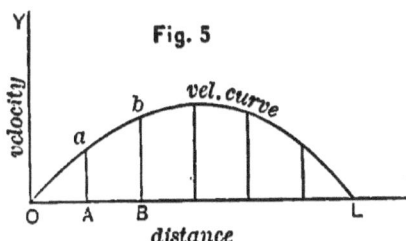

A familiar illustration is afforded by the motion of the

piston of a steam-engine. At the beginning and end of its stroke the velocity is zero, at the middle of the stroke the velocity is greatest, and it varies from this value to the end values. The curve of velocity, if plotted, is found to be of a form such as *Oabc* ... *L* in Fig. 5.

11. In uniform motion the velocity v at any instant is equal to s/t. In variable motion the corresponding relation would be ds/dt, since the velocity v may be assumed to be uniform for an indefinitely small distance ds, and during an indefinitely small time dt. Hence

$$ds = vdt.$$

The total distance passed over in the time t is found by summing the distances ds, that is, by the integration ($=$ *summation*) of the expression vdt; or

$$s = \int_0^t vdt,$$

which includes all possible cases.

If, for example, the velocity v is constant, then

$$s = vt + c$$

when c is the constant of integration. If we suppose that the point starts from rest (or $s = 0$ when $t = 0$) we have

$$s = vt,$$

as found above.

Ex. 1. A velocity of 60 miles an hour is 88 ft. per sec.

2. A bicycle rider makes m miles in h hours: find his average velocity. *Ans.* $22m/15h$ ft. per sec.

3. A train runs 29 miles for 2 hours, 30 miles for 3 hours, and 32 miles for 1 hour: find its average velocity.

Ans. 30 m. an hour.

4. The velocity of a particle in a rectilinear path varies

as its distance from the starting-point ($= cs$): find its position at the end of a time t. *Ans.* $s = e^{ct}$, where e is the base of the natural system of logarithms.

12. Acceleration.—In variable motion the rate of change of velocity is called the acceleration. If the velocity changes uniformly with the time, the motion is said to be uniformly accelerated. The measure of an acceleration is the change of velocity in unit time. Thus, if a point moves with a velocity of 1 ft. per sec., 3 ft. per sec., 5 ft. per sec., etc., in consecutive seconds, the acceleration is 2 ft. per sec. in every second of the motion. Hence acceleration is distance-per-second per second, the unit being 1 foot (or 1 meter) per-second per second.

This method of expressing acceleration, though strictly correct, is cumbersome. If it is understood that both velocity and rate of change of velocity are referred to the same unit of time, it will be sufficient if we express acceleration as distance per second. This is the more ordinary method, and with the above understanding can cause no confusion.*

If the velocities of the point had been 5 ft. per sec., 3 ft. per sec., . . . the change of velocity is numerically the same as before, but in the *opposite sense* to that of the original velocity. The nature of an acceleration may therefore be indicated by the signs + and −, as the change of velocity is in the same sense or in the opposite sense to that of the original velocity. Hence an acceleration is + if the velocity increases algebraically, and − if it decreases algebraically. To a negative acceleration the name *retardation* is sometimes given.

13. Just as rate of change of position or velocity is uniform or variable, so may rate of change of velocity or accel-

---

* A single word for unit-acceleration is needed, and one also for unit-velocity.

eration be uniform or variable. In uniformly accelerated motion, the rate of change of velocity being constant, if u denotes the initial velocity, and v the final velocity, the change in the whole interval of time t being $v - u$, the change per second or the acceleration a is $(v - u)/t$, and therefore

$$v = u + at. \quad \ldots \ldots \quad (1)$$

Also, since the rate of change of velocity is constant from beginning to end, the average velocity occurs half-way; that is,

average vel. = initial vel. + ½ change of vel.

$$= u + \tfrac{1}{2}(v - u)$$

$$= \tfrac{1}{2}(u + v).$$

Hence the distance s passed over is found from

$$s = \tfrac{1}{2}(u + v) \times t$$

$$= ut + \tfrac{1}{2}at^2, \quad \text{from eq. (1).} \quad (2)$$

The two equations (1) and (2) contain relations between the quantities involved which are independent of one another. Other relations may be deduced from them which are convenient, but which contain no new principle. Thus, eliminating t, we find

$$v^2 = u^2 + 2as,$$

a useful formula.

If the point had started from rest, then $u = 0$, and the equations become

$$v = at, \qquad v^2 = 2as,$$
$$s = \tfrac{1}{2}at^2, \qquad s = \tfrac{1}{2}vt.$$

14. If the acceleration is variable, the relation corresponding to $a = (v - u)/t$ would be $a = dv/dt$, since the acceleration may be assumed to be uniform during an indefinitely small change of velocity dv in the indefinitely small time dt. Putting $v = ds/dt$, we have

$$a = d^2s/dt^2.$$

The formulas found above follow at once from this equation. Thus, let a particle start from a point O with a velocity u: it is required to find its velocity v and distance s from O at the end of a time t, the acceleration being constant. Here

$$d^2s/dt^2 = a.$$

Integrating,

$$ds/dt = at + c,$$

c being the constant of integration. But when $t = 0$, ds/dt or $v = u$; hence

$$v = ds/dt = at + u,$$

which gives the velocity at the end of the time t.

Integrating a second time,

$$s = \tfrac{1}{2}at^2 + ut,$$

since when $t = 0$, $s = 0$, and therefore the constant of integration is 0.

15. *Curve of Acceleration.*—We have seen how to construct the curve of velocity of a point in motion, either by taking the times as abscissas or the distances as abscissas. Both are convenient at times. We proceed now to show

how to construct the curve of acceleration when the curve of velocity has been plotted.

First take the case of a motion in which the times are plotted as abscissas. Let the velocity change uniformly from u to v in the time t. The rate of change of velocity being constant, the velocity curve ab . . . of Fig. 4 becomes a straight line, as in Fig. 6. The acceleration $a = (v-u)/t$ is represented in the figure by $\tan \theta$, that is, by the tangent of inclination of the line ab . . . to OX. Hence if the distances OA, AB, . . . represent one second, the accelerations measured on the velocity scale would be represented from second to second by aa_1, bb_1, . . . all of which are equal to one another. If, therefore, a line be drawn parallel to OX, and at a distance a from it measured on the velocity scale, it will represent the curve of acceleration.

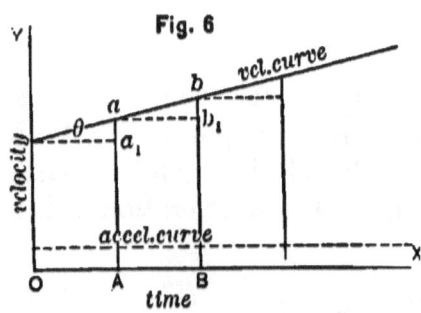
Fig. 6

If the rate of velocity is not constant, so that the curve of velocity is curvilinear, then since $a = dv/dt$, the acceleration at a point P (whose co-ordinates are v, t) is represented by $\tan \theta$ when θ is the inclination of the tangent at P to OX. Hence, to plot the acceleration curve, draw tangents to the velocity curve from second to second, and lay off as the ordinates the rise or fall of the tangent measured on the velocity scale. The curve may thus be plotted from point to point.

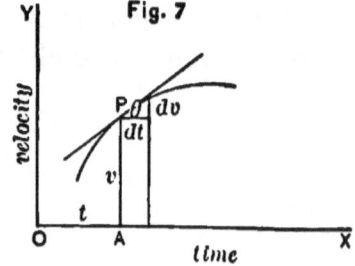
Fig. 7

Next consider the case in which the distances are plotted as abscissas: for example, the curve of acceleration of the piston of a steam-engine. From any point P in the velocity curve (Art. 10), let fall PM perpendicular to OX, and draw PQ at right angles to the tangent at P. Then

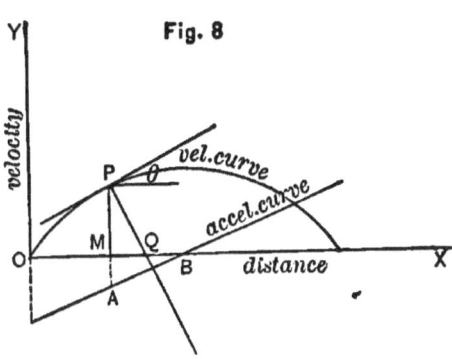

Fig. 8

$$a = dv/dt = \frac{dv}{ds} \times \frac{ds}{dt} = \tan \theta \times PM = MQ.$$

Prolong PM to A, so that $MA = MQ$, and A is a point on the required curve. Similarly other points may be found. Hence the curve of acceleration is the line AB.

Comparing the curves of velocity and acceleration in this case, we see that when the velocity is zero the acceleration is a maximum. As the velocity increases the acceleration decreases; when the velocity is greatest the acceleration is zero, and at that point it changes sign.

Ex. 1. If the acceleration is constant, prove that the velocity curve is a parabola.

2. If the acceleration increases uniformly, prove that the velocity curve is a straight line.

16. The relations found for the motion of a particle hold also for the motion of a body, provided its motion is a motion of *translation;* that is, if all the particles of the body describe paths that are precisely alike. We therefore determine the translation of a body by determining the translation of a single particle of the body. The kinematics of body translation is therefore the kinematics of a point.

Ex. 1. In 5 seconds the velocity of a point changes from 200 ft. to 100 ft. per sec. Find the acceleration.

Ans. $a = -20$.

2. The velocity of a point changes from 20 ft. to 10 ft. per second in passing over 75 ft. Find the acceleration and time of motion. *Ans.* $a = -2$, $t = 5$ sec. Draw a figure illustrating the motion.

3. A point starts from rest. Show that the accel. if const. is equal to twice the distance described in the first second.

4. A point describes 160 ft. in the first two seconds of its motion, and 50 ft. in the next second. When will it come to rest? When has it a velocity of 20 ft. per second? When of -20 ft. per second? *Ans.* 5 sec.; 4 sec.; 6 sec.

5. A point starts with a velocity u and under a constant acceleration $-a$. Show that it will come to rest in u/a sec., after describing a distance $u^2/2a$.

6. In the Westinghouse air-brake trials (1887) on the P. R. R., a train of 50 freight cars running at 36 miles an hour was stopped in 593.5 ft. Find the acceleration of the brake. *Ans.* $a = -2.3$ ft. per sec.

7. A point starts from a position A with a velocity u; to find its velocity and its distance from A at the end of a time t, the acceleration being proportional to the time ($= ct$) and in the direction of the velocity u.

Ans. $v = u + \tfrac{1}{2}ct^2$, $s = ut + \tfrac{1}{6}ct^3$.

17. Composition of Motions.—Thus far we have considered the case of a point which has received a displacement in a single direction. But a point may receive several displacements at the same time either in the same direction or in different directions.

As only one single path results, these displacements must combine into a single displacement to which the path is due. To this single displacement the name of **Resultant Displacement** is given, and to the separate displacements the name of **Components**.

Thus, conceive a point P in motion along a straight line AB (as a ring sliding along a wire), and that at the same time the line is also moved. If the displacement of the line is in the same direction as that of the point, the point

Fig. 9

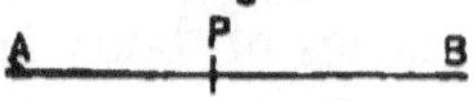

COMPOSITION OF VELOCITIES.

receives two simultaneous displacements or a single total displacement equal to their sum, if in the opposite direction to their difference.

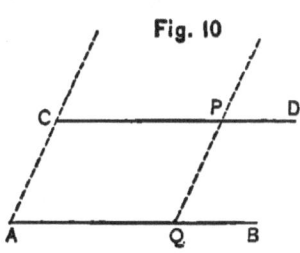

Fig. 10

If the line is moved in the direction AC while the point is moved along AB, the point has two simultaneous motions—one along AB and one along AC. The law of the displacements being known, the position of the point may be found at the end of any assigned time. For the motion along AB alone would carry it a distance AQ in this time. But the motion along AC has carried the line AB to the parallel position CD, and P will therefore be the position of the point at the end of the motion. Hence the final position P is the opposite angular point to the initial position A of the parallelogram CQ, constructed on the lines AQ, AC, representing the distances due to the single motions. This proposition is called the **Parallelogram of Displacements**.

18. Now velocities and accelerations being quantities having direction and magnitude, and capable of being represented by finite straight lines, may be treated in a manner analogous to displacements. This we proceed to do.

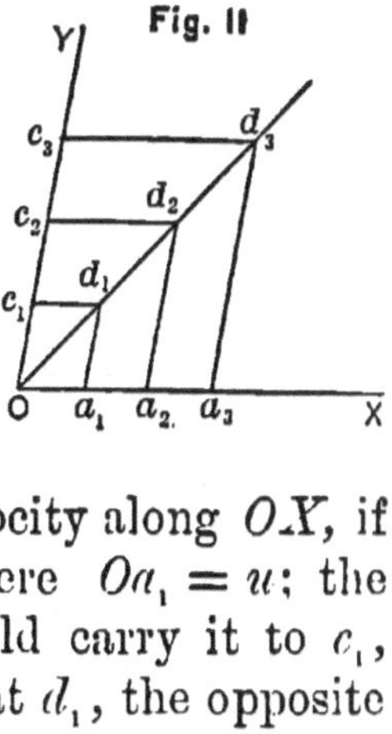

(*a*) *Composition of Constant Velocities.*—Suppose a point O has two simultaneous constant velocities u, v in the directions OX, OY not in the same line.

Fig. 11

At the end of the first second the velocity along OX, if acting alone, would carry it to a_1, where $Oa_1 = u$; the velocity along OY, if acting alone, would carry it to c_1, where $Oc_1 = v$; when both act, it arrives at d_1, the opposite angle of the parallelogram Od_1 to O. Similarly, at the end of the second second it arrives at d_2, where $Oa_2 = 2u$, $Oc_2 = 2v$; and so on. The path is thus *some* line passing through O, d_1, d_2, ... To find its form we notice that

$$c_2 d_2 = 2c_1 d_1, \quad Oc_2 = 2 Oc_1,$$
$$\therefore Oc_1 : c_1 d_1 = Oc_2 : c_2 d_2;$$

and hence $Od_1 d_2$ ... must be a straight line.

Hence the path of the point is along the diagonal Od_2; and since the distance Od_1 passed over in the first second is equal to the distances $d_1 d_2$, ... passed over in the second ... seconds, the resultant velocity is constant, and is represented by the line $Od_1 d_2$ .... This proposition is called the **Parallelogram of Velocities**.

(*b*) *Composition of Constant Accelerations.* The same method of reasoning as in (*a*) may be applied to the combination of two constant accelerations. The statement is this: *If a point experiences simultaneously two constant accelerations, represented in magnitude and direction by two straight lines AB, AC, the resultant motion has a constant acceleration, which is represented in magnitude and direction by the concurrent diagonal AD of the parallelogram AD.* This is the **Parallelogram of Accelerations**.

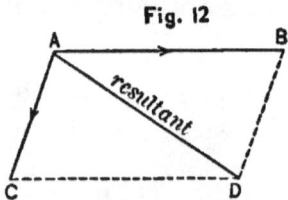
Fig. 12

Ex. 1. The velocity along AB is 9 ft. per sec. and along AC 12 ft. per sec. If the angle $BAC = 90°$, find the resultant velocity.

[*Solution.*—Draw AB, AC at right angles. Plot on a scale of 12 ft. = 1 in. Then $AB = \frac{3}{4}$ in., $AC = 1$ in. Complete the parallelogram $ABCD$. Scale off AD. It measures $1\frac{1}{4}$ in. Hence resultant velocity $= 1\frac{1}{4} \times 12 = 15$ ft. per sec.]

2. If the angle $BAC = 60°$, find the resultant.

RESOLUTION OF MOTIONS.

3. A ball moving with a velocity of 15 ft. per sec. is struck so as to move off at right angles with a velocity of 20 ft. per sec.: find the velocity given to it.

Ans. 25 ft. per sec.

19. The above examples having been solved from drawings made, that is, graphically, solve them a second time by computation.

Ex. 1. This is the same as finding the hypotenuse of a right-angled triangle of which the sides are given. Hence,

$$AD = \sqrt{AB^2 + AC^2} = \sqrt{9^2 + 12^2} = 15, \text{ as before.}$$

2. This is the same as finding the third side of a triangle of which the other two sides and the contained angle are given. Hence

$$AD = \sqrt{AB^2 + AC^2 + 2AB \times AC \cos 60°}.$$

20. Resolution of Motions. Conversely, a velocity or an acceleration represented by AD may be broken up or *resolved* into two components AB, AC, being the adjacent sides of the parallelogram constructed on AD as diagonal. This may be done in an indefinitely great number of ways, as an indefinitely great number of parallelograms may be constructed on the same diagonal. Other conditions must be added to render the problem determinate.

Fig. 13

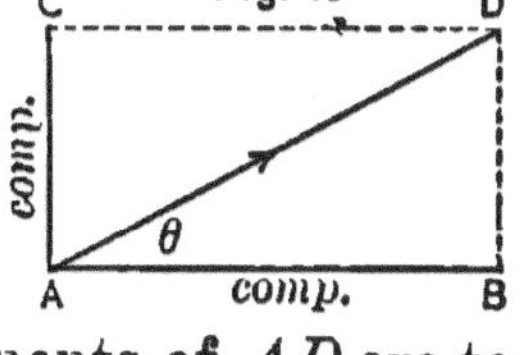

Suppose, for example, that the components of AD are to be at right angles and the angle BAD ($= \theta$) is given. Then CAD is known, and the components AB, AC can be plotted. They are thus determined *graphically*.

Since $BD = AC$, it is evident that the magnitudes of the components of AD could be represented by the two sides AB, BD of the triangle ABD. Their values may be found by solving the triangle ABD *trigonometrically*.

24   MOTION.

Ex. 1. A ship is sailing N. 30° E. at 8 miles an hour: find its easterly velocity and its northerly velocity.

Ans. 4 m., 4 $\sqrt{3}$ m. per hour.

2. Find the vertical velocity of a train when moving up a 1% gradient at 30 m. an hour.   Ans. 0.3 m. an hour.

3. Solve (1) and (2) by computing the values required.

4. Show that the components of a velocity v in two directions, making angles of 30°, 60° with it, are $v/2$, $v\sqrt{3}/2$.

21. If a particle is at the point x, y at a time t, and if ds/dt, dx/dt, dy/dt are the velocity of the particle and its components parallel to the axes of X, Y respectively, and θ the angle which the direction of motion makes with the axes of x, then

$$\frac{dx}{dt} = \frac{ds}{dt}\cos\theta, \qquad \frac{dy}{dt} = \frac{ds}{dt}\sin\theta,$$

$$\left(\frac{ds}{dt}\right)^2 = \left(\frac{dx}{dt}\right)^2 + \left(\frac{dy}{dt}\right)^2.$$

Similarly, if d^2s/dt^2 is the acceleration of the particle in its path and the corresponding accelerations parallel to the axes are d^2x/dt^2, d^2y/dt^2, then if θ is the angle which the direction of motion makes with the axes of x,

$$\frac{d^2x}{dt^2} = \frac{d^2s}{dt^2}\cos\theta, \qquad \frac{d^2y}{dt^2} = \frac{d^2s}{dt^2}\sin\theta,$$

$$\left(\frac{d^2s}{dt^2}\right)^2 = \left(\frac{d^2x}{dt^2}\right)^2 + \left(\frac{d^2y}{dt^2}\right)^2.$$

MOTION IN A CURVE.

22. A point P in motion instead of proceeding in the same direction may be continually changing the direction

MOTION IN A CURVE.

of its motion so that the path is a curve. The direction of motion of P at any point A of a curvilinear path ABC being the line joining that point to the consecutive point in the path, will be in the direction of the tangent AA_1 to the curve at A. Similarly, at B the direction of motion is along the tangent BB_1, so that in moving from A to B the direction of motion has changed from AA_1 to BB_1, or through the angle A_1CB_1.

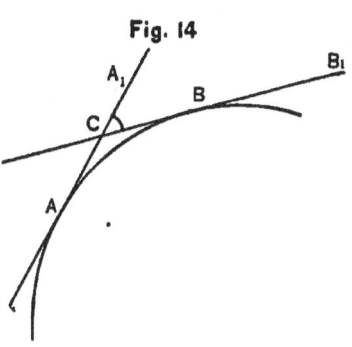

Fig. 14

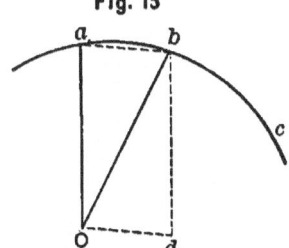

Fig. 15

From any point O draw a line Oa to represent the velocity at A in magnitude and direction, and suppose a to move so that the line joining it to O will represent in magnitude and direction the successive velocities of P as it moves in its path. Then a will trace out a continuous curve.

Consider two positions A and B of P in its path at which the velocities are Oa, Ob. The velocity Oa combined with the *change* of velocity between A and B must give the velocity Ob at B. But by completing the parallelogram $Oabd$ we see that Oa, Od combined will give Ob. Hence the change of velocity is represented by Od or by its equal ab in the triangle Oab. Now if A and B are indefinitely near each other, Oa and Ob represent the values of the velocity of P at A and at the next point in the path. Hence ab represents the instantaneous change of velocity or the acceleration in the path at A. Hence the velocity in the curve ab . . . represents the acceleration in the original path AB . . . Also the direction of ab is the tangent at a. Hence at any point in abc the tangent is parallel to the direction of the acceleration at the corresponding point of the path ABC. To the curve abc the name of **Hodograph*** is given.

23. For example, suppose a point to move with a uniform velocity v in a circular path of radius r. Draw $Oa, Ob, Oc,$

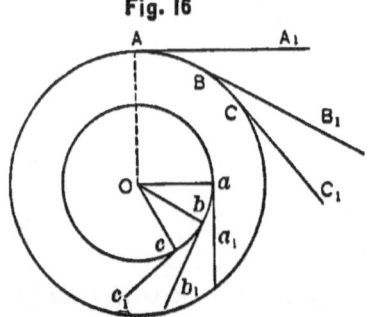

Fig. 16

... to represent the velocities at $A, B, C, \ldots$ in magnitude and direction. Each of these velocities being equal to v, the points $a, b, c \ldots$ will lie on a circle of centre O. Also the velocity in the circle ABC, ... being uniform, the arcs $AB, BC, \ldots$ described in equal times are equal, and therefore the angles $AOB, BOC,$ ... are equal. Hence the angles $aOb, bOc, \ldots$ are equal, and the arcs $ab, bc, \ldots$ described in equal times are equal, or the hodograph is described with uniform velocity.

Hence the hodograph of a point moving with uniform velocity in a circle is a circle described with uniform velocity.

Ex. 1. A point moves with uniform velocity in a straight line: find the hodograph. *Ans.* A point.

2. A point moves with uniformly accelerated motion in a straight line: find the hodograph. *Ans.* A straight line.

3. Show that the direction of motion of any point B on the rim of a wheel running with velocity v on a straight track is perpendicular to AB when A is the point of the wheel in contact with the track at the instant considered.

[For B has two velocities each $= v$, one along the tangent BE and the other along

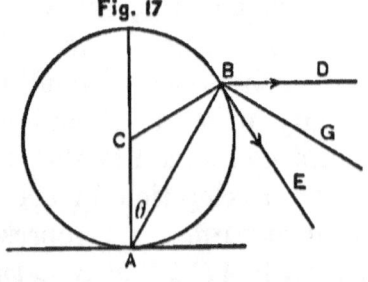

Fig. 17

---

* By Sir W. R. Hamilton (1805–1865).

BD parallel to the path of C. The resultant BG bisects the angle EBD. $\therefore ABG = 90°$. The resultant velocity $= 2v \cos \theta/2$.]

The solution also follows at once from Art. 145.

RELATIVE MOTION.

24. The motion of a point P has been defined by its change of position with reference to another point O regarded as fixed. This gave the *absolute* motion of P. But if the point O is also in motion, or has an absolute motion with respect to a third point, the motion of P is no longer said to be absolute, but *relative*. This is really the case of bodies in nature, as no point in space is known to be fixed absolutely. Still, for the purpose considered, an assumed point may be regarded as fixed, and in this sense motion is said to be absolute.

The problem of relative motion is really an example of the composition of motions. Suppose, for example, a body A to move with an absolute velocity u, and B with an absolute velocity v, both being referred to the same fixed point O, and in the same straight line; it is required to find the relative velocity of A and B. Conceive both A and B to move in a medium which itself moves with a velocity v, but in the opposite direction to the motion of B. Then B is at rest with reference to the fixed point O. But as the motion of the medium affects A and B alike, their relative motion is unchanged. Hence as a velocity v has been imparted to A, the velocity of A relative to B will be $u - v$ if both were originally moving in the same direction and $u + v$ if in opposite directions.

As an illustration, take two men A and B walking on a boat's deck from bow to stern, and that the velocity of the boat is equal to the velocity of B. Then B is at rest relative to the shore, and the motion of A relative to B is the same as if the boat were at rest.

Ex. 1. Interpret the motion when $u - v$ is $+$, when $-$.

2. If the motions are parallel instead of being in the same straight line, are the relative velocities the same as before?

3. Two trains at a depot are on parallel tracks. Why is it difficult for a passenger to tell whether his own or the other is in motion?

[It is not to be wondered at that it took mankind so long to discover that the earth moves round the sun.]

25. Consider next when the velocities u, v of the two points A, B are *not* in the same straight line. Suppose the lines OX, OY to represent these velocities in magnitude and direction. As before, conceive the motion to take place in a medium which itself moves with a velocity v, but in the opposite direction to B, and represented by OZ. The point B is now at rest. The velocity of A is the resultant of the velocities OZ, OX, that is, is equal to the diagonal OW, which therefore represents the velocity of A relative to B.

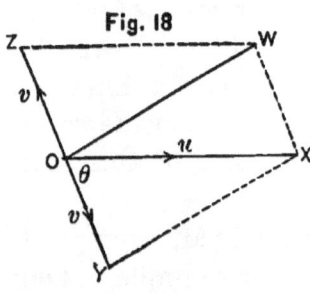

Fig. 18

The three velocities are represented by the sides of the triangle OXW, the directions being indicated by arrows. Hence, if in a triangle one side OX represent the velocity of A, XW a velocity equal to and opposite that of B, and OX, XW are in the same sense around the triangle, the third side OW taken in the opposite sense around the triangle will represent the velocity of A relative to B.

Conversely, if the absolute velocity of A and the relative velocity of A to B were given, we should have from the same triangle XW to represent the absolute velocity of B, but in the contrary sense.

Any mechanism may be employed to illustrate relative motion by putting a sheet of paper on one of its moving pieces, and a pencil on another moving piece, when the curve traced by the pencil on the paper will represent the relative motion of the two pieces.

Ex. 1. Two vessels start at the same time from the same harbor, one sailing east at 12 miles an hour, the other south at 9 miles an hour: find the velocity of one relative to the other. *Ans.* 15 m. an hour.

2. Two railroad tracks intersect at 60°, and two trains start at the same instant from the junction at 30 miles an hour each: find their relative velocity in magnitude and direction.

3. Two bodies A, B move with velocities u, v inclined at an angle θ: show that the velocity of B with respect to A is $\sqrt{u^2 + v^2 - 2uv \cos \theta}$, and inclined at an angle $\tan^{-1} v \sin \theta / (v \cos \theta - u)$ to the direction of A.

4. Two railroad tracks intersect at 90°. To a passenger in one train travelling at the rate of 32 miles an hour the other seems to have a velocity of 40 miles an hour: find its absolute velocity. *Ans.* 24 miles an hour.

5. A boat is propelled at 12 miles an hour across a stream flowing at 5 miles an hour, in a direction perpendicular to the current: find the velocity of the boat with reference to the bottom of the channel.
Ans. 13 miles an hour, up stream.

6. A man travelling eastward in a wind apparently from the north, doubles his speed when the wind appears to blow from the northeast. Show that the wind is really southeast, and blowing with a velocity of $4\sqrt{2}$ miles an hour.

CHAPTER II.

FORCE AND MOTION.

26. Common experience shows that to put a body in motion or to stop it if in motion requires a certain muscular effort (push or pull) or some equivalent. To this effort or its equivalent we give, as already stated, the name *force*.

Hitherto we have considered motion apart from the body moved and apart also from the force acting. This was an ideal case, and gave us the geometrical side of the question (**Kinematics**). In an actual case we must consider the motion with reference to the body moved and to the force acting as well. This gives us the physical side, and is known as **Dynamics**. In doing this and to lay the foundation for an extension of the kinematical treatment of motion to dynamical questions, we are compelled to call in the aid of experiment.

The science of dynamics rests upon three principles or laws, known as Newton's laws of motion.* Before stating them, certain rude experiments will be indicated which are sufficient to suggest the laws but not to establish their truth. No direct proof is possible. The proof is indirect, and is made in this way. Assume the laws true, and certain consequences follow which can be tested experimentally. This has been done in so many ways and by so many

---

* "... Though Newton's laws of motion are a much clearer and more general statement of the grounds of Mechanics than had appeared before his time, they do not involve any doctrines which had not been previously stated or taken for granted by other mathematicians."—*Whewell.*

independent observers, particularly in astronomical work, that we are justified in accepting them as true. So complete have been the tests and so firm is the conviction of the truth of the laws, that results deduced from them which cannot be verified in any way are accepted without hesitation.

27. Stress.—In order to exert force the agent acting must meet a resistance. Thus the hand in motion does not exert force until it meets some object. The object reacts on the hand. Press the table and the table will press the hand. Force is always a *mutual* action: in other words, forces are never single, but act in pairs—one the *action* and the other the *reaction*. This pair of actions is known as a **Stress**. If it is of the nature of a push, as in cracking a nut, the name *compression* (or pressure) is given to it; if of the nature of a pull, as in breaking a string, the name *tension* is given.

A stress can never occur except between two bodies or two parts of the same body, and is always exerted over the surfaces coming in contact. If we divide the total stress by the area of this surface we obtain the stress per unit area, as per sq. in., for instance. Thus we are accustomed to speak of the stress of steam in a boiler as pressure per sq. in. Or we may consider stress without reference to area, looking to the total magnitude only, and consider it acting at a point.

In some cases the relation between the action of the agent and the reaction of the resistance is sufficiently evident. Thus if one body rests upon another, it will be granted that the pressure exerted by the upper is equal to the counter-pressure exerted by the lower : if a horse hauls a canal-boat to which he is attached by a rope, the pull of the rope on the horse is equal to its pull on the boat, and so on. But when a stone falls from a height it is not evident whether the action of the earth on the stone is equal to the action of stone on the earth. Nor is the relation evident between the actions of a magnet and a piece of iron, nor between bodies widely separated, as the earth and moon.

The results of experiments direct and indirect on the mutual actions of bodies are summed up in what is known as the law of stress : *To every action there exists always a reaction equal in magnitude and opposite in direction ;* or as it may be expressed : *The mutual actions of two bodies are always equal, and act in opposite directions.*

28. Force being thus always double may be looked at from the point of view of the body acted on or of the body (as agent) exerting the action. The two components being equal and opposite, either will suffice for a numerical measure of the *magnitude* of the force.

Suppose a body at rest on a level floor. If let alone it will remain at rest. If a push is given to it (= force applied) so as to cause it to move along the floor, it will come to rest after going a short distance. If the floor is waxed, it will go a greater distance for the same push. The smoother the surface the farther it goes, and the more nearly in a straight line. If the floor were perfectly smooth, we can conceive of no reason why the body should not continue to move in a straight line forever.

Now our minds are so constituted that we cannot conceive of a change occurring without a cause. On the rough floor the change of motion is accounted for by the action between the floor and the body—an action outside the body. But on the smooth floor this outside action is removed. Still, in this case, to make the body change its velocity or change the direction of motion, some outside action is found to be necessary. We say then that the body has within itself no power of making any change in its state, either of motion or of rest. To this property of inability of a body to change its state we give the name **Inertia**.* It

---

* The term *inertia* or *vis inertiæ* was introduced by Kepler (1571-1630).

is to be regarded as an inherent or characteristic property of matter. The law of inertia was enunciated by Newton as follows : *Every body continues in its state of rest or of uniform motion in a straight line except in so far as it is compelled by impressed forces to change that state.*

It thus appears that force causes not merely change of place in the body moved, but change of velocity as well. We may therefore extend the definition from muscular effort to this: *Force is whatever causes deviation from uniformity or rectilinearity of motion in the body acted on.*

29. The force exerted by an agent on a body being one component of the stress, the other component, the reaction of the body or the "kick against change of motion," depends on the inertia of the body, and may be called *inertia-resistance*. Being equal to the action of the agent, if we can measure it we have a measure of the stress, which term includes both components.

We have many familiar illustrations of inertia-resistance. Thus, on jumping from a train in motion, on reaching the ground we are hurled forward. In jumping on a train in motion, a jerk is received. So a sudden change of velocity will make itself known to the passengers by a thrust or jerk. The intensity of the thrust or jerk depends on the difference of velocity of train and passenger, thus showing that the inertia-resistance called into play is proportional to the instantaneous change of velocity or the acceleration a communicated. We may therefore write

$$inertia\text{-}resistance = ma$$

when m is a constant. This constant may be called the *coefficient of inertia*.

30. The comparison of forces is thus reduced to a comparison of distances and times, and by assuming a unit of force all forces may be expressed in terms of this unit so long as we keep to the *same* body.

Mass.—But in general the question is not regarding the comparison of forces acting on the same body, but of forces acting on different bodies. Suppose two passengers to jump on the same train, the larger will receive the greater jerk. We explain this by saying that the two bodies are of different **Mass**. We may therefore compare the masses of bodies by communicating the same acceleration to each body when the ratio of the masses will be the ratio of the coefficients of inertia. A rude measurement would be afforded by having each passenger grasp at the instant of jumping on the train a spring-balance: the ratio of the pulls would indicate the ratio of the masses.

We may observe the effects of the same force on blocks of the same substance of different sizes. It is found that the larger the block the smaller the acceleration imparted by the force, that is, the greater the mass. The mass would in this case depend on the size of the block, or, as is sometimes said, the *quantity of matter* in it. And when we come to blocks of different materials we agree *conventionally* to ascribe the greater mass to the body to which the smaller acceleration is imparted. If the same force gives the same acceleration to two different bodies, we say conventionally that they are of the same mass; and if the acceleration given to one is n times that given to the other, we say that the mass of the second is n times that of the first. Hence, *the masses of bodies are inversely proportional to the accelerations imparted to them by the same force.*

31. Unit of Mass.—It follows that masses may be compared by a measurement of accelerations. The operation may be called *massing*. It enables us to express all masses in terms of *some one* standard mass, and so make a quantitative measurement of mass. This one mass we may choose for unit-mass, and we may make it what we please. As in the case of the other fundamental units already assumed, the units of distance and time, all that is necessary is that having once chosen it we must be consistent in its use.

The units employed are the British unit, which is a certain lump of platinum called a **Pound** (lb.), and the metric unit, which is also a lump of platinum called a **Kilogram** (kg.). The masses of all bodies may now be expressed in pounds or kilograms by comparing the accelerations due to the action of the same force on the unit mass and on the bodies in question. Multiples or submultiples of the standard units, such as the ton, ounce, gram, etc., are often employed as being more convenient in certain cases than the standard units themselves.

32. *Unit of Force.*—We have seen that forces may be compared by comparing the accelerations produced in the same mass. This enables us to express all forces in terms of a unit force. The units of acceleration and mass being already defined, the *unit force* may be conveniently expressed in terms of them as the force producing unit-acceleration in unit mass. If we take unit acceleration to be one ft. per sec., and unit mass to be one lb., the name **Poundal** is given to unit force; if unit acceleration be one cm. per sec. and unit mass be one gram, the name **Dyne** is given to it.

33. We may find a numerical expression for any force in terms of the unit force, say the poundal. For by our definition, to impart to a mass of one lb. an acceleration of one ft. per sec. requires a force of one poundal, and the preceding makes it reasonable to suppose that to impart to a mass m an acceleration a would require a force of ma poundals. Denoting the force by F, we may write

$$F = ma,$$

which means that the force which produces an acceleration a ft. per sec. in a mass of m lb. is ma poundals.

Now the force F and the inertia-resistance of the body

being opposite aspects of the same stress, it follows from Art. 30 that with this system of units the coefficient of inertia is equal to the number of units of mass contained in the body, and the inertia-resistance is equal to the mass-acceleration ma of the body.

If now u is the velocity of a body of mass m at the beginning of time t and v the velocity at the end of this time under the action of a constant force F, the acceleration a is equal to $(v-u)/t$ (Art. 13). Hence, substituting for a in $F = ma$, we have

$$Ft = mv - mu.$$

The product Ft is called the *impulse* of the force during the time t, and the product mv or mu is called the *momentum* of the mass m in the direction of the velocity v or u. Hence $mv - mu$ is the change of momentum due to the impulse.

We may now appreciate more clearly the meaning of Newton's second law of motion, which states that: *The change of momentum of a body is numerically equal to the impulse which produces it, and is in the same direction.*

34. From the law we have the relation

$$Ft = mv - mu,$$

as its statement in symbolic form.

Writing this in the form $F = (mv - mu)/t$, we see that force may be defined as *rate of change of momentum*.

Putting the rate of change of velocity $(v-u)/t = a$, the acceleration, we have

$$F = ma,$$

a convenient form, and which is called the *general equation of motion*.

Whether the acceleration be uniform or variable, we may write (Art. 14)
$$a = d^2s/dt^2,$$
and hence
$$F = m d^2s/dt^2,$$
which is also called the *general equation of motion*.

The general equation of motion, which is the algebraic statement of the second law of motion, is the connecting link between motion and force. It enables us to pass from the kinematical properties of motion already laid down to questions involving force and mass. It is the link between the ideal and the actual, the geometrical and the physical.

35. From this law we infer, too, that since change of momentum per second is proportional to the magnitude only of the force acting, this change is the same whether the body is at rest or in motion.

Hence, too, for the same body force and acceleration are simultaneously constant, being connected by the relation $F = ma$; or, as it may be stated, a constant force constitutes constant acceleration to the body acted on by it.

A *variable force* may be considered to consist of a succession of constant forces varying in magnitude and direction, and acting for indefinitely small intervals. The accelerations contributed may be considered uniform during these intervals, and the total acceleration in any time found by summation.

The law also implies that when two or more forces act on a body at the same time, each force produces an acceleration in its own direction without reference to the others. It therefore follows that forces may be combined by the rules already laid down for the combination of accelerations (Art. 18).

Ex. 1. Explain why by striking the handle of a hammer against a wall the head may be fixed on firmly.

2. A man stumbling can save himself more easily on land than on smooth ice. Explain.

3. In suburban-passenger traffic the trains must stop and start quickly. The boiler and machinery are placed over the driving-wheels. Why?

4. Show that it necessarily follows from the second law of motion that forces can be represented by straight lines.

5. What are the tests of the equality (1) of two forces, (2) of two masses?

6. State the parallelogram of momenta.

7. A man with a hod on his shoulder falls off a ladder: find the pressure on his shoulder during the fall.

36. Gravitation Measure of Force.—The unit of mass being assumed, we have seen how all masses may be expressed in terms of the unit by measuring the accelerations contributed by equal forces. This is a strictly scientific method of measuring mass, and is sufficient. But though easily described in general terms, it is difficult of performance in practice. Accordingly we give another method more easily put in operation.

It is a fact of common observation, that a body free to move falls towards the earth. It acts as if the earth attracted it. It is assumed as a convenient explanation of the observed phenomenon that there exists an attraction between the earth and the body, and to this attractive force the name *force of gravity* is given.

A body free to move if exposed to the action of the force of gravity is uniformly accelerated. Experiment* shows that at the same place it acts on all bodies in the same way; that is, the acceleration g produced by it has no relation to the magnitude of the bodies or to the material of which they are composed.

---

* Drop simultaneously pieces of lead, iron, paper, etc., etc., from a shelf in a glass vessel from which the air has been exhausted. All will be observed to strike the bottom of the vessel simultaneously. The only force acting is the force of gravity, and since all strike the bottom at once, they must have the same acceleration, as each has passed over the same distance in the same time.

Experiment shows, too, that the value of g is constant so long as we keep to the same place on the earth's surface. It varies, however, from place to place.* This is explained by the fact that the earth is not a perfect sphere, and is not homogeneous in structure. For latitude 45° at sea-level its value is 32.2 ft., or 9.81 meters nearly. This may be taken as an average value.

37. We may make a rough comparison of any force with the gravity force of a body in this way. Place the body on a spring-balance and note the compression of the spring. If the force produces the same compression of the spring we say it is equal to the gravity force of the body.

The *unit force* is naturally assumed to be equal to the gravity force of the unit mass, one lb. or one gram. This force causes, as explained above, an acceleration g in one lb. But the force causing an acceleration g in one lb. is g poundals. Hence the unit force is equivalent to g poundals. As, however, it is convenient to have a distinct name, the unit is called a **Pound**, so that a force of one pound is equivalent to the attractive force between one pound mass and the earth, and is equal to g poundals. Hence we may convert poundals to pounds by dividing by the value of g at the place in question.

38. The use of the word pound in the double sense of mass and force is objectionable, but it is sanctioned by ordinary custom, and the context must decide in which sense it is used. To aid in making the distinction we shall use for mass the symbol *lb.*, and for force the word *pound*.†

The pound is called the *gravitation unit of force*, because it depends on the force of gravity, which is not constant in

---

* "When Halley in 1677 went to the island of St. Helena to observe the stars of the southern hemisphere he found his clock lose so much that the screw at the bottom of the pendulum did not enable him to shorten it sufficiently."

† Suggested by Supt. Mendenhall of the United States Coast and Geodetic Survey.

value over the earth's surface. The other unit of force, the poundal (or dyne), does not involve g, and is known as the *absolute unit*. The first being the older and more easily applied, is the unit of daily life; the second being the more comprehensive is used in astronomical and electrical work, and in precise physical investigations in general.

39. Weight.—The gravity forces of two bodies of masses m, m_1 being as mg poundals to $m_1 g$ poundals or as m to m_1 are in the ratio of the masses. If the bodies are placed in the scale-pans of a common balance and the balance remains in the same position, the gravity force of each is the same, and the two bodies have equal mass, or, as we say in common language, have equal **Weight**.* The process is called *weighing*, and hence, by assuming a body of standard mass, we may express all bodies in terms of this standard. We may therefore, in comparing masses, substitute for the complicated process of massing (Art. 31) the simple operation of weighing.

In ordinary language the word weight is used in the double sense of mass and force. The original signification of the term was what we now call mass, and its extension to force was a later development. "The word weight must be understood to mean the quantity of the thing as determined by the process of weighing against standard weights." Thus in buying a barrel of flour we buy the mass that weighs 196 pounds.

The builder and machinist find it necessary to use it in the other sense, as in computing the force necessary to support a load of given weight (= balancing the gravity force of a load), or in computing the stresses in a structure designed to support a given load.

It is unfortunate that the term is ambiguous, but there is no help for it—any more than for the ambiguity of the term

---

* On the effect of "centrifugal force" on the weight of a body see Art. 69, with the examples appended, particularly 9–11 inclusive.

pound. In fact the two go together—pound weight (mass) originally, and pound weight (force) secondarily.

To prevent confusion, we shall express all dynamical formulas in terms of the absolute units. The passage to the gravitation units and the use of the terms weight, pound, etc., in the examples can give no trouble if the explanations given are kept in mind. The context will always make clear the sense intended.

Ex. 1. How many poundals are equal to [the gravity force of] one ton? *Ans.* 2000 g poundals.

2. Show that one poundal is equivalent to $\frac{1}{2}$ oz.

3. Would it be advantageous for a merchant to use a spring-balance for buying groceries in New York to sell in Cuba? How would a pair of scales answer?

40. Note on Units.—The three fundamental units in Mechanics are the units of time, distance, and mass. Being fundamental, they are arbitrary, and are chosen for convenience, or as the result of circumstances. Their definitions have already been given; but we shall here repeat, collect, and go into a little more detail.

The unit of time is the **Second**. It is derived from observations of the earth's rotation. The assumption of this unit therefore really amounts to making the motion of the earth on its axis the standard motion, and by means of the second all motions are tacitly compared with this standard.

The standards of length are the **Yard** and the **Meter**. The yard is the distance between two lines on a certain bronze bar kept in London, England, when the bar is at the temperature 62° F. The *foot* is $\frac{1}{3}$ of this distance, and the *inch* $\frac{1}{36}$ of the same distance. The meter is the distance between the ends of a certain platinum bar kept in Paris, France, when at the temperature 0° C. It was intended to be the ten-millionth part of the meridian distance between the equator and the pole, and is nearly equal to this distance, but not exactly. A meter is equal to 39.37 inches, or 3.28 ft. The *centimeter* is $\frac{1}{100}$ of the meter.

FORCE AND MOTION.

The standards of mass are the **Pound** (lb.) and the **Kilogram**. The pound is a certain piece of platinum kept at London, England. The *ounce* is $\frac{1}{16}$ of the pound. The kilogram is a certain piece of platinum kept at Paris, France. The *gram* is $\frac{1}{1000}$ of the kilogram, and was intended to be of the same mass (which it is very nearly) as a cubic centimeter of water at 3°.9 C., the temperature of maximum density of water.

The units used in any investigation are multiples or subdivisions of the standard units as found most convenient. The system of units involving the centimeter, gram, and second, with the dyne as unit of force, is called the *C.G.S.* system. It forms a sort of international system, and is being largely adopted by physicists, astronomers, and electricians. The British (absolute) system of the foot, lb., and second, with the poundal as unit of force, is known as the *F.P.S.* system; and the British (gravitation) system of the foot, lb., and second, with the pound as unit of force, is the system of every-day life. In engineering work, the inch, ton, and minute are very often the units employed.

The following table of relative magnitudes will be found convenient:

1 lb. =	453.59 grams.	1 gram =	0.0022 lb.
1 inch =	2.54 centimeters.	1 centimeter =	0.3937 inch.
1 foot =	30.48 centimeters.	1 meter =	3.2809 feet.
1 mile =	1609.33 meters.	1 gram =	15.432 grains.

41. *Dimensions of Units.*—All mechanical quantities are expressed in terms of some system of units. The two leading systems in use in this country, the F.P.S. and the C.G.S., have been explained. It is convenient to be able to pass rapidly from the one system to the other, or from one system to any other. Of course the quantity itself is quite independent of the unit employed to measure it,—just as the matter of this book is in no way affected by the size of the type used by the printer.

NOTE ON UNITS.

The fundamental units are those of distance, time, and mass. Let L, T, M denote the magnitudes of these units. Then if we say a distance is l units in length, the complete symbol representing this would be lL. Usually it is written l only, the unit being tacitly assumed.

All derived units may be expressed in terms of the fundamental units. Thus unit velocity being the velocity of a point which describes unit distance in unit time, we have

$$\text{unit vel.} = \text{unit dis.} / \text{unit time} = L/T.$$

Similarly,

$$\text{unit accel.} = \text{unit vel.} / \text{unit time} = L/T^2;$$
$$\text{unit force} = \text{unit mass} \times \text{unit accel.} = ML/T^2;$$
$$\text{unit mom.} = \text{unit mass} \times \text{unit vel.} = ML/T;$$

and unit impulse being measured by the number of units of momentum generated is of the same dimensions as unit momentum.

Ex. 1. How many dynes in a poundal?
[1 poundal $= ML/T^2 =$ lb. $\times$ ft./sec.^{2} = 453.59 grams $\times$ 30.48 cm./sec.^{2} = 13825.3 dynes.]

2. Show that the foot per sec. and mile per hour units of velocity are as 15:22.

3. Show that one mile per hour is 44.7 cm. per sec.

4. Reduce a velocity of 100 ft. per min. to cm. per sec.

5. How many dynes in [the force of] an imperial pound?
Ans. 445,000 dynes, about $= \frac{2}{5}$ megadyne.

6. Show that [the force of] 1 gram = 981 dynes.

7. Show that [the force of] 1 grain = 63.58 dynes.

8. Prove that a pressure of 1 pound per sq. ft. is equivalent to 479 dynes per sq. cm.

9. Find the value of g if one minute is taken as the unit of time. *Ans.* 115,200 ft.

10. Find the unit of time if g is taken as unity, one ft. being the unit of length. *Ans.* 0.25 $\sqrt{5}$ sec.

11. How many dynes in the unit of force if the meter, minute, and kilogram are taken as the units of distance, time, and mass respectively?
Ans. 100 $\times$ 1000 $\times$ 60^2 dynes.

CHAPTER III.

DYNAMICS OF A PARTICLE.

42. HAVING considered the geometrical properties of motion, and also the methods of measuring mass and force, we are ready to study the motion produced in a body of given mass by forces of given magnitude.

When a body is acted on by forces, experience shows that various forms of motion may arise. If all of the component particles of the body move through equal distances in the same direction, the motion is said to be a motion of **Translation**. The motion of any particle would in this case give the motion of the body. In a motion of rotation the particles do not move through equal distances in the same direction, those nearest the axis of rotation moving the shortest distance. If a body consisted of a single particle, it would, in its rotation about an axis passing through it, remain in the same position. We shall therefore exclude rotation, and be able to study the translation of a body if we consider the motion of a single particle only. We may conceive the whole body concentrated as it were into a single particle of equivalent mass.

43. Composition of Forces.—The number of forces acting on a particle may be one or more than one. If we can combine the separate forces into an equivalent single force, we can reduce all cases to that of the action of a single force. The method of combining forces will be our first step, and next we shall consider the motion of a particle under the action of a force.

If several forces act on a particle at rest or in motion, the

COMPOSITION OF FORCES. 45

accelerations communicated are the same as if each force acted separately on the particle at rest. In other words, the acceleration produced by a force on a particle is independent of any motion it may have and independent of motions produced by other forces acting simultaneously. This is involved in the statement of the second law of motion, but is repeated and expanded here for greater clearness. It is sometimes known as the *principle of the independence of forces*.

44. Representation of Force.—When a force acts on a particle its line of action must pass through the particle. The force itself contains a certain number of poundals or dynes. We may say that the elements of the force are three—the geometrical position of the particle acted on, the direction of the force, and the number of units it contains or its magnitude. It may therefore be represented by a straight line AB, the length of AB representing the magnitude of the force, the direction from A to B the direction of the force, and the point A the point of application. Each unit of length of AB will represent unit force. But the length of the unit is arbitrary. Hence we may plot forces to any scale we please, as 1 poundal $= 1$ inch, 10 poundals $= 1$ inch, etc.

The direction of a force may be indicated by its sign. Thus a force of 2 units acting at A towards the right might be written $+2$, an equal force in the opposite direction -2. The choice of signs is arbitrary, and it is only necessary to remember that if one direction is assumed to be $+$, the opposite direction must be $-$. In a diagram the direction is conveniently indicated by an arrow-head.

Fig. 19

Ex. On a scale of 100 pounds per in. what force would be represented by a line 20 in. long? *Ans.* 2000 pounds.

45. Resultant of Two Forces.—Suppose that F_1, F_2 are two forces which act on a particle A of mass m. The accelerations a_1, a_2 produced by these forces are (Art. 34) F_1/m, F_2/m respectively, and the resultant acceleration a in direction and magnitude is represented (Art. 18) by the diagonal of the parallelogram of which a_1, a_2 are adjacent sides. Hence, if R denotes the force which would produce the acceleration a, that is, if $R = ma$, it must represent in magnitude and direction a force which produces the same acceleration on A as F_1 and F_2. To the force R the name **Resultant Force** is given, and conversely F_1, F_2 are the **Components** of R.

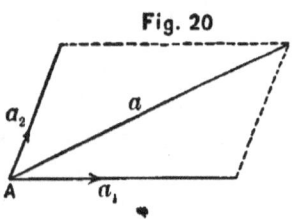

Fig. 20

We may represent this graphically. Let AB, AC represent the forces F_1, F_2 in magnitude and direction (scale, say, 1 poundal = 1 in.); then AD the concurrent diagonal of the parallelogram constructed on AB, AC as adjacent sides will represent in magnitude and direction the resultant R of the two forces on the same scale. This principle is called the **Parallelogram of Forces.*** Hence, instead of finding the accelerations due to the forces and combining them into a single acceleration, and thence finding the force which would produce this acceleration, we may combine the forces themselves directly.

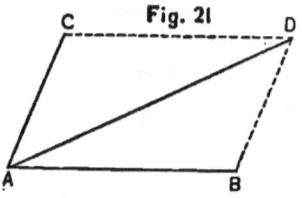

Fig. 21

Ex. 1. If the two forces act in the same straight line, find their resultant. *Ans.* $F_1 \pm F_2$. Why the double sign?

2. Explain the action of the forces by which an arrow is discharged from a bow.

3. Explain (by a drawing) the action of the forces by which a kite rises in the air.

4. Show by a drawing that the value of R decreases as the angle between the forces increases.

---

* The parallelogram of forces was first formulated by Newton (1642–1727).

COMPOSITION OF FORCES.

5. A satchel is carried by a strap slung over the shoulder: show that the longer the strap the less its tension.

46. Instead of finding the diagonal of the parallelogram by a geometrical construction, as just explained, we would obtain the same result if we computed its value from the known values of the sides AB, AC and the contained angle $BAC\ (=\theta)$. Thus from trigonometry we have in the triangle ABD [note $AC = BD$; $BAC + ABD = 180°$].

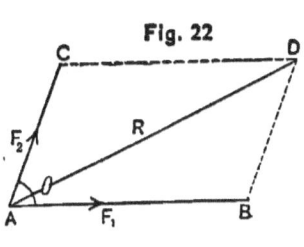

Fig. 22

$$AD^2 = AB^2 + BD^2 - 2AB \cdot BD \cos ABD$$
$$= AB^2 + AC^2 + 2AB \cdot AC \cos BAC,$$
or $\qquad R^2 = F_1^2 + F_2^2 + 2F_1 F_2 \cos \theta,$

which gives the *magnitude* of the resultant. The *direction* may be found by solving the triangle ABD to find the angle BAD. The *position* is known since the force acts at A. Hence R is completely determined.

The special case of the forces acting in directions at right angles is important. The parallelogram becomes a rectangle, and from the figure

$$R^2 = F_1^2 + F_2^2, \quad \cos BAD = F_1/R,$$

whence both the magnitude and direction of the resultant are determined.

Ex. 1. If two equal forces F, F are at right angles to one another, then $R = F\sqrt{2}$.

2. If two equal forces F, F are inclined at an angle 2θ, then $R = 2F \cos \theta$.

3. Prove that the value of R increases as the angle between the forces diminishes, and *vice versa*.

4. When the angle BAC is 180° the forces are in the same straight line, and the formula, if correct, should reduce to the sum or difference of the forces. Examine, and see if it does.

5. Two equal forces F act at an angle of 60°: find their resultant.

6. Find the resultant of two equal forces, each of 10 pounds, acting at an angle of 30°.   *Ans.* 19.3 pounds.

47. Consider in Fig. 22 the manner in which the resultant is formed. The forces F_1, F_2 drawn to scale are represented by the lines AB, AC. From B the line BD is drawn parallel to AC, and from C the line CD is drawn parallel to AB. The diagonal AD of the parallelogram represents the resultant in magnitude, direction, and position.

Fig. 23

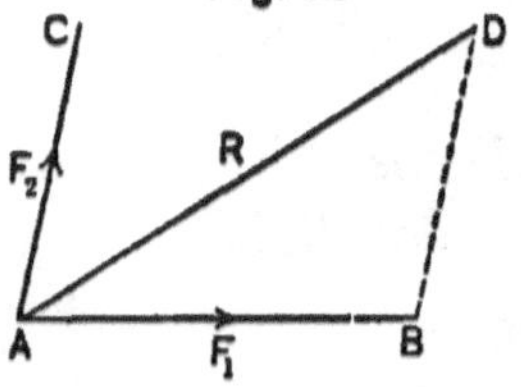

This construction is equivalent to that shown in Fig. 23. Plot the forces F_1, F_2 as before. From B draw BD parallel and equal to AC. Join AD, which represents the resultant.

Still better, by breaking the figure into two parts (Figs. 24, 25). Let F_1, F_2 be the forces acting at O. From any point A draw AB to scale equal and parallel to F_1. From B draw BD to scale equal and parallel to F_2. Join AD, which will represent the resultant in *magnitude* and *direction*. To find its *position:* We know that it must pass through O, and hence if through O we draw a line equal and parallel to AD, we have R in magnitude, direction, and position. We have therefore a **Force Diagram** (Fig. 24) and a **Construction Diagram** purely geometrical (Fig. 25). In Fig. 23 the two overlap, and in simple cases there is no confusion in their being so drawn; but in complicated cases it is better to keep them separate, as we shall see later.

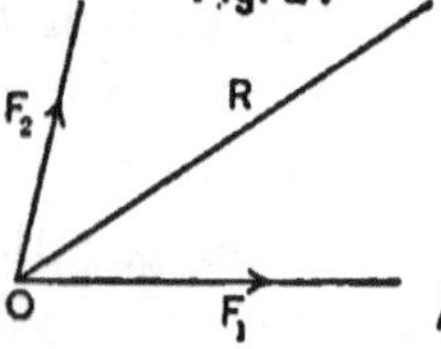

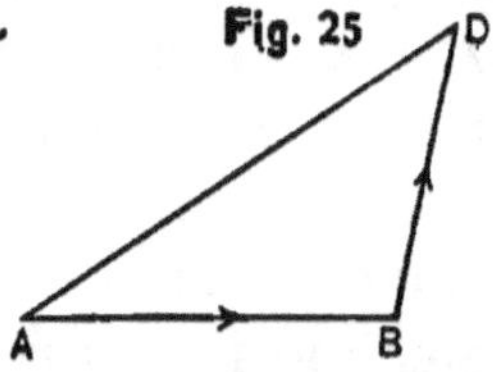

48. *Resultant of more than two Forces.*—Let F_1, F_2, F_3, F_4 represent forces acting on a particle at O: it is required to find their resultant.

COMPOSITION OF FORCES.

Following the method of Art. 47, from a point A we draw AB equal and parallel to F_1, BC equal and parallel to F_2, CD equal and parallel to F_3, DE equal and parallel to F_4. Join AE, which will represent the resultant in magnitude and direction. In the force diagram draw R equal and parallel to AE, and we have the resultant in magnitude, direction, and position.

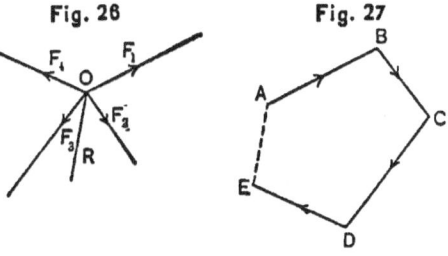

Fig. 26   Fig. 27

For join AC, AD. Then AC is the resultant of AB, BC, that is, of F_1, F_2; AD is the resultant of AC, CD, that is, of F_1, F_2, F_3; AE is the resultant of AD, DE, that is, of F_1, F_2, F_3, F_4; which proves the proposition.

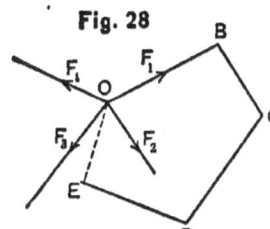

Fig. 28

We might have combined the two diagrams as shown in Fig. 28, or we might have derived the resultant directly from the parallelogram of forces as shown in Fig. 29.

Notice that in any method we may take the forces in *any order*, and we shall always find the same value of AE. Test this statement by making drawings to a large scale.

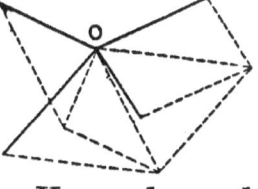

Fig. 29

Ex. 1. Three forces of 6, 8, 10 pounds act at angles of 120° with each other: find their resultant. Draw to scale by different methods, and compare results. Vary order, and compare.

2. Forces of 1, 2, 3, 4, 5, 6 act at angles of 60°: find R. Test as in Ex. 1.

3. Forces of 20, 20, 21 pounds act at a point. The angle between the first and second is 120° and between the second and third 30°: find R.   *Ans.* 29 pounds.

4. Is it necessary that force and construction diagrams be drawn to the same scale?

5. In the construction diagram the lines are drawn parallel to the forces : would it be allowable to draw them perpendicular to the forces, or inclined at any (the same) angle, θ for example? Test by a drawing.

6. If the forces are in the same straight line, what does the force polygon become? what the construction diagram?

49. Resolution of Forces.—By means of the parallelogram of forces, a force R can be found equivalent to two forces F_1, F_2, acting on a particle A. Conversely, the force R acting at A may be resolved into two component forces F_1, F_2 acting at A, by constructing on R as diagonal a parallelogram, and taking the sides to represent the components. The problem is similar to that already discussed in Art. 20.

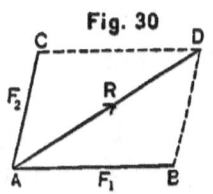
Fig. 30

Ex. 1. If a force is resolved into two components, prove that the greater component always makes the smaller angle with the force.

2. Resolve a force of 20 pounds into two components each of which makes an angle of 60° with it.

Ans. Each = 20 pounds.

3. Resolve a force of 10 pounds into two equal components, one of them making an angle of 45° with the force.

Ans. 7 pounds, nearly.

4. Find that rectangular component of a force of 10 pounds which makes an angle of 60° with the force.

Ans. 5 pounds.

5. Explain the boatmen's saying, that there is greater "power" in hauling a canal-boat with a long rope than with a short one.

The values of the rectangular components X, Y of a force R may readily be computed analytically. Thus in the right-angled triangles ABD, ACD,

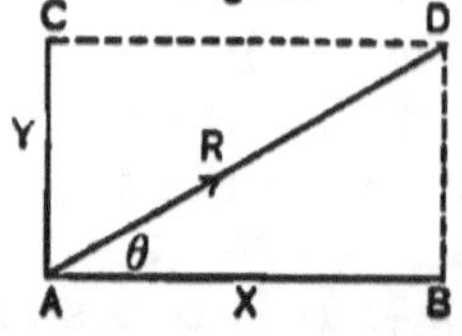

$X = AB = R \cos \theta$,

$Y = AC = R \sin \theta = R \cos \overline{90° - \theta}$,

which give the values of the two components X and Y. Hence the rectangular component of a

Fig. 31

RESOLUTION OF FORCES. 51

force R in a given direction is equal to $R \times \cos$ (angle between component and R). As a check,

$$X^2 + Y^2 = R^2 \cos^2 \theta + R^2 \sin^2 \theta = R^2,$$

which is also evident from the figure.

Ex. 1. Find the components of a force 10 when $\theta = 60°$, 90°, 120°, 180°, 240°, 270°, 300°. *Ans.* 5, 5 $\sqrt{3}$; 0, 10; − 5, 5 $\sqrt{3}$; − 10, 0; − 5, − 5 $\sqrt{3}$; 0, − 10; 5, − 5 $\sqrt{3}$. [Draw a figure for each case, and explain the sign of the result.]

2. The rectangular components of a force are each equal to p poundals: what is the force?

3. Show that the components of a force F in two directions making angles β, γ with it are $F \sin \beta / \sin (\beta + \gamma)$, $F \sin \gamma / \sin (\beta + \gamma)$.

4. In a direct-acting steam-engine the piston pressure P is equivalent to $P \tan \theta$ perpendicular to its line of action and $P \sec \theta$ along the connecting-rod, θ being the angle of inclination of the connecting-rod to the line of action of the piston (see Fig. 119).

50. The analytical solution leads us to a method of *combining* forces which is often more convenient than the graphic method given in Art. 48. The two methods may be used to check one another.

Take three forces F_1, F_2, F_3, acting on a particle O. Through O draw *any* two lines OX, OY at right angles to each other, and let θ_1, θ_2, θ_3 denote the angles which the directions of F_1, F_2, F_3 make with OX. The components of

F_1 are $F_1 \cos \theta_1$ along OX; $F_1 \sin \theta_1$ along OY;
F_2 are $F_2 \cos \theta_2$ along OX; $F_2 \sin \theta_2$ along OY;
F_3 are $F_3 \cos \theta_3$ along OX; $F_3 \sin \theta_3$ along OY.

The components along OX being in the same straight line, may be combined by addition into a single force X (Art. 48); that is,

$$F_1 \cos \theta_1 + F_2 \cos \theta_2 + F_3 \cos \theta_3 = X. \quad \ldots \quad (1)$$

Similarly, the components along OY, being in the same straight line, may be combined into a single force Y, or

$$F_1 \sin \theta_1 + F_2 \sin \theta_2 + F_3 \sin \theta_3 = Y. \quad \ldots \quad (2)$$

Hence the original forces are equivalent to two forces X, Y acting in directions OX, OY at right angles to each other. The resultant of X, Y must therefore be the resultant of the original forces. Call it R, and let θ be the angle it makes with the axis of X; then

$$R \cos \theta = X, \quad R \sin \theta = Y. \quad \ldots \ldots \quad (3)$$

Square and add (remembering that $\cos^2 \theta + \sin^2 \theta = 1$), and

$$R = \sqrt{X^2 + Y^2},$$

which gives the *magnitude* of the resultant. Divide the second of equations (3) by the first, and

$$\tan \theta = Y/X,$$

which gives the *direction* of the resultant.

Hence, since the resultant acts at O, it is known in position, magnitude, and direction, and is completely determined.

If we equate the values of X, Y in equations 1, 2, 3, we find

$$R \cos \theta = F_1 \cos \theta_1 + F_2 \cos \theta_2 + F_3 \cos \theta_3 ;$$
$$R \sin \theta = F_1 \sin \theta_1 + F_2 \sin \theta_2 + F_3 \sin \theta_3 .$$

Now OX, OY are *any* two rectangular axes. Hence *the component in any direction of the resultant of a number of forces is equal to the sum of their components in the same direction.*

Ex. 1. Three forces of 6, 8, 10 pounds act on a particle at angles of 120° to each other: find the resultant in magnitude and direction.

RESOLUTION OF FORCES.

[Since the direction of OX is arbitrary, we may take it along any of the forces.
(1) Take OX along the force 6. Then
$X = 6 - 8\cos 60° - 10\cos 60° = -3$;
$Y = 8\cos 30° - 10\cos 30° = -\sqrt{3}$;
and $R = \sqrt{9+3} = 2\sqrt{3}$;
$\tan \theta = -\sqrt{3}/-3 = 1/\sqrt{3}$ or $\theta = 210°$.
(2) Take OX to fall along the force 8. Then
$X = 8 - 6\cos 60° - 10\cos 60° = 0$;
$Y = 10\sin 60° - 6\sin 60° = 2\sqrt{3}$;
$R = 2\sqrt{3}$, as before;
$\tan \theta = 2\sqrt{3}/0 = \infty$ and $\theta = 90°$;
or the resultant is perpendicular to the force 8, showing it to be in the same *relative* position with reference to the other forces as before.]

2. Solve with OX along the force 10.

51. Having now the means of combining the forces that act on a particle into a single force giving the same motion, we proceed to study this motion.

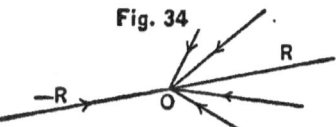

Fig. 34

Conceive a particle O acted on by a number of forces whose resultant is R. If a force equal and opposite to R be added, the whole system of forces acting on the particle will balance. The resultant of the forces is *nil,* and the system is said to be in **Equilibrium**. From the relation $F = ma$, it follows when $F = 0$ that $a = 0$. Hence a system of forces in equilibrium implies that there is no acceleration. Thus the velocity of the body, if it had any before the forces commenced to act, would be unchanged, and the motion would continue uniform and in a straight line; if at rest, it would remain at rest. Equilibrium, therefore, does not imply rest, but rest implies equilibrium. The branch of dynamics which considers the circumstances for which equilibrium is possible is called **Statics**.

When the forces do not balance, an acceleration arises from the resultant force, and the particle moves with a motion compounded of the motion in its original path, and that due to the resultant. The branch of dynamics which considers the circumstances under which change of motion takes place is called **Kinetics**.

STATICS OF A PARTICLE.

52. When a particle is in equilibrium under forces acting in the same straight line, the total acceleration produced by the forces is *nil*, and therefore the sum of the accelerations in one direction is equal to the sum in the opposite direction. Hence the sum of the forces acting in one direction must be equal to the sum in the opposite direction. In other words, the forces must reduce to *two* forces equal in magnitude and opposite in direction.

Next, let *three* forces not in the same straight line act on the particle. Find the resultant R of any two F_1, F_2. For equilibrium to exist, R and F_3 must be equal and opposite. Hence if three forces acting on a particle are in equilibrium, any one of them is equal and opposite to the resultant of the other two.

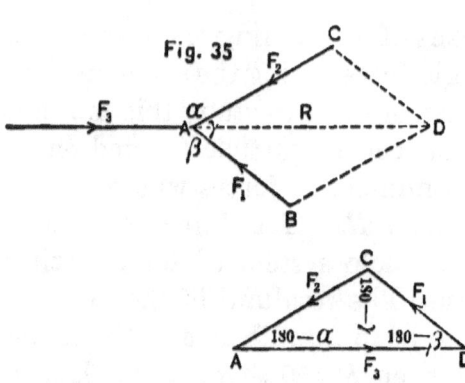

Fig. 35

The sides of the construction triangle ACD are parallel to the three forces F_1, F_2, F_3, and proportional to them in magnitude (Art. 47). Notice that their directions are the same way round the triangle. Hence *three forces acting on a particle will be in equilibrium if they can be represented by the three sides of a triangle drawn parallel to the forces, and taken the same way round.* This proposition is known as the **Triangle of Forces**.

It may be expressed analytically. If α, β, γ be the

POLYGON OF FORCES. 55

angles between the directions of the forces, then in the construction triangle the angles are evidently $180° - \alpha$, $180° - \beta$, $180° - \gamma$; and since the sides of a triangle are as the sides of the opposite angles,

$$DC/\sin(180° - \alpha) = CA/\sin(180° - \beta)$$
$$= AD/\sin(180° - \gamma),$$

or

$$F_1/\sin \alpha = F_2/\sin \beta = F_3/\sin \gamma;$$

that is, *when three forces acting on a particle are in equilibrium, each is proportional to the sine of the angle between the directions of the other two forces.*

Illustration.—Take a piece of board, and drive in three smooth pegs A, B, C, or place three pulleys at A, B, C. Run strings over the pegs, and knot together as at O. Suspend weights from the strings. Draw lines along the strings on the board, and plot the triangle abc with sides parallel to these lines. The sides of this triangle will be found to be proportional to the weights.

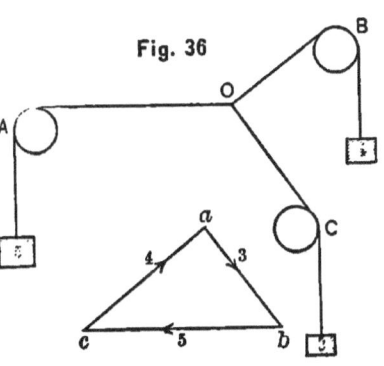

Fig. 36

Ex. 1. Make the weights 3, 4, 5 oz., and it will be found that one angle of the triangle abc will be 90°.

2. Could the three weights be equal to one another? Plot abc in this case, if possible.

53. Polygon of Forces.—If in the force diagram of Art. 48 the direction of R be reversed, the particle will be in equilibrium under the action of F_1, F_2, F_3, F_4, $-R$. Indicate the directions of these forces on the construction diagram, and notice that they are the same way round. Hence *any number of forces in the same plane acting on a particle will be in equilibrium if they can be represented by* *the sides of a polygon drawn parallel to the forces, and taken the same way round.* This is known as the **Polygon of Forces.**

Ex. In the polygon of forces any side represents in magnitude and direction the resultant of the remaining forces, but with sign reversed.

54. The analytical equivalent of the polygon of forces may be deduced from Art. 50. For if the forces acting at O are in equilibrium, the resultant R must be equal to zero. Hence
$$X^2 + Y^2 = 0,$$
which, since X^2 and Y^2 are both positive, can only be satisfied by $X = 0$, $Y = 0$, that is, by
$$F_1 \cos \theta_1 + F_2 \cos \theta_2 + \ldots = 0,$$
$$F_1 \sin \theta_1 + F_2 \sin \theta_2 + \ldots = 0.$$

Hence *if any number of forces in the same plane acting on a particle are in equilibrium, the sums of the components of the forces along any two straight lines at right angles to each other through the particle are equal to zero.*

Ex. 1. State the analytical conditions of equilibrium, when 2, 3, ... n forces act on a particle.

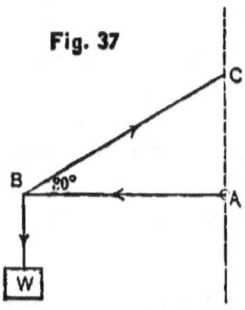

Fig. 37

2. A rod AB whose weight may be neglected is hinged at A, and supports a weight W at B. It is held up by a string BC fastened to a fixed point C vertically above A. If AB is horizontal and angle $ABC = 30°$, find the tension T_1 of the string, and the thrust T_2 along AB.

[The point B is in equilibrium under T_1, T_2, W. Resolve vertically and horizontally, then
$$T_1 \cos 60° - W = 0,$$
$$T_1 \cos 30° - T_2 = 0;$$
$$\therefore T_1 = 2W, \; T_2 = W \sqrt{3}.]$$

3. In a canal with parallel banks, a boat is moored by two ropes attached to posts on the banks. If the ropes are in-

clined at angles of 30°, 60° to the banks, compare the pulls on them, both ropes being in the same horizontal plane.

Ans. 1: $\sqrt{3}$.

KINETICS OF A PARTICLE.

55. If a number of forces act on a particle and the resultant be found, a certain motion is due to this resultant. If the particle has this motion, it is said to be *free*; if it has some other motion, the deviation must be owing to the entrance of some cause not accounted for, and the motion is said to be *constrained*. In free motion the particle is isolated from all causes tending to affect its motion except the acting forces, while in constrained motion this is not the case.

We have seen (Art. 5) that the position of a particle is defined by its coördinates with reference to certain axes assumed to be fixed. A change in position is represented by changes in these coördinates. Hence the coördinates being either a distance and two angles or three distances, a point is said to have three degrees of freedom to move.

If the point is compelled to remain in an assigned plane (as the plane of the paper), its position is defined by two coördinates, and it is said to have two degrees of freedom and one degree of constraint. Similarly, if compelled to remain at the same distance from a fixed point it would move on the surface of a sphere, and have two degrees of freedom and one of constraint.

Again, if the point were compelled to remain in two planes, that is, in their line of intersection, it would have one degree of freedom and two of constraint: so also if compelled to remain in one plane and keep at the same distance from a fixed point, that is, to move in a circular path.

If compelled to remain in three planes, it can have only

one position, their point of intersection, and is therefore wholly constrained.

Ex. How many degrees of freedom has a curling-stone on smooth ice; a stone in a sling; a compass joined to a tripod by a ball-and-socket joint?

56. Free Motion.—By means of the relation $F = ma$ connecting force acting, mass acted on, and acceleration produced, we are able to extend the geometrical properties of motion to particles acted on by given forces. Various paths may result, depending on the motion of the particle at the time the force begins to act. We shall first of all consider the particle to be unconstrained, and have all degrees of freedom.

Suppose the particle to have an initial velocity u, and that the force F acts in the direction of this velocity, causing an acceleration a. Then the resultant velocity at the end of a time t is composed of that due to u and that due to the acceleration a. Hence if v is the final velocity and s the distance passed over, we have (Art. 13)

$$v = u + at, \qquad s = ut + \tfrac{1}{2}at^2,$$
$$= u + Ft/m, \qquad = ut + \tfrac{1}{2}Ft^2/m,$$

in terms of the absolute units.

Ex. 1. A mass of 10 lbs. is moved along a smooth table by a weight of 6 pounds attached to a string which passes over a smooth peg on the edge of the table: find the distance passed over in 2 sec., and the velocity acquired.

[Effective force = 6 pounds = $6g$ poundals; mass moved = $10 + 6 = 16$ lbs.; $\therefore a = 6g/16 = 12$ ft.; $v = 2 \times 12 = 24$ ft. per sec.; $s = \tfrac{1}{2} \times 12 \times 2^2 = 24$ ft.].

2. An ice-boat weighing 1000 lbs. is driven for 30 sec. by a force of 100 pounds: find the velocity acquired and the distance passed over, supposing it starts (1) with a velocity of 10 ft. per sec., (2) from rest.

3. Find the tension P of the string in Ex. 1.

[Effective force on mass $10 = 10g - P$;
$\therefore$ accel. $= (10g - P)/10$.

FREE MOTION. 59

Effective force on mass $6 = P - 6g$;
$\therefore$ accel. $= (P - 6g)/6$.
Hence $P = 7\frac{1}{2}$ pounds.]

4. An elevator weighing m lbs. is lifted by a force of n pounds: find the acceleration and tension of the lifting chain. $Ans.\ a = \dfrac{m-n}{m+n}g;\ P = \dfrac{2mn}{m+n}g.$

5. A bucket weighing 25 lbs. is let down into a well with a uniform velocity: find tension of rope.
$Ans.$ 25 pounds.

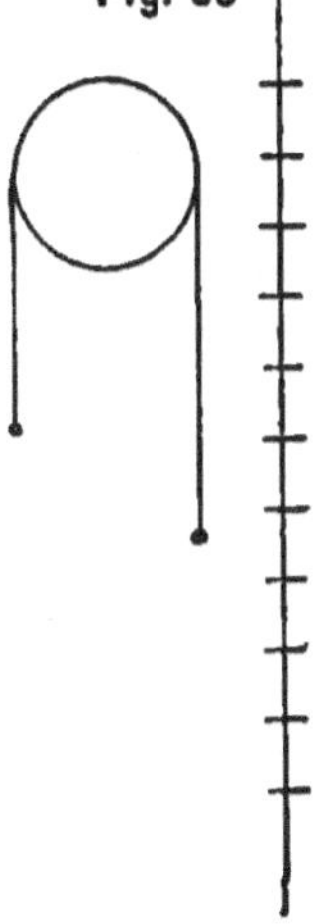

6. Two bodies of weights w_1 and w_2 pounds are fastened to a string which passes over a smooth peg: find the acceleration and tension of the string. $Ans.\ a = \dfrac{w_1 - w_2}{w_1 + w_2}g;\ \dfrac{2}{T} = \dfrac{1}{w_1} + \dfrac{1}{w_2}.$

Fig. 38

[If the value of a is observed, we have the value of g from $\dfrac{(w_1 + w_2)a}{w_1 - w_2}$, all of the quantities in this expression being now known. By making the differences between w_1 and w_2 small, the acceleration a may be made as small as we please. The smaller it is the easier it is to observe. In this consists the advantage of using two weights instead of a single weight falling freely to determine g.

To find a we observe the distance s passed over in t sec. by means of a graduated scale placed vertically. Then, since $s = \frac{1}{2}at^2$, we have a at once.

For example, let $w_1 = 21$ oz., $w_2 = 20$ oz., and suppose that in 5 sec. the weight w has fallen 9.8 ft. Then

$a = \dfrac{19.6}{25} = 0.784$, and $g = \dfrac{20 + 21}{21 - 20} \times 0.784 = 32 +$ ft.

An apparatus constructed on this principle, but with certain mechanical contrivances for lessening friction and giving convenient means of measuring the heights fallen through, is known as *Atwood's machine*. It is to be found in most physical laboratories.]

7. A train of 100 tons is running at the rate of 45 miles

an hour: find what constant force is required to bring it to rest in (1) one minute, (2) one mile.

Ans. (1) 220,000 poundals ; (2) 165,000 poundals.

8. What pressure will a man weighing 150 pounds exert on the floor of an elevator descending with an acceleration of 4 ft. per sec. ? *Ans.* $131\frac{1}{4}$ pounds.

9. How is it that as an elevator comes to rest in its descent one feels as if he were being lifted up?

10. A man who is just strong enough to lift 150 lbs. can lift a barrel of flour of 200 lbs. from the floor of an elevator while going down with an acceleration of 8 ft. per sec.

11. The pull of the engine on a train whose weight is 100 tons is 1000 pounds. In what time will the train acquire a velocity of 45 m. an hour? *Ans.* 7 min. 42 sec.

12. An express engine weighing a lbs. starts from a depot with a train of n cars of b lbs. each, with an acceleration of c ft. per sec.: find (1) the pull the engine is exerting; (2) the pulls on the successive couplers from the engine to the rear of the train.

Ans. Pull on engine coupler $= bcn$ poundals.

57. *Falling Bodies.*—A case of special interest is when the acting force is the force of gravity. This force acts vertically downwards, and being constant, produces a constant acceleration g ($=32.2$ ft. or 981 cm.) vertically downwards. Hence if a particle has a velocity u, its motion is compounded of two motions,—one due to this velocity, and the other to the acceleration g. Suppose the velocity u to be vertical. Then the two motions are in the same vertical, and we have the case of *falling bodies*. The resultant velocity v, at the end of a time t, would be the sum of the original (or initial) velocity u and the velocity gt acquired under the force of gravity in this time, that is,

$$v = u \pm gt,$$

according as the initial velocity of projection u is vertically downwards or vertically upwards.

Also, as in Art. 13, we have
$$s = ut \pm \tfrac{1}{2}gt^2$$
for the distance fallen or height acquired in the time t.

By eliminating t we have a direct relation between v, g, u, s,
$$v^2 = u^2 \pm 2gs,$$
which is often convenient.

If the body falls from rest, there is no initial velocity, and
$$v = gt, \qquad s = \tfrac{1}{2}gt^2, \qquad v^2 = 2gs.$$

This naturally follows from the statement in Art. 36, that the acceleration contributed by the force of gravitation is independent of the mass of the body.* Hence the whole question is one of kinematics.

It is of course understood that the action of the atmosphere is not taken into account. The motion is conceived to take place in a vacuum.

58. The general equation of motion for a falling body would be
$$d^2s/dt^2 = -g,$$
which may be developed as in Art. 14, and the results found above will be obtained.

Ex. 1. A body is projected vertically upwards with a velocity of 161 ft. per sec.: find (1) when it will come to rest; (2) the height to which it will rise.

[(1) When it comes to rest $v = 0$; $\therefore$ substitute $v = 0$, $u = 161$, $g = 32.2$ in $v = u - gt$ and $t = 5$ sec.; (2) substitute $t = 5$, $u = 161$, in $s = ut - \tfrac{1}{2}gt^2$ and $s = 402.5$ ft. Or substitute $v = 0$, $u = 161$ in $v^2 = u^2 - 2gs$ and $s = 402.5$ ft.]

---

* Galileo (1564–1642) was the first who appealed to experiment in all physical inquiries. Until his time it was taught that the velocities of falling bodies are proportional to their weights. He argued that if this were true two crown pieces must fall faster when sticking together than when unconnected, *which is contrary to experience.*

2. In Ex. 1, find the velocity when the body is at a height of 257.6 ft.

Ans. $v = \pm 96.6$ ft. per sec.; the plus sign indicating the velocity of ascent, and the minus sign the velocity of descent, each at 257.6 ft. from the point of projection.

3. A body is projected vertically upwards with a velocity of 161 ft. per. sec.; find at what times it is 257.6 ft. above the starting point. Explain both answers.

4. In Ex. 3, find the total time of flight.

5. Find the distance passed over by a body falling freely during the sixth second of its fall. *Ans.* 176 ft.

6. It is required to project a body vertically to a height of 36 ft.; find the velocity of projection. *Ans.* 48 ft. per sec.

7. A stone thrown vertically upwards is observed to be at a height of 96 ft. in 2 sec.; how much higher will it rise?
Ans. 4 ft.

8. Two bodies are dropped from a height at an interval of 2 sec.; find the distance between them at the end of the next 2 sec. *Ans.* 192 ft.

9. A falling body describes s ft. in the nth sec. of its fall; show that the initial velocity is $s - g(n - 0.5)$ ft. per sec.

10. If s_1, s_2, s_3 are the distances described by a falling body in t_1, t_2, t_3 seconds, prove that

$$s_1(t_2 - t_3) + s_2(t_3 - t_1) + s_3(t_1 - t_2) = 0.$$

59. *Projectiles.* If a particle is projected from a given point in a given direction, and is acted on by the force of gravity only, it is called a projectile. If the direction of projection is vertical, the initial velocity and the acceleration due to gravity are in the same direction and the path is a straight line. This case has already been considered under falling bodies.

But if the direction of projection is not vertical, the path is a curve which must be in the vertical plane containing the direction of projection, there being no force to cause it to move out of this plane. This case we proceed to discuss.

Let the velocity of projection u make an angle θ with the horizontal line OX. Resolve u into vertical and horizontal components, that is, into $u \cos \theta$ along OX and $u \sin \theta$ along OY. The total vertical velocity v_1, at the end of a

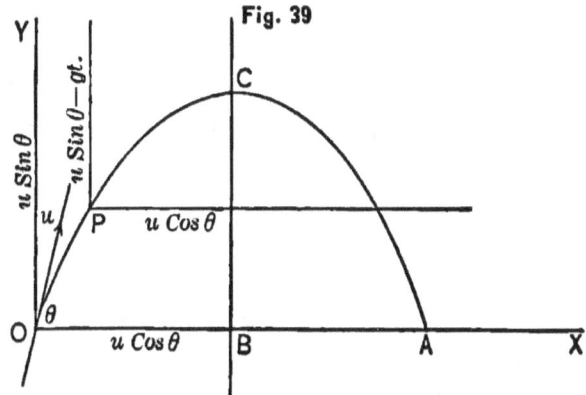

Fig. 39

time t when the particle has reached a point P, say, is (Art. 57)

$$v_1 = u \sin \theta - gt, \quad \ldots \ldots (1)$$

and the distance $PQ (= y)$ passed over in a vertical direction is

$$y = tu \sin \theta - \tfrac{1}{2} gt^2. \quad \ldots \ldots (2)$$

The horizontal velocity v_2 is, since gravity has no effect on the horizontal motion,

$$v_2 = u \cos \theta, \quad \ldots \ldots (3)$$

and the distance $OQ (= x)$ passed over at the end of the time t is

$$x = tu \cos \theta. \quad \ldots \ldots (4)$$

From these four equations the motion is determined.

To find the *path* of the particle. By ascribing to t different values and computing the values of x and y the positions of as many points in the path can be found as desired. Or by eliminating t between equations (2) and (4) we find a relation between the co-ordinates x, y which holds for all values of t and is therefore the equation of the path. This gives

$$y = x \tan \theta - gx^2/2u^2 \cos^2 \theta,$$

which represents a parabola.*

To find the *time of flight*, that is, the time in which the particle will reach the line OX. When this happens $y = 0$, and

$$\therefore 0 = tu \sin \theta - \tfrac{1}{2} gt^2,$$

whence $\quad\quad t = 0, \; t = 2u \sin \theta/g;$

which shows that the particle is twice on the line OX, once at O, the beginning of the motion, when $t = 0$, and again at A, the end of the motion, when $t = 2u \sin \theta/g$. The latter, being the time from the beginning to the end of the motion, is the time of flight.

The horizontal distance OA, or the *range*, is the value of x at the end of the time of flight. Hence

$$\text{range } OA = u \cos \theta \times 2u \sin \theta/g = u^2 \sin 2\theta/g.$$

The greatest value $\sin 2\theta$ can have is unity, and this occurs when $2\theta = 90°$ or $\theta = 45°$. Hence the horizontal range is greatest when the angle of projection is $45°$. This result is not true in practice, as we have not taken into account the resistance of the air. Experiment gives an angle of about $34°$ instead of $45°$.

To find the *greatest height* consider that at the highest point the vertical velocity is *nil*. For, if not, the particle could rise higher. This gives the relation

$$0 = u \sin \theta - gt$$

and

$$t = u \sin \theta/g,$$

---

* This is the *great* discovery of Galileo. No attempt had been made up to his time to explain curvilinear motion of any kind.

FREE MOTION. 65

showing that the greatest height is reached in half the time of flight. Substitute in the value of y which gives the height at *any* time this value of t, and

greatest height $BC = u^2 \sin^2 \theta / 2g$.

Also, $OB = u \cos \theta \times u \sin \theta / g = u^2 \sin 2\theta / 2g$,

which is half the range.

The resultant velocity v at any point P on the path is

$$v = \sqrt{v_1^2 + v_2^2}$$
$$= \sqrt{u^2 - 2ugt \sin \theta + g^2 t^2}.$$

It will be noticed that, as in the case of a falling body, all results are independent of the mass of the body. Hence they are true whether the mass projected is large or small, and the problem may be considered as kinematical.

60. The differential equations of motion in the case of a projectile are

$$d^2x/dt^2 = 0, \qquad d^2y/dt^2 = -g,$$

x, y being the coördinates of the particle in its path at the end of a time t. Integrating between the limits 0 and t, remembering that $v \cos \theta$ is the initial velocity along the axis of X, and $v \sin \theta$ that along the axis of Y we have

$$dx/dt = v \cos \theta, \qquad dy/dt = v \sin \theta - gt.$$

Integrating a second time,

$$x = tv \cos \theta, \qquad y = tv \sin \theta - \tfrac{1}{2} gt^2,$$

the results already found.

Ex. 1. If the velocity and acceleration take place in the same straight line, what is the equation of the path?

2. A balloon floating in a horizontal current of air with

a uniform velocity of 45 miles per hour suddenly collapses and descends with an acceleration of 32 ft. per sec.; trace its path.

3. A ball is thrown horizontally from a height of 10 meters with a velocity of 20 meters per sec.: find when it strikes the ground; the range; the final velocity; and the inclination of the direction of motion at the point of striking the ground.

4. Prove that the range for an elevation of 30° is the same as for an elevation of 60°, and for an elevation of $45° + \theta$ the same as for $45° - \theta$.

5. Compare the greatest elevations in the two cases.

6. Prove that the height of the vertex in feet is nearly 4 times the square of the time of flight in seconds.

7. A body is projected horizontally from a given height h with a velocity u; prove that the equation to the path is

$$2u^2 y = gx^2.$$

Show that the range is equal to $u\sqrt{h}/4$ nearly.

8. A ball is fired at an angle of 45° so as just to pass over a wall 10 ft. high at a distance of 100 yards. How far from the wall will it strike the ground? *Ans.* 10.34 ft.

9. "Swift of foot was Hiawatha:
   He could shoot an arrow from him
   And run forward with such fleetness
   That the arrow fell behind him!
   Strong of arm was Hiawatha:
   He could shoot ten arrows upward,
   Shoot them with such strength and swiftness
   That the tenth had left the bowstring
   Ere the first to earth had fallen."

If one second elapsed between the discharge of each of the arrows and Hiawatha shot at his greatest range, prove that he must have been able to run at the rate of 99 miles an hour.

10. Show that for parabolic motion the hodograph is a straight line.

61. *Central Forces.*—If the acting force F is constantly directed towards a fixed point or centre it is said to be central.

FREE MOTION.

The most important case is that of attractive forces in which the law of attraction is that of the inverse square of the distance r of the particle from the centre, or $F = C/r^2$ where C is a constant.

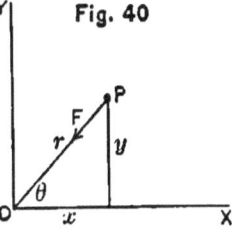
Fig. 40

Let O be the centre; OX, OY the axes of coördinates; and x, y the coördinates of the particle P at a time t. Let $OP = r$, m the mass of the particle, and the angle $POX = \theta$.

The general equations of motion are

$$\frac{d^2x}{dt^2} = -\frac{F}{m}\cos\theta, \qquad \frac{d^2y}{dt^2} = -\frac{F}{m}\sin\theta,$$

or

$$\frac{d^2x}{dt^2} = -\frac{cx}{r^3}, \quad \ldots (1) \qquad \frac{d^2y}{dt^2} = -\frac{cy}{r^3}, \quad \ldots (2)$$

if we place $F/m = C/r^2 m = c/r^2$ where $c = C/m$.

The relation between x and y will give the equation to the path of the particle. To find it:

Multiply the first equation by y, the second by x, and subtract.

$$\therefore x\frac{d^2y}{dt^2} - y\frac{d^2x}{dt^2} = 0;$$

and by integration

$$x\frac{dy}{dt} - y\frac{dx}{dt} = k, \text{ a constant.}$$

Also, since $x = r\cos\theta$, $y = r\sin\theta$,

$$x\frac{dy}{dt} - y\frac{dx}{dt} = r^2\frac{d\theta}{dt}. \qquad \ldots \ldots (3)$$

Hence, eliminating r^2,

$$\frac{d^2x}{dt^2} = -\frac{c}{k}\cos\theta\,\frac{d\theta}{dt}, \qquad \frac{d^2y}{dt^2} = -\frac{c}{k}\sin\theta\,\frac{d\theta}{dt};$$

and by integration

$$\frac{dx}{dt} - c_1 = -\frac{c}{k}\sin\theta, \qquad \frac{dy}{dt} - c_2 = \frac{c}{k}\cos\theta$$

$$= -cy/kr, \quad (4) \qquad\qquad = cx/kr, \quad (5)$$

when c_1, c_2 are constants.

Multiply the fourth equation by y, the fifth by x, and subtract, and we have

$$k + c_1 y - c_2 x = cr/k = c\sqrt{x^2 + y^2}/k,$$

the equation to a conic section with the origin at the focus.

Hence the path described by a particle under the action of a central force varying inversely as the square of the distance is a conic section, whose focus is the centre of force.

This is the case of planetary motion, the sun being at the centre of force.

The further discussion of this problem will be found in works on mathematical astronomy.*

62. Constrained Motion.—To a particle acted on by a force F in an assigned direction a certain path results. If the path differs from this, it must be owing to some cause which changes the motion, that is, to the action of another force. Hence if the path is prescribed we may, by adding forces which with the original force will give a resultant which can produce this path, consider the motion free. The discussion will therefore come under the principles already laid down.

---

* The development of this subject is due to Sir Isaac Newton.

63. *Motion on a Horizontal Plane.*—Resolve every given force F into its two components $F\cos\theta$ along the plane AB and $F\sin\theta$ at right angles to it, θ being the inclination of F to the plane. To each of these forces an

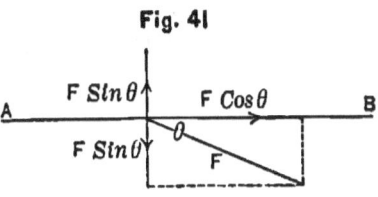

Fig. 41

acceleration is due. But the particle is constrained so as not to move in the direction of the force $F\sin\theta$. This can be brought about by assuming that the plane exerts an equal force $F\sin\theta$ in the opposite direction.

As regards the horizontal stress between the particle and the plane, we can say nothing *à priori*. Experiment shows that it depends on the nature of the surfaces in contact. We shall for the present assume that the stress between the particle and the plane is normal only, or, as it is often expressed, that the plane is *smooth*.

If therefore a particle slides on a smooth plane under the action of a force F inclined at an angle θ, the reaction of the plane is $F\sin\theta$ and the force acting along the plane is $F\cos\theta$, which latter being that to which the motion is due, is the effective force.

64. *Motion on an Inclined Plane.*—Suppose a particle of

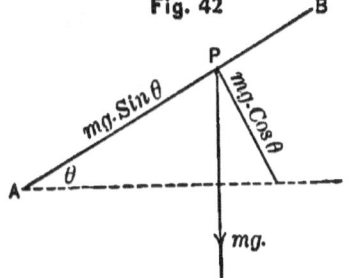

Fig. 42

mass m lbs. on an inclined plane, and acted on by gravity only. The force acting is mg poundals vertically downward.

Resolve mg into components $mg\sin\theta$ along the plane, and $mg\cos\theta$ at right angles to it. The reaction of the plane is $mg\cos\theta$, and the effective force along the plane is $mg\sin\theta$. The acceleration along the plane is therefore $mg\sin\theta/m = g\sin\theta$.

If the initial velocity is in the direction of the acceleration along the plane, the path is a straight line. If u denote the velocity at B, the velocity v attained on reaching A at the foot of the plane is given by

$$v^2 = u^2 + 2g \sin \theta \times AB$$
$$= u^2 + 2gh,$$

when h is the height of the plane. Hence the final velocity is independent of the inclination of the plane.

If the initial velocity is not in the direction of the acceleration along the plane, the path is a parabola, whose equation may be found from Art. 59 by substituting $g \sin \theta$ for g.

65. The above results may also be deduced from the general equation of motion of a particle on an inclined plane,

$$d^2s/dt^2 = -g \sin \theta,$$

where θ is the inclination of the plane to the horizontal, and s the distance of the particle P from the point O at the time t. The solution is similar to that of Art. 14.

Ex. 1. A body starts from rest and falls down a plane of height h: prove that the velocity acquired is $\sqrt{2gh}$ and the distance passed over in t sec. is $\frac{1}{2}gt^2 \sin \theta$.

2. Prove that the velocity of a particle on reaching A (Fig. 42) from B by moving on the plane is equal to that acquired by falling freely through the height h of the plane. If t_1, t_2 are the times required to attain these velocities, prove $t_2 = t_1 \sin \theta$.

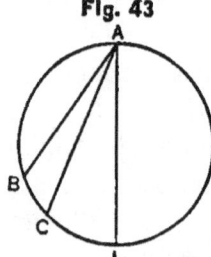

Fig. 43

3. Prove that the times of descent of a particle starting from the extremity A of a vertical diameter AL is the same along all chords $AB, AC, \ldots$ of the circle.

Hence find the line of quickest descent from a given point to a given straight line.

4. Find the line of quickest descent from a given point to a given vertical circle.

66. In the case of a particle of mass m sliding down a plane from rest, the motion along the plane is uniformly accelerated, the moving force being $mg \sin \theta$. For *equilibrium* a force must be applied such that the resultant force along the plane is *nil*. Hence if a force F be applied *parallel to the plane*, it will hold the particle in equilibrium if

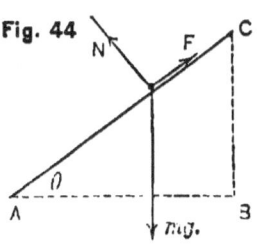

Fig. 44

$F = mg \sin \theta$ or $F : mg = BC : AC =$ height : length.*

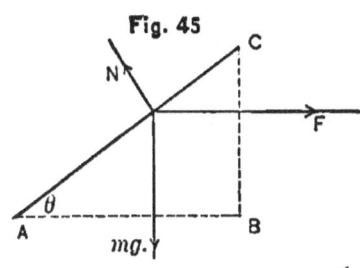

Fig. 45

If the force F be applied *parallel to the base*, the condition of equilibrium would be

$F \cos \theta = mg \sin \theta$,

or $F : mg = BC : AB$

= height : base.

The normal pressure in the first case would be

$N = mg \cos \theta$,

and in the second

$N = mg \cos \theta + F \sin \theta = mg \sec \theta$.

Ex. 1. Show that the values of F and N are the same if the particle moves uniformly upward or downward, or is at rest.

2. Show that the force F is most efficient when acting parallel to the plane.

3. A weight of m lbs. is placed on a smooth inclined plane, and is acted on by a horizontal force of mp poundals : find the acceleration.   *Ans.* $a = (g \sin \theta \pm p \cos \theta)$.

4. On an inclined plane a horizontal force P supports a

---

* This is of special interest, as being the problem of oblique forces first solved. The solution is due to Simon Stevinus of Bruges, Belgium (1548-1620). It may be found in *Whewell*, Mechanics, p. 44.

weight W, and a force Q parallel to the plane will also support W; prove
$$P^{-2} - Q^{-2} = W^{-2}.$$

5. On an inclined plane a force P acting parallel to the plane can support a weight W_1, and acting horizontally a weight W_2; prove
$$W_1^2 - W_2^2 = P^2.$$

67. *Motion in a Circle.*—Suppose a particle of mass m to move with constant velocity in the circumference of a circle of radius r. As in Art. 23, draw the hodograph of the particle, and let this be the circle abc with centre O (Fig. 16). The velocity at a is perpendicular to Oa which is parallel OA and equal in value to a constant quantity a. But the velocity at any point of the hodograph is equal to the acceleration at the corresponding point of the original path. Hence the acceleration in the path ABC is always directed to the centre O of the path; in other words, the particle as it moves in its circular path is acted on by a constant force F directed to the centre of the circle, and therefore with its direction always perpendicular to the direction of motion.

To find the magnitude of this force. Let t be the time in which the circle ABC is described, then $tv = 2\pi r$. Also, since the circle abc is described in the same time, $ta = 2\pi v$. Hence by eliminating t
$$a = v^2/r$$
and $$F = ma = mv^2/r.$$

To this force F acting constantly towards the centre of the circle as the particle moves uniformly in the circumference the name of **Centripetal Force** is given. The velocity being constant, the acceleration contributed by the centripetal force is completely spent in changing the direction of motion from point to point.

It may be illustrated by supposing a particle attached by a string to an axis through O and made to revolve about this axis with uniform velocity in a region from which the effect of gravity is conceived to be eliminated. The circular motion is thus due to the initial velocity v and to the pull of the string, and to these alone.

Suppose that the string is cut when the particle reaches A. Since there is no force now acting, the particle will move in the straight line AA_1 tangent to the circle at A and with velocity v. This follows from the law of inertia. The constant pull of the string therefore acts only in changing the motion from uniform rectilinear to uniform circular motion.

Suppose next the string removed and the constant pull replaced by a force F. This force must act towards the centre O, must act constantly, must continually change its direction as the particle changes place, and must produce a constant acceleration a, which, combining with the constant velocity v along the tangent, changes at every moment the direction of the velocity v without changing its magnitude.

Consider further. The pull in the string is a stress, the action *on* the particle towards the centre and the reaction *of* the particle from the centre. The two are equal. The first is the centripetal force, and to the other the name **Centrifugal Force*** is given. The centripetal force being the force required for producing the change of direction, the centrifugal force is therefore really the inertia-resistance of the particle.

68. The centrifugal force may be expressed in terms of the number of revolutions made in a given time. Thus if n is the number of revolutions per second, then $v = 2\pi r n$ and
$$F = m \times 4\pi^2 r^2 n^2 / r$$
$$= 39.48 \, mrn^2 \text{ poundals.}$$

---

* Term introduced by Huygens (1629-1695).

If n is the number of revolutions per minute, and we call the weight of the body w lbs., this reduces to

$$F = 0.00034\ wrn^2 \text{ pounds,}$$

the rule used in practice.

69. A very remarkable application of the idea of centripetal force was made by Newton to test the truth of the law that the acceleration of gravity varies inversely as the square of the distance from the earth's centre. Observation shows that the moon revolves round the earth in an orbit nearly circular and with uniform velocity. If $v=$ velocity of moon, $R=$ radius of orbit, then the acceleration of the moon directed to the centre of the earth is v^2/R. If this acceleration is due to gravity, we have

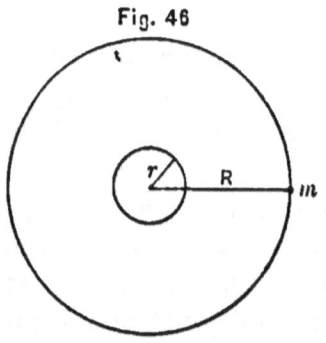

Fig. 46

$$g' = v^2/R$$

when g' is the value of g at the distance R from the earth's centre. Also, if the acceleration of gravity varies inversely as the square of the distance from the earth's centre,

$$g'/g = r^2/R^2$$

when r is the earth's radius.

Hence, eliminating g', we have, as the condition to be satisfied if the hypothesis is true,

$$v^2 R = r^2 g.$$

Now from measurement, $R = 240,000$ miles, $r = 4000$ miles, $g = 32$ ft., time of revolution of moon $= 27$ days 8 hours $= 2,360,000$ seconds nearly, whence $v = 3375$ ft. per sec. Substituting these values, the expression will be found to check.

CONSTRAINED MOTION. 75

Also, we may find the difference between the true and the apparent weight of a body at the equator as affected by centrifugal force. For the true weight being the pull of the earth if at rest differs from the apparent weight or actual pull of the earth by the centrifugal force. Hence if m is the mass of the body,

$$mg - mg_1 = mv^2/r$$

when g_1 is the actual acceleration due to gravity. If, for example, $m = 1$ lb., a simple reduction will show that the centrifugal force will amount to 24 grains, giving the difference of weight.

Also, we have

$$vt = 2\pi r$$

when $t = 24$ hours and $r = 4000$ miles. Hence

$$g - g_1 = 0.111 \text{ ft.},$$

or the acceleration of a particle falling freely at the equator is 1/9 ft. less than it would be if the earth did not revolve on its axis.

The actual acceleration of gravity at the equator is *observed* to be 32.09 ft. per sec. Hence if the earth did not revolve on its axis the acceleration of gravity there would be $32.09 + 0.11 = 32.20$ ft. per sec.

Ex. 1. Why cannot the centripetal force increase the velocity of the moving particle? [∵ always perpendicular to the direction of motion.]

2. Explain how it is that although the particle constantly *gains* velocity along the radius it never *possesses* any such velocity.

3. A stone of 1¾ lbs. is whirled 90 times a minute at the end of a string 3½ ft. long: find the tension of the string.
    Ans. 544 poundals, or 17 pounds nearly.

4. The distance of the moon from the earth is 240,000 miles and she revolves round the earth once in 27 days 8 hours. Find the acceleration relative to the earth.

5. Find the velocity of projection in order that a bullet

shot horizontally may travel round the earth continually. [From $v^2/r = g$, $v = 5$ miles per second nearly.]

6. Show that the centrifugal pressure on the rails by a locomotive of w lbs. moving at the rate of v miles per hour in a curve of r feet radius is $0.0669\ wv^2/r$ pounds.

6a. The driving-wheels of a locomotive are 5 ft. in diameter and the cylinders 2 ft. stroke. If the velocity is 50 miles an hour, find the centrifugal force developed by the counterweight, supposing it to weigh 300 lbs. and that the distance of its centre of gravity from the center of the axle is 20 in. *Ans.* 13,328 pounds.

8. Show that in lat. 60° the normal component of the centrifugal force of the earth's rotation is one fourth of what it is at the equator.

9. Show that the centrifugal force at the equator is $1/289$ of what the force of gravity would be if the earth did not revolve on its axis.

10. Show that if the earth were to revolve on its axis 17 times faster than it does, all bodies at the equator would be without weight.

11. Show that " a body weighing 1 lb. avoir. on a spring-balance at the earth's equator would weigh only 2.6534 ounces upon the same spring-balance at the moon's equator."

70. *Simple Harmonic Motion.*—Suppose that while the particle P moves in a circle of radius r with uniform velocity v, another particle M moves along the diameter AB in such a way that PM is always perpendicular to AB. Both P and M must start from the same point A, both will reach B at the same time, and while P makes a complete revolution, M will move from A to B and back again. The motion of M is called simple harmonic motion*

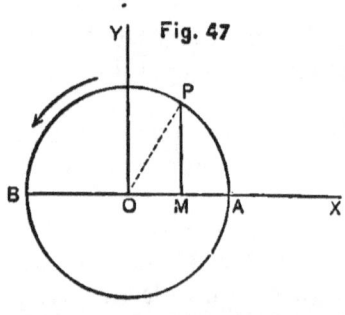

Fig. 47

---

* " Physically, the interest of such motions consists in the fact of their being approximately those of the simplest vibrations of sound-

(S. H. M.). The time of oscillating from A to B and back again, being the same as that required for passing once round the circumference in the corresponding circular motion, is $2\pi r/v$, and is called the **Period** of the S. H. M.

The velocity of M being equal to the component of the velocity of P in the direction AB, is $v \sin POA$. The acceleration of M is the component of the acceleration of P in the direction AB. But the acceleration of P is along PO, and is equal to v^2/r. Hence the acceleration of $M = \dfrac{v^2}{r} \cos POA = \dfrac{v^2}{r^2} \times OM$, and therefore $v^2/r^2 =$ acceleration of M/OM. The distance OM of the particle M from the centre is called the **Displacement**.

We may therefore write
$$\text{period } T = 2\pi r/v$$
$$= 2\pi \sqrt{\text{displacement/acceleration}}.$$

71. This may e proved otherwise. Let the particle start from A, and let P be its position in the circular path at the end of a time t. The angle POA expressed in circular measure is $2\pi t/T = \omega t$, where ω is the circular measure of the angle described in one second. Hence
$$x = OM = OP \cos POA = r \cos \omega t.$$
Also $\quad v = dx/dt = -\omega r \sin \omega t,$
and $\quad a = d^2x/dt^2 = -\omega^2 r \cos \omega t = -\omega^2 x,$
or the acceleration along OX varies as the displacement x, the result found above.

72. The distance OA or OB of the extreme position of the particle from the mean position O is called the **Amplitude** of the S. H. M., and the fraction of the period which has elapsed since the particle M left its initial position A is called the **Phase** of M at the time t.

---

ing bodies, such as a tuning-fork or pianoforte wire,—whence their name,—and of the various media in which waves of sound, heat, light, etc., are propagated."—*Tait*.

Ex. 1. The motion of the piston of a steam-engine is the more nearly harmonic the greater the ratio of the connecting-rod to the crank axis. (See Fig. 119.)

2. Combine two S. H. M.'s of equal period and which take place in the same straight line.

Ans. Amplitude $= (r + r') \cos \omega t$, a S. H. M.

3. Combine two S. H. M.'s in directions at right angles to each other if the periods are the same.

[Take them parallel to the axes of X, Y: then

$$x = r \cos \omega t, \qquad y = r' \cos \omega t.$$

Eliminate t and the locus results. It is $x/r - y/r' = 0$, a straight line.]

4. From P (Fig. 47) let fall PN perpendicular to OY. Show that N has a S. H. M. differing $\tfrac{1}{4}$ in phase from M but of the same amplitude and period.

[For $ON = r \sin \omega t = r \cos (\omega t - \pi/2)$.]

5. Show that a uniform circular motion is equivalent to two simultaneous S. H. M.'s of equal amplitude and period but differing $\tfrac{1}{4}$ in phase.

6. Combine two S. H. M.'s in directions at right angles to each other if the periods are as 1 to 2. *Ans.* A parabola.

These loci and others more complex may be traced out mechanically by Blackburn's pendulum, an instrument to be found in most physical laboratories.

73. Simple Pendulum. Consider the motion of a particle of mass m suspended from a point C by a string of length l, the force of gravity being the acting force. The arrangement is known as a simple pendulum.

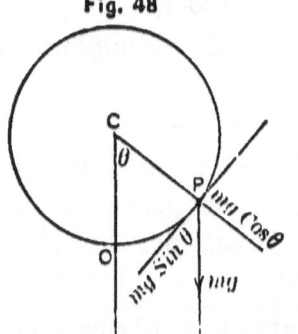

Fig. 48

Let P be the position of the particle at any time. Denote the angle between CP and the vertical CO by θ. The acting force mg may be resolved into $mg \sin \theta$ along the tangent at P and $mg \cos \theta$ at right angles to it.

The motion is due to the tangential component only as the other being equal to the pull of the string cannot affect it.

CONSTRAINED MOTION. 79

Now accel. along tang. $= mg \sin \theta / m$

$\qquad = g\theta$, if θ is small

$\qquad = OP \times g/l$;

or, the acceleration is proportional to the displacement OP, and therefore the motion in the small arc OP is a S. H. M. The time t of an oscillation being one-half the period, we have

$$t = \pi \sqrt{\text{displac.}/\text{accel.}}$$
$$= \pi \sqrt{l/g},$$

a result independent of the length of the arc. Hence in all small arcs the times of oscillation are the same, and the vibrations of a pendulum are therefore said to be *isochronous*.

74. We may now find the length l of a pendulum beating seconds at any place. For take a pendulum of length l, and count the number of oscillations n, in a day. The number of seconds in this time is 86,400. But if $t, t,$ are the times of oscillation of the two pendulums, we have

$$86,400/n_{,} = t_{,}/t = \sqrt{l_{,}/l},$$

and therefore l is found.

We have now at once the means of computing the value of g at the place in question.* Thus

$$g = \pi^2 l.$$

Another method of finding g is given in Ex. 6, Art. 55. The pendulum method is the more accurate. See also Art. 156.

---

* In measuring the accelerating force of gravity Galileo was led to the invention of the pendulum as a means of measuring small portions of time. He found $g = 31$ ft. The true value was first found by Huygens—who also gave us the pendulum clock.

75. If a pendulum of length l makes n oscillations in a given time τ at a place where the acceleration of gravity is g, then
$$\tau/n = t = \pi \sqrt{l/g}.$$
Suppose (1) the length of the pendulum slightly changed by an amount λ. By differentiation
$$-\tau\, dn/n^2 = \frac{\pi}{2} \sqrt{1/gl}\, dl$$
and
$$-dn = n\, dl/2l = n\lambda/2l,$$
giving the *loss* in the number of oscillations.

Suppose (2) the pendulum carried to a place where g is different by an amount γ, the length remaining the same; then
$$\tau\, dn/n^2 = \frac{\pi}{2} \sqrt{l/g^3}\, dg$$
and
$$dn = n\, dg/2g = n\gamma/2g,$$
giving the *gain* in the number of oscillations.

Suppose (3) the pendulum carried to a height h above the earth's surface; then, since g varies as $1/r^2$, r being the earth's radius, we have
$$\tau/n = cr\sqrt{l}, \qquad \text{where } c \text{ is a constant.}$$
Hence
$$-\tau\, dn/n^2 = c\sqrt{l}\, dr,$$
$$-dn = n\, dr/r = nh/r,$$
giving the *loss* in the number of oscillations.

Similarly if carried to a depth h below the surface the *gain* in the number of oscillations would be nh/r.

Ex. 1. If a pendulum, length l, vibrates n times in s seconds, prove
$$l\pi^2 n^2 = g s^2.$$

2. Find the number of oscillations made by a pendulum a yard long in one minute. *Ans.* 62.57.

CONSTRAINED MOTION. 81

3. A particle attached to a fine wire vibrates 60 times in 3 minutes: find the length of the wire.   *Ans.* 29.36 ft.

4. A seconds pendulum makes 10 oscillations more in 24 hours at the foot of a mountain than at the top: find the height h of the mountain.   *Ans.* ½ mile nearly.

5. A pendulum which beats seconds at the surface when carried to the bottom of a mine gains 5 beats in 24 hours: find the depth of the mine.

6. At New York the value of g is 32.16 ft.: find the length of the seconds pendulum there.   *Ans.* 39.1 in.

7. A clock gains 30 m. per week: how much should the pendulum be shortened for correct time.
   Ans. 0.006 of its length.

8. A clock keeps correct time at a place where g is 32.24 ft.: show that it will gain 3 m. 20 sec. per day at a place where g is 32.09 ft.

76. The problem of the pendulum is a special case of the motion of a particle constrained to move on a smooth vertical circle under the action of gravity.

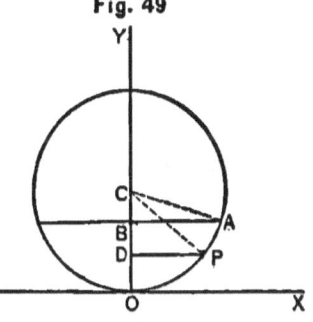

Fig. 49

Take the origin at O, the lowest point of the circle; OX horizontal, OY vertical, and let x, y denote the co-ordinates of P any position of the particle. Let A be its initial position, $AP = s$, and $OCP = \theta$, $OCA = \beta$, both expressed in circular measure. Draw AB, PD parallel to OX.

Then for an indefinitely small distance ds, the path may be regarded as a straight line and the general equation of motion is

$$d^2s/dt^2 = -g \sin \theta.$$

Integrating, we find

$$v^2 = (ds/dt)^2 = 2gr (\cos \theta - \cos \beta) = 2g \times BD,$$

or the velocity at any point P is the same as that acquired in falling through the height BD, that is in falling from the horizontal line AB.*

To find the time of motion from A to P. We have $ds = rd\theta$, and therefore, from the preceding equation,

$$(d\theta/dt)^2 = 2g(\cos\theta - \cos\beta)/r,$$

and $$t\sqrt{2g/r} = -\int_\beta^\theta d\theta/\sqrt{\cos\theta - \cos\beta},$$

the $-$ sign being taken because θ decreases as t increases. This equation cannot be integrated by the ordinary methods. If, however, β is so small that powers above the second may be neglected, we have $\cos\theta - \cos\beta = (\beta^2 - \theta^2)/2$, and

$$t\sqrt{g/r} = -\int_\beta^\theta d\theta/\sqrt{\beta^2 - \theta^2} = \cos^{-1}(\theta/\beta),$$

which gives the value of t.

If $\theta = 0$, we get the time of reaching the lowest point to be $\dfrac{\pi}{2}\sqrt{r/g}$, the result already found in Art. 71 for the pendulum.

The *pressure* N of the particle on the circle at P is due

---

* The following is Galileo's experimental proof of this principle. "In Fig. 50 let a string AC with a weight C appended be fastened to a point A in the vertical plane ACB, so that the weight may swing in the circular arc CBD. If the weight be let fall from D it will descend to B and rise again to C, the velocity at the lowest point B acquired by falling down DB exactly sufficing to carry it up to the horizontal line from which it fell. Now let a nail be fixed at E in the vertical line AB so that on the side of D the weight may be compelled to move in the circular arc GB of which the centre is E. Then G being in the horizontal line CD, let the weight fall from G and it will be found that it still rises exactly to C before its velocity is extinguished."—*Whewell*.

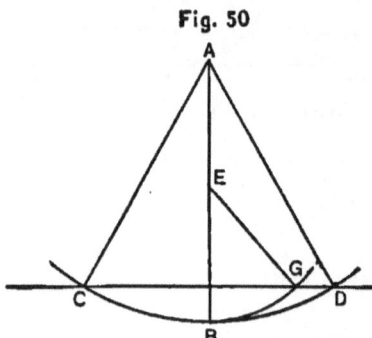

Fig. 50

both to the centrifugal force and to the weight of the particle. Hence if m is the mass of the particle,

$$N = mv^2/r + mg \cos \theta.$$

Ex. 1. Compare the times of a particle sliding down a small arc AO of a vertical circle to the time of sliding down the chord AO. *Ans.* $\pi : 4$.

2. A particle starts from the highest point of a smooth vertical circle and slides down the convex side under the action of gravity: find where it leaves the circle.
Ans. At a depth $=$ radius/3.

3. If particles start from the common highest point of a series of vertical circles down their convex sides, find the locus of the points of departure from the circles.
Ans. A straight line.

4. A mass m hanging at the end of a string of length l is projected with a velocity u so as to describe a vertical circle. Show that the tension of the string T and the velocity v at any point in the path whose vertical height is h are found from

$$u^2 = v^2 + 2gh;$$
$$Tl/m = u^2 + g(l - 3h).$$

Hence show that if $u^2 > 5gl$ the particle will perform complete revolutions; if $u^2 < 2gl$ it will oscillate in an arc less than a semi-circumference; and if $u^2 > 2gl$ and $< 5gl$ it will cease to describe a circle and the motion become parabolic.

77. *Centrifugal Pendulum*.— Suppose a particle of mass m suspended by a string from a point O and caused to swing about the vertical axis OA with a uniform velocity v in a circular path. Such an arrangement is called a *centrifugal pendulum*.

Let B be the position of the particle at any time. Denote the angle between OB and the vertical OA by θ.

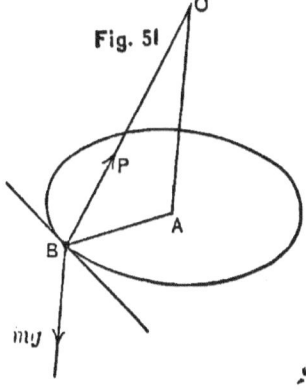

Fig. 51

The particle is acted on by two forces, the gravity force mg and the pull P in the string directed to the point O. Since the resultant motion is the same as in the case of a particle acted on by a centripetal force (directed to A), it follows that the resultant of the acting forces must be directed along the radius $BA\,(=r)$ and form a centripetal force. Hence, there being no resultant vertical force, we have
$$P\cos\theta - mg = 0;$$
$$\text{centrip. force} = P\sin\theta = mg\tan\theta;$$
and the acceleration a due to the centripetal force is thus $g\tan\theta$.

But since v is the velocity in the circular path,
$$a = v^2/r.$$
Eliminating a,
$$v^2 = rg\tan\theta,$$
or
$$hv^2 = gr^2,$$
if we put the height $OA = h$; which gives the relation between h, v, r.

The time T in which the particle makes a revolution, or the period, is given by
$$T = \text{circum. of path/velocity}$$
$$= 2\pi r/v$$
$$= 2\pi\sqrt{h/g}\ \text{seconds.}$$

Also, we may determine h so that the number of revolutions per second may be any desired number, n for example. Then
$$v = 2\pi r \times n.$$
But
$$v\sqrt{h} = r\sqrt{g}.$$
Whence eliminating v, and putting $g = 32.2$,
$$hn^2 = 0.815\ \text{feet,}$$
the relation required.

Ex. In going round a ring 100 ft. in diameter on a 50-in. bicycle a velocity of 10 ft. per sec. is attained. Find the distance of the highest point of the wheel from the vertical through the lowest point. *Ans.* 3 in. nearly.

78. The centrifugal pendulum may be used as a regulator of mechanical motion. An apparatus of this kind, known as the **Governor**, was applied by James Watt to the steam-engine.*

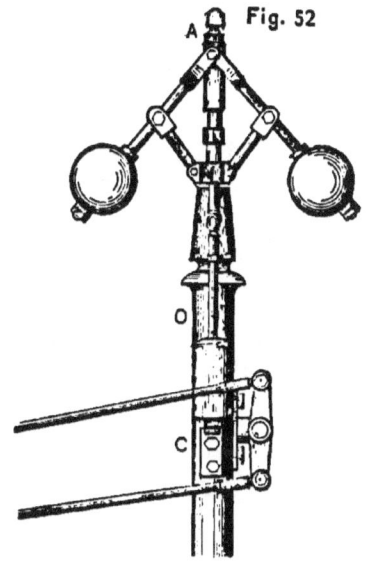

Fig. 52

In Fig. 52, which represents a Corliss-engine governor, as the speed of the engine increases the spindle, AO revolves more quickly, and the balls separate; as it diminishes, the balls come together. The slide O rises and falls accordingly, and by means of a set of levers C the steam-valves of the engine are acted on, and the supply of steam admitted to the cylinder regulated.

Ex. 1. Explain clearly the *pendulum motion* in the governor.

2. Does the Watt governor prevent increase of speed?

3. Find the length of a Watt governor that will run 60 revolutions per minute. *Ans.* 9.78 in.

---

* "If a pair of common fire-tongs suspended by a cord from the top be made to turn by the twisting or untwisting of the cord the legs will separate from each other with force proportioned to the speed of rotation. Mr. Watt adapted this fact most ingeniously to the regulation of the speed of his steam-engine."

CHAPTER IV.

STATICS OF A RIGID BODY.

79. Having studied the behavior of a particle under the action of forces, we proceed to study the behavior of a body of finite size, a body being regarded as a collection of particles.

The directions of the forces applied to a particle must necessarily all pass through the particle. In a body the directions need not all pass through one point. Besides, forces applied to a body may cause it to change its *shape* as well as to change its position. To exclude the former, we shall for the present assume that the body cannot be made to change its form or be distorted by the action of the forces applied. To such a body the name of **Rigid Body** is given. Though bodies differ more or less as regards rigidity, we are not acquainted with one perfectly rigid; so that a result deduced on the hypothesis of a body being perfectly rigid can only be regarded as an approximation to the actual state of the case in practice. The hypothesis is made only for convenience of study, as it is simpler to discuss the properties of bodies one at a time than to attempt to grasp all at one time.

As in particle motion, the first step will be to combine the acting forces, all of which are supposed to lie in the same plane.

80. Composition of Forces.—Suppose forces F_1, F_2, F_3, F_4 in one plane to act on a body at different points A, B, C, D. Each particle acts on the particle next it, and is acted on by it in return. These internal forces forming actions and reactions occur always in pairs, and being equal in magnitude and opposite in sense, are themselves in equilibrium.

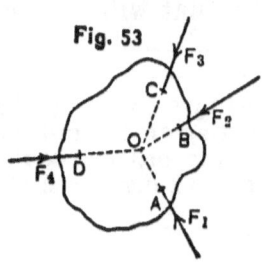

Fig. 53

COMPOSITION OF FORCES.   87

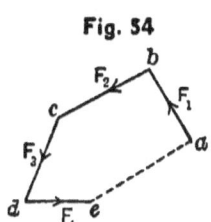
Fig. 54

Hence we need only consider the external forces F_1, F_2, F_3, F_4 so far as the motion of the body is concerned.

Prolong the directions of all the forces, and suppose these directions to meet in a common point O. All of the forces may be conceived to act at this point. The motion will consequently be the same as if the whole body were concentrated into a single particle at O and the resultant force R would be found graphically as in Art. 47 by plotting the polygon $abcde$, whose closing side ae would be this resultant in magnitude and direction; or by analysis, as in Art. 49, by resolving the forces along two axes through O in directions at right angles to each other, and making the sums of the components in each direction equal to zero.

81. If the directions of the forces do *not* all meet in a point, we can still find the resultant by repeated applications of the parallelogram of forces. For the resultant of F_1 at A and F_2 at B is the resultant R_1 of these forces acting at D; the resultant of R_1 at D and F_3 at C is the resultant R_2 of R_1 and F_3 at E. Hence R_2 is the resultant of F_1, F_2, F_3 acting at A, B, C respectively.

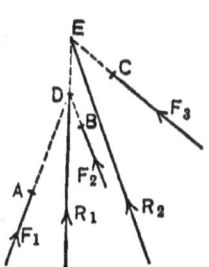
Fig. 55

This construction is often inconvenient. The following modification or rather combination of it and the preceding is more practical: Plot to scale the forces F_1, F_2, F_3 in order, the line ab representing F_1, bc representing F_2, and cd representing F_3. The line ad closing the polygon will on the same scale represent the resultant R of the forces in *magnitude* and *direction*. To prove this, join ac. Then ac is the resultant of ab, bc, and ad is the resultant of ac, cd, that is, of ab, bc, cd. Hence the resultant is determined in magnitude and direction.

To find its *position*, that is, some point in its line of action. At any point p in the line of action of F_1 apply any two equal forces R_1, R_2 in opposite directions. Let R_3 along qp be the resultant of F_1 and R_1; R_4 along rq of F_2 and R_3; and R_5 of F_3 and R_4. Hence the two forces R_2, R_5 are equiva-

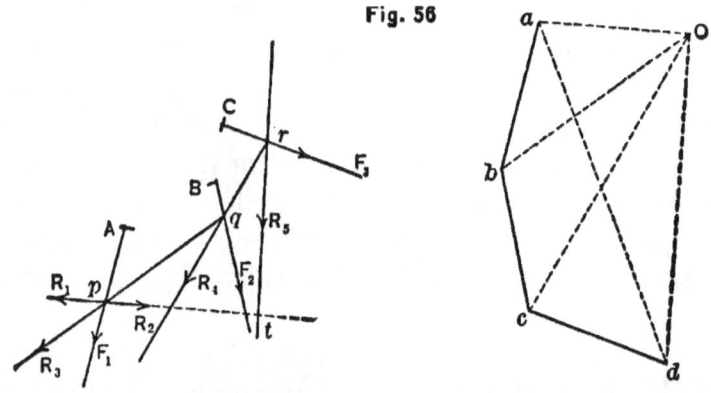

Fig. 56

lent to the three forces F_1, F_2, F_3. The resultant R of R_2, R_5 passes through the point t, in which their directions intersect. Hence if through t a line equal and parallel to ad be drawn, it will represent the resultant R of F_1, F_2, F_3 in magnitude, direction, and position.

Again, since ab represents the force F_1, if we draw aO, bO parallel to R_1, R_3, the sides of the triangle Oab will represent the forces R_1, F_1, R_3 acting at p. Similarly, the sides of the triangles Obc, Ocd will represent the forces at q, r. But R_1 is *any* force. Hence Oa is any line, and the position of the point O is arbitrary. The point O is called the **Pole**.

This gives us the key to the following rule for finding *graphically* the resultant of any number of forces acting in one plane on a rigid body. Construct a polygon $abcd$ to scale, whose sides are parallel to and in the same sense as the forces; the closing side will represent the resultant in magnitude and direction.

From any point O, draw lines Oa, Ob, Oc, Od to the angular points of the force polygon. From any point p in F_1 draw pq parallel to Ob to meet F_2 in q, and draw qr parallel to Oc. A line through t, the intersection of pt parallel to Oa, and rt parallel to Od, will give the resultant in position. Hence it is completely determined.

82. It is evident that a force equal and opposite to the resultant R would hold the forces F_1, F_2, F_3 in equilibrium. Hence forces in equilibrium in a plane may be represented by the sides of a closed polygon $abcd$, whose sides are parallel and in the same sense as the forces.

The converse of this, that if forces acting in a plane can be represented by the sides of a closed polygon which are parallel to and in the same sense as the forces, they are in equilibrium, is not true. For the polygon would be the same, no matter what the position of the forces may be. This condition, in fact, provides against translation only. An additional condition to provide against rotation is necessary. (See Art. 88.)

Ex. 1. Three forces P, Q, R are represented in direction by the sides of an equilateral triangle taken the same way round: show that their resultant is

$$\sqrt{(P^2 + Q^2 + R^2 - PQ - QR - RP)}.$$

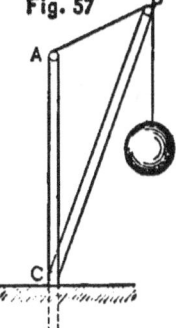

Fig. 57

2. If R is the resultant of two forces P and Q, and S the resultant of P and R, show that the resultant of Q and S is $2R$.

3. In a jib-crane a weight of 20 tons hangs at rest: find the pull P of the chain AB if $AC = 2AB$. Ans. $P = 10$ tons.

4. A square frame has a force 4 acting from A to B, 5 from B to C, 6 from A to D, and 7 from D to C: find the resultant in magnitude and position.

5. An interesting application of the triangle of forces is afforded by the suspension-bridge

with the roadway uniformly loaded. One half of the bridge is represented in the figure.

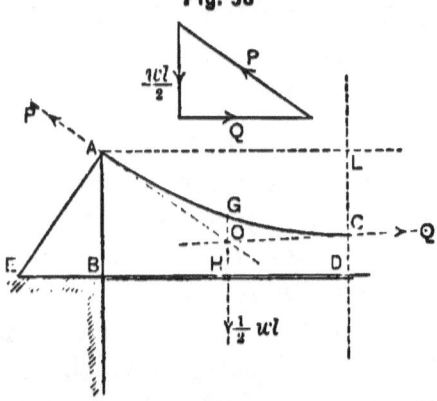

Fig. 58

[Let AB represent the pier, AC the suspension cable, BD the roadway, and AE the anchorage cable. The roadway is suspended by rods from the cable, and the weight on the cable may therefore be assumed to be uniform per foot length, and its direction GH to pass through H, the middle point of BD. If l is the span and w the weight per unit of length, the load acting at G is $wl/2$. The forces acting on AC are the weight $wl/2$ and the tensions PQ at its ends, which act along the tangents at those points. The tangent CO at C is horizontal, and the direction GOH of $wl/2$ is vertical. Hence AO is the direction of P.

If d is the deflection CL of the span, draw the triangle of forces, and show that $Q = wl^2/8d$.

What is the value of P?

Also prove that the curve of the chain AC is a parabola. (Take C as origin, CL, CO axes; then equation to curve will be found to be $4dx^2 = l^2y$, a parabola.)]

83. *Parallel Forces*.—The case of the forces being parallel is of special importance. Draw ab, bc to scale, to represent the parallel forces F_1, F_2: the line ca closing the polygon (in this case a straight line) will represent a force equal and opposite to the resultant. Hence

Fig. 59

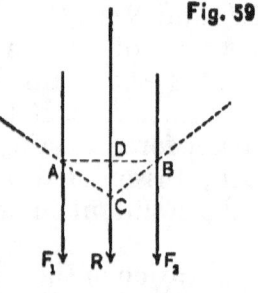
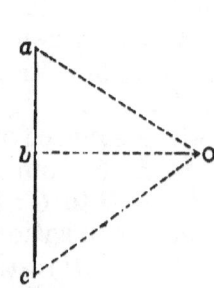

the *magnitude of* the resultant is equal to the sum of the forces.

COMPOSITION OF FORCES. 91

To find its *position*. Take any point O, and join Oa, Ob, Oc. Draw CA parallel to Oa, AB parallel Ob, BC parallel Oc. Then C, the intersection of AC and BC, is a point on the resultant. A line through C equal and parallel to ac, that is, parallel to F_1 or F_2, will therefore give the resultant in magnitude, direction, and position.

We may readily find an expression for the position of the point D, in which the resultant cuts AB. From similar triangles Oab, ACD; Ocb, BCD;

$$CD/AD = ab/Ob, \qquad CD/BD = cb/Ob.$$

Eliminate CD and Ob, and

$$BD/AD = ab/cb = F_1/F_2,$$

or

$$F_1 \times AD = F_2 \times BD;$$

which, since the whole distance AB is known, gives the position of D.

Illustration.—Make an apparatus as in Fig. 60, and find the point A of balancing of known weights by trial. Compute its position and compare results.

Compare W with the sum of the weights strung along the rod.

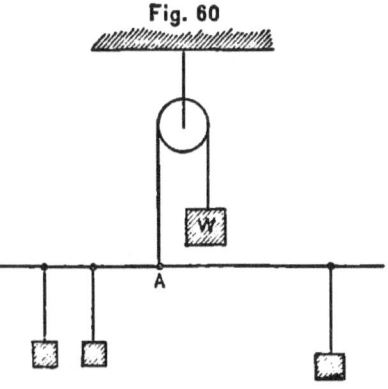
Fig. 60

1. Draw the figure corresponding to Fig. 59 when F_1, F_2 act in opposite directions. Show that $R = F_1 - F_2$.

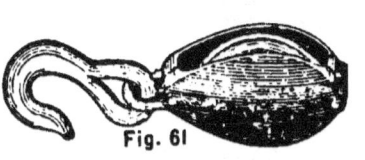
Fig. 61

2. A pulley is a wheel or *sheaf* with a groove round its outer edge, and capable of revolving freely about an axis through its centre O. This axis is fixed in a frame or *block* to which a hook is attached.

In a *fixed* pulley let a cord passing over the sheaf, support a weight W. The pull F on the string being the same throughout its length, $F = W$; and if P is the pressure on the support, we have the pulley acted on by 4 forces, F, W, P, and its weight w. Hence for equilibrium

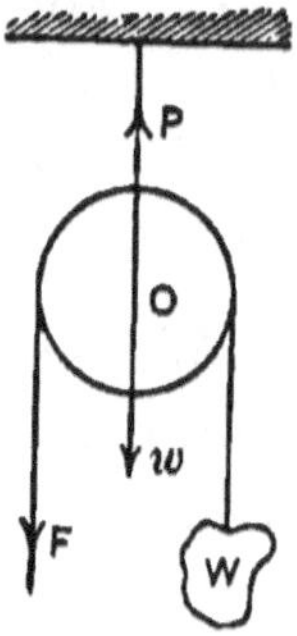

$$P = F + W + w = 2W + w,$$

Fig. 62

In a *movable* pulley the block is supported by a cord passing under the sheaf.

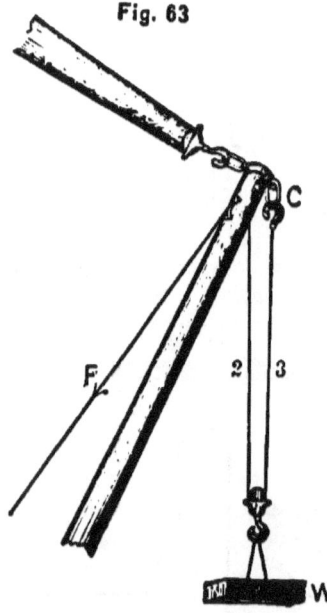

Fig. 63

3. In Fig.63 we have a single fixed and a single movable pulley. If the ropes 2 and 3 are parallel, and W is the weight of the movable pulley, prove

$$W + w = 2F.$$

Find the pull on the hook at C.

4. In a pulley tackle the upper and lower blocks each contain two sheaves, and the same rope passes round all: prove

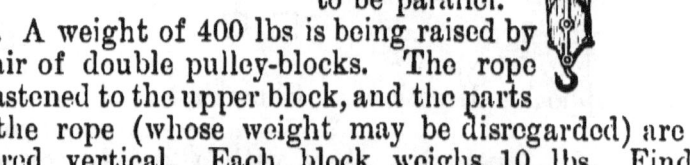

Fig. 64

W + wt. lower block = $4F$,

supposing all of the cords to be parallel.

5. A weight of 400 lbs is being raised by a pair of double pulley-blocks. The rope is fastened to the upper block, and the parts of the rope (whose weight may be disregarded) are considered vertical. Each block weighs 10 lbs. Find the pressure on the axle of the upper block. *Ans.* 522.5 pounds.

84. Moments.—If, besides acting in opposite directions, F_1, F_2 are equal, the points a and c in the construction diagram (Fig. 59) coincide, and the resultant is zero. The lines AC, BC become parallel, and therefore do not intersect.

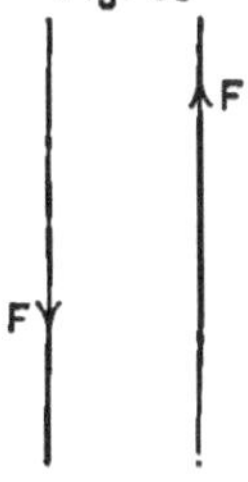

A consideration of Fig. 65 will show that the tendency of the forces is to turn the body round an axis. We are thus led to discuss the case of forces that cause turning.

Fig. 65

Suppose a force F in the plane of the paper acting on a body, and causing it to turn about an axis through a point O perpendicular to the plane of the paper. The turning effect depends on the magnitude of the force and on its distance from the axis, and the product of the two may be regarded as a measure of the importance of the force in producing turning. This product is called the **Moment of the Force about the Point**, so that we may define the moment of a force about a point to be numerically equal to *the product of the force and the perpendicular let fall from the point on its line of action*. Thus the moment of F about a fixed point O is Fp, p being the perpendicular let fall from O on F.

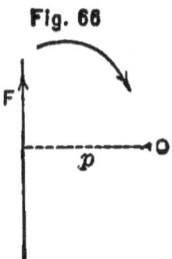

Fig. 66

The *unit of moment* depends on the units of force and distance, and is named a foot-poundal, a foot-pound, an inch-ton, etc., according to the units of force and distance employed. (See Art. 130.)

It is evident that the direction of turning about O is as indicated by the arrow in the figure. Reverse the direction of the force, and the direction of turning is reversed. To indicate the sense of the turning it is usual to call the moment of a force about a point negative when the tendency to produce turning is in the direction in which the hands of a clock move, and positive when the tendency is in the opposite direction. Thus in the figure the moment is $-Fp$.

85. The moment of a force F with reference to a fixed point O may be represented *graphically*. For if ab represent F plotted to scale and Oc the distance p, then the moment Fp is represented by $ab \times Oc$, that is, by twice the area of the triangle Oab, which has ab for base and Oc for altitude.

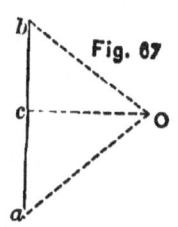

Fig. 67

We may now find the relation between the moment of a force AD about a given point O, and the moments of its components AB, AC about the same point. For from geometry

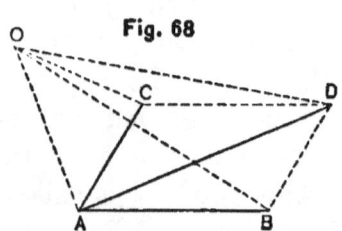

Fig. 68

$$OAD = OAC + OCD + ADC$$
$$= OAC + OAB;$$

that is, the moment of AD about O is equal to the sum of the moments of AB, AC about O.

This very important proposition may be proved more generally as follows: Let $F_1, F_2, \ldots$ be the forces acting at A, R their resultant, and O any point in the plane of the forces. From O let fall the perpendiculars $Oa, Ob, \ldots Ol$ on $F_1, F_2, \ldots R$. Join AO. Then, since the component of R in any direction is equal to the sum of the components of $F_1, F_2, \ldots$ in the same direction (Art. 49), take the direction AY at right angles to AO, and we have

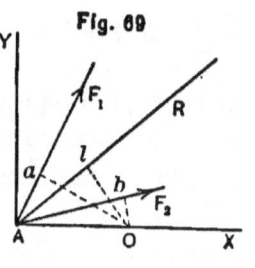

Fig. 69

$$R \sin OAl = F_1 \sin OAa + F_2 \sin OAb + \ldots, \quad (1)$$

or
$$R \times Ol = F_1 \times Oa + F_2 \times Ob + \ldots; \quad (2)$$

MOMENTS. 95

which shows that *the moment of the force R about O is equal to the sum of the moments of its component forces about the same point.*

Two important consequences follow:

(a) If the direction of R is reversed, the forces F_1, F_2, ... $-R$ are in equilibrium, and we have

$$0 = R \times Ol + F_1 \times Oa + F_2 \times Ob + \ldots;$$

or, *when forces acting at a point are in equilibrium, the algebraic sum of their moments about any point in their plane is zero.*

(b) When forces acting at a point A are in equilibrium, their moment about any point O gives the same relation as the resolution of the forces about an axis through A perpendicular to AO. One equation is a multiple of the other, equation (2) being deduced from (1) by multiplying by AO. See Art. 100 for an illustration of this.

Ex. 1. Find the moment of a force about any point in its line of action.

2. Compare in magnitude and direction the moments of two forces about any point on their resultant.

2a. Hence find the algebraic sum of the moments of two or more forces about any point situated on their resultant.

3. Is there any reason why a man should put his shoulder to the spoke rather than to the body of a wagon in helping it up hill?

4. If R is the resultant of two parallel forces F_1, F_2, and abc is any line perpendicular to their lines of action, prove independently of Art. 85 that

$R \times al = F_1 \times ab + F_2 \times ac.$

[Follows from $F_1 \times bl = F_2 \times cl$; $F_1 + F_2 = R$. Art. 83.]

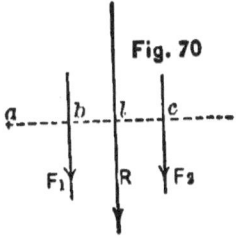
Fig. 70

5. Show that the dimensions of the moment of a force about a point are ML^2/T^2.

86. Couples.—Let us return to the two equal and opposite parallel forces, Art. 84. The moments of the forces about any point a are $-F \times ab$ and $+F \times ac$, respectively. Hence the measure of the turning effect of the two forces would be $-F \times ab + F \times ac$ or $F \times bc$, that is, the product of one of the forces by the distance between the directions of the forces.

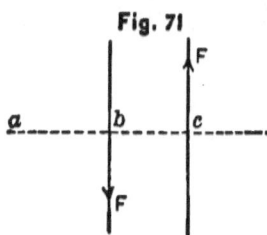

Fig. 71

To the system of two equal parallel forces acting in opposite directions but not in the same straight line the name **Couple** is given. The line bc being the distance between the lines of action of the forces is called the **Arm** of the couple, and the product $F \times bc$, or force × arm, is called the **Moment of the couple**, or the **Torque**.

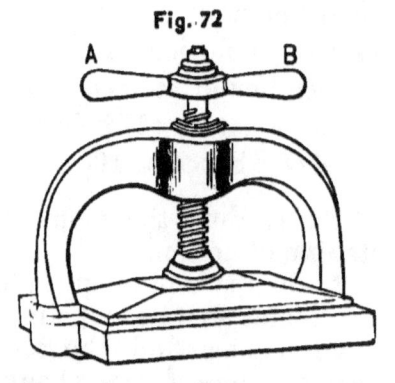

Fig. 72

An example of a couple is seen in the copying-press. The handle is pushed at A and pulled at B, the push and pull forming a couple. In consequence the screw rotates.

It requires a couple to wind a watch.

87. The moment of a couple depending only on the magnitude of the forces and the distance between them, the effect of a couple is not altered by turning the arm through any angle about one end, nor by moving the arm parallel to itself in the plane of the couple, nor by changing the couple into another couple having the same moment.

It hence follows that the resultant of a number of couples in a plane is a couple whose moment is equal to the sum of their moments.

It also follows that a single force F and a couple P, P acting on a body cannot be in equilibrium. For let the moment of the couple be Pa, a being its arm. Replace the couple P, P by a couple F, F of arm b, so that $Fb = Pa$, and place it in the plane so that one of its forces F is opposite to the single force F. The two forces F, F at C are in equilibrium, leaving the single force F at D unbalanced. Hence there cannot be equilibrium.

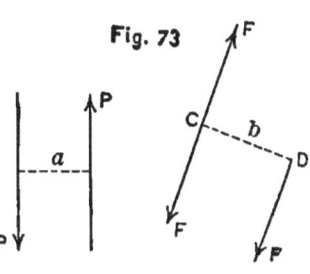

Fig. 73

Ex. 1. Three forces are represented in magnitude, direction, and position by the sides of a triangle taken the same way round: show that they form a couple whose moment is numerically equal to twice the area of the triangle.

2. Four forces are represented in magnitude, direction, and position by the sides of a square taken the same way round: prove that they form a couple whose moment is numerically equal to twice the area of the square.

88. Remembering that the turning effect of a force is measured by the moment of the force, we can now find the conditions of equilibrium when any number of forces F_1, F_2, ... act on a rigid body at different points A, B, ..., all of the forces being in the same plane. For the reasons stated in Art. 80, it is necessary to consider the external forces only.

At any point O introduce two forces F_1, F_1', each equal to F_1, and of opposite directions. This will not disturb the equilibrium. Now F_1 and F_1' form a couple of moment $F_1 p_1$, if p_1 is the distance of O from the line of action of F_1. Thus F_1 at A is equivalent to F_1 at O, and a couple $F_1 p_1$. Treating the other forces in the same way, we have the forces F_1 at A, F_2 at B, ... equivalent to F_1, F_2, ... at O, and the couples $F_1 p_1$, $F_2 p_2$, ...

Fig. 74

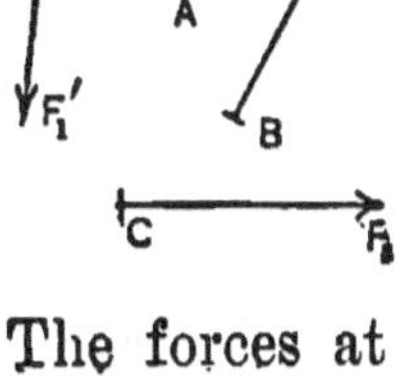

The forces at O may be combined into a single resultant

R and the couples into a single couple G whose moment is equal to the sum of their moments. But a single force and a single couple cannot be in equilibrium. Hence for equilibrium we must have
$$R = 0, \quad G = 0,$$
the conditions sought.

These conditions may be put in a form more convenient for computation. Through O draw two lines OX, OY, forming axes of coördinates, and let each force be resolved into components parallel to these axes. Denote the components by X_1, Y_1; X_2, Y_2; ... respectively.

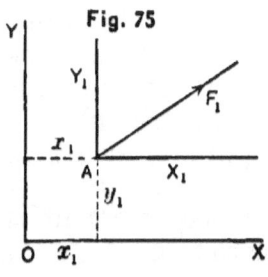
Fig. 75

Now if ΣX, ΣY denote the sums of the forces X_1, X_2, ...; Y_1, Y_2, ... along the axes of X and Y, then
$$(\Sigma X)^2 + (\Sigma Y)^2 = R^2$$
and $R = 0$ can only be satisfied by
$$\Sigma X = 0, \quad \Sigma Y = 0.$$

Also, since the moment of the resultant about any point is equal to the sum of the moments of its components about the same point, the moment $F_1 p_1$ must be equal to $Y_1 x_1 - X_1 y_1$ where x_1, y_1 are the coördinates of A. Hence $G = \Sigma (Yx - Xy)$, and if $G = 0$, we must have
$$\Sigma (Yx - Xy) = 0.$$

Hence the conditions of equilibrium may be stated—

(a) *The sums of the components of the forces along lines parallel to each of two rectangular axes drawn through any point in their plane is zero.*

(b) *The sum of the moments of the forces about any point in the plane is zero.*

From these conditions three unknowns may be determined, and no more. Hence, in order that a problem of this kind be determinate, the number of unknown forces that enter cannot exceed three. An important application of this principle occurs in finding stresses in roof and bridge trusses.

Ex. 1. What are the conditions of equilibrium of two forces? Also of three forces, two of which are parallel?

2. Show that parallel forces are in equilibrium when the sum of the forces $= 0$, and the sum of their moments about every point in their plane $= 0$.

3. In the single movable pulley (Fig. 63) if the ropes are inclined at an angle θ, prove $W = 2F\cos\theta/2$.

4. If the sum of the moments of a number of forces acting at a point in a plane about each of three points not in the same straight line is zero, the forces are in equilibrium. Prove this.

5. Let AB represent a rigid rod (as a crowbar) turning on a fixed support C. Let a force F be applied at A, and let W be the resistance to be balanced at C. Given the lengths of AC, CB, it is required to find the relation between F, W when in equilibrium.

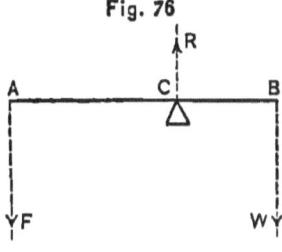

Fig. 76

[Neglect for the present the weight of the rod. Let F and W be vertical, and let R denote the vertical pressure at C; then R must be the resultant of F and W, and therefore

$$R = F + W.$$

Take moments about C, and

$$F \times AC - W \times BC = 0.$$

Hence the ratios of F, W, R are found.

The rod AB is known as a *lever*, the support C the *fulcrum*, and the distances AC, CB the *arms* of the lever. The equation $F \times AC - W \times BC = 0$ is sometimes called *the principle of the lever*.*]

6. Show by sketch the positions of force, resistance, and

---

* The properties of the lever were first given by Archimedes (B.C. 287–212).

fulcrum in the following levers: wheelbarrow, spade, claw-hammer, rowboat, pair of scissors, pair of nut-crackers, the forearm.

7. A lever is 2 ft. long: where must the fulcrum be placed that 10 pounds at one end may balance 30 pounds at the other end?

8. From a pole resting on the shoulders of two men a weight W is suspended. It is n times as far from one man as from the other; what does each support?

Ans. $W/(n+1)$, $nW/(n+1)$.

Fig. 77

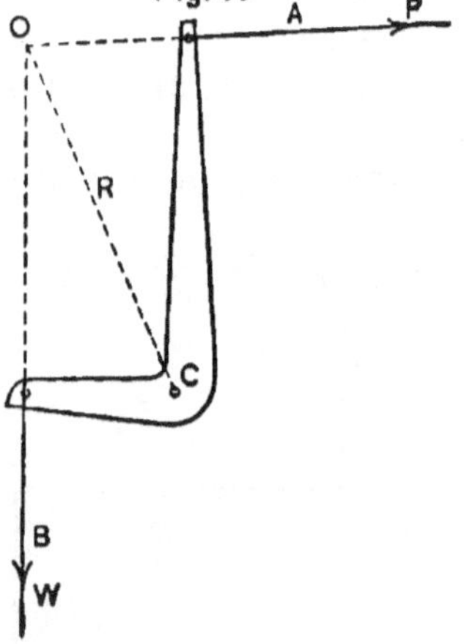

9. Find the relation between F and W in a bell-crank lever. A and B the bell wires, C the pivot about which the lever turns.

[The directions of F, W, and the reaction R of the pivot meet in a point O. Hence take moments about C.]

10. A pair of nut-crackers is a inches in length and a pressure of p pounds will crack a nut placed b inches from the hinge: what weight placed on the nut would crack it?

Ans. pa/b pounds.

11. Show that a single fixed pulley is equivalent to a lever with equal arms (Fig. 62).

12. Two cylinders fastened together move freely on a common axis O which is horizontal. A force F acts by a cord coiled round the larger cylinder (or *wheel*), and balances a weight W hanging from a cord coiled round the smaller cylinder (or *axle*).

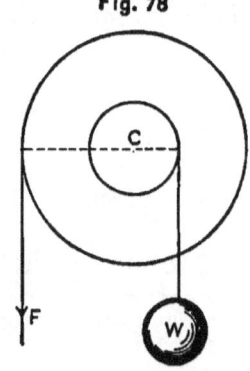

Fig. 78

[The apparatus is equivalent to a lever with *unequal* arms, the axis corresponding to the fulcrum of the lever, and the radii to the arms. It is called the *wheel and axle.*

We have

$$F + W = \text{pressure on axis,}$$
$$F \times \text{radius wheel} = W \times \text{radius axle.}]$$

COUPLES. 101

13. The axle of a capstan is 2 ft. in diameter. If four sailors push with a force of 40 pounds each at the ends of

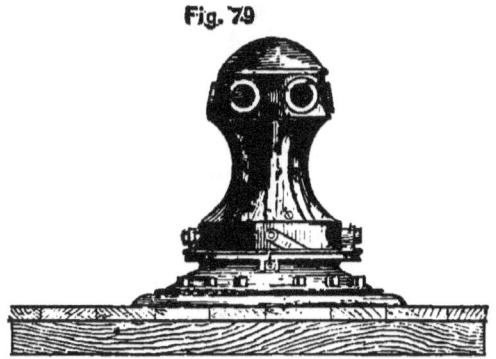
Fig. 79

spikes 4 ft. long, find the weight of the anchor that is lifted.

14. If the force is transmitted by toothed wheels, the teeth work in each other, so that the motion takes place as

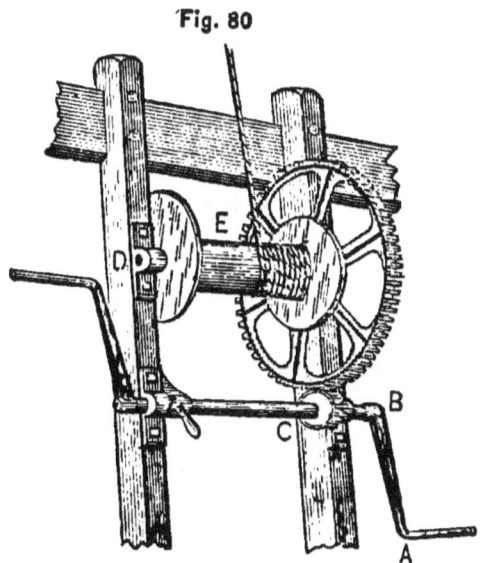
Fig. 80

if between two circles (called *pitch circles*) in rolling contact. We therefore replace the wheels by the pitch circles, and consider the force to be tangential to these circles at the successive points of contact.

Fig. 81

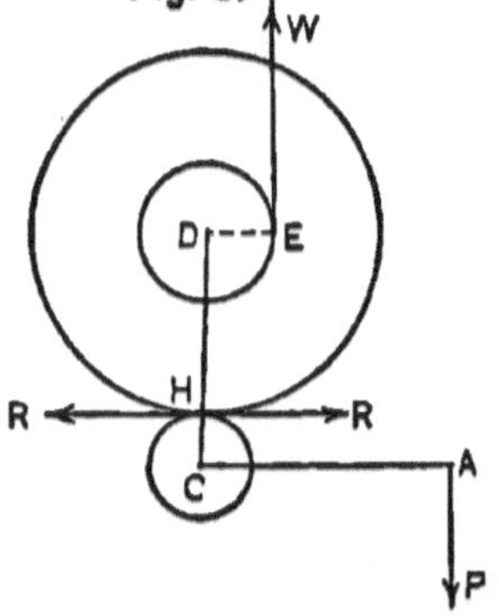

[In a *winch* we have a lever AB combined with toothed wheels, and a drum round which the rope attached to the weight W is moved. Replace the toothed wheels by pitch circles, and the mechanism in outline with the forces acting is as in Fig. 81. We have
$$F \times AC = R \times CH,$$
$$R \times HD = W \times DE;$$
$$\therefore \frac{F}{W} = \frac{DE}{AC} \times \frac{CH}{HD} = \frac{\text{rad. drum}}{\text{length arm}} \times \frac{\text{no. teeth in pinion}}{\text{no. teeth in wheel}}.]$$

15. Given that the cranks have 18 in. leverage, the gears are 4 to 1, the drum 6 in. in diameter, and the capacity with two-man power is 3 tons: find the force exerted by each man.

89. Centre of Parallel Forces.—We have seen (Art. 83) that two parallel forces F_1, F_2 acting at A, B are equivalent to a single force $F_1 + F_2$ acting at a point D on the line AB, such that

$$F_1 \times AD = F_2 \times BD.$$

Similarly, if F_3 is a third force acting at C, the three forces are equivalent to $F_1 + F_2$ at D and F_3 at C, or to a single force $F_1 + F_2 + F_3$ at G, such that

$$(F_1 + F_2) \times DG = F_3 \times CG;$$

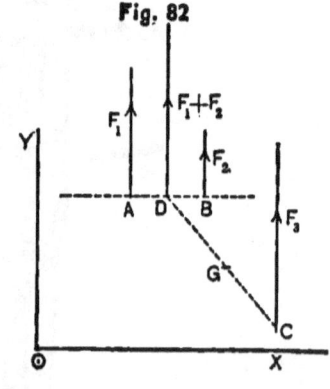

Fig. 82

and so on.

This result is entirely independent of the directions of the forces, so that the point G will be in the same position if the forces are turned in the same sense through the same

CENTRE OF PARALLEL FORCES. 103

angle about A, B, so as to remain parallel to one another. The fixed point G being the centre of the points of application of the parallel forces, is called the **Centre of Parallel Forces**.

It is convenient to express the coördinates $\bar{x}$, $\bar{y}$ of G, the centre of parallel forces, in terms of the coördinates x_1, y_1; x_2, y_2; ... of A, B, ... referred to axes OX, OY drawn through any point O in the plane of the forces.

Since G is in the same position no matter what the directions of the forces may be, let them be parallel to OY. Take moments about O, and

$$(F_1 + F_2 + F_3)\bar{x} = F_1 x_1 + F_2 x_2 + F_3 x_3,$$

and $\bar{x}$ is found.

Next take them parallel to OX, and take moments about O; then

$$(F_1 + F_2 + F_3)\bar{y} = F_1 y_1 + F_2 y_2 + F_3 y_3,$$

and $\bar{y}$ is found.

The values of $\bar{x}$, $\bar{y}$ may be written for any number of forces,

$$\bar{x} = \Sigma Fx / \Sigma F, \quad \bar{y} = \Sigma Fy / \Sigma F,$$

when Σ is the symbol of summation.

It is evident that the same reasoning would apply if the points A, B, ... were not in the same plane, the forces still being parallel. If z_1, z_2 denote their distances from a fixed plane, the distance $\bar{z}$ of G from this plane would be given by

$$\bar{z} = \Sigma Fz / \Sigma F.$$

90. *Centre of Gravity.*—As an illustration of parallel forces, consider the force of gravity acting on the particles of a body. A body may be regarded as built up of particles, the weights of the particles forming a system of forces whose lines of action, passing through the earth's centre, are so nearly parallel in a body of ordinary size that we may consider them to be so. If m_1, m_2, ... lbs. are the masses of the particles, the parallel forces acting downwards on them are $m_1 g$, $m_2 g$, ... poundals, and the resultant force would be found by adding the forces. To G, the centre of these parallel forces, the name of **Centre of Gravity*** is given. Its distance $\bar{z}$ from the plane of X, Y may be written $\bar{z} = \Sigma mgz / \Sigma mg$. This may also be written

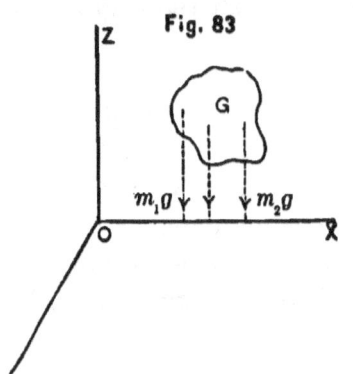

Fig. 83

$$\bar{z} = \Sigma mz / \Sigma m,$$

and hence the centre of gravity is also called the *centre of mass*, or by some the *centroid*.

91. That the line of action of the resultant force of gravity passes through the centre of gravity in all positions of a body, suggests an experimental method of finding the centre of gravity. Thus conceive the body suspended by a string from a point P. The forces acting are the resultant force of gravity at the centre of gravity, and the tension (pull) of the string. The lines of action of these forces must lie in the vertical through P. Hence, to find G, suspend from P, and strike the vertical PH; next suspend from any other point Q, and strike the vertical QK: the point

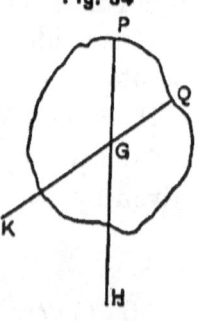

Fig. 84

---

* The idea of the centre of gravity of bodies is due to Archimedes.

of intersection of PH and QK will be the centre of gravity G required.

92. When the particles of a body are so distributed that there are always the same number in the same volume, the body is said to be of uniform density. The *unit of density* is taken to be the mass of unit volume. Thus, if m is the mass and V the volume, then the density $\rho = m/V$.

If the density is not uniform, we must estimate it at every point. Thus for an indefinitely small mass dm of volume dv about a point, the density at the point is dm/dv.

We shall consider bodies of uniform density only.

Ex. 1. The C. of G. of a uniform straight rod is at its middle point.

[The rod being uniform, is such that the number of particles on one side of the centre C is equal to that on the other side, and the C. of G. of every pair being at C, the C. of G. of the whole is at C.]

2. Find the C. of G. of a triangular lamina of uniform thickness and density.

[Conceive it divided into strips by lines parallel to AB. The C. of G. of each strip will be at its middle point. Hence the C. of G. of the whole will lie on the line CD joining C to D, the middle point of AB. Similarly, it will lie on the line joining A to E, the middle point of BC. Hence it is at G, the intersection of CD and AE.

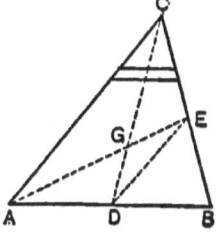

Fig. 85

Join DE. The triangles DGE, AGC are similar, and $DE = \tfrac{1}{2}AC$. $\therefore DG = \tfrac{1}{2}CG = \tfrac{1}{3}CD$.]

3. Prove that the C. of G. of a triangle (triangular lamina, strictly) coincides with that of three equal weights placed at its angular points.

4. Three men support a heavy triangular board at its corners: compare the weights supported by each man.

5. The sides of a triangle are 3, 4, 5: find the distance of the C. of G. from the angles.

$Ans.$ $\sqrt{13/3}$, $2\sqrt{13/3}$, $5/3$.

6. Explain how an instrument which stands on three

screws can be "levelled" by means of these screws. Take a galvanometer, for example.

Fig. 86

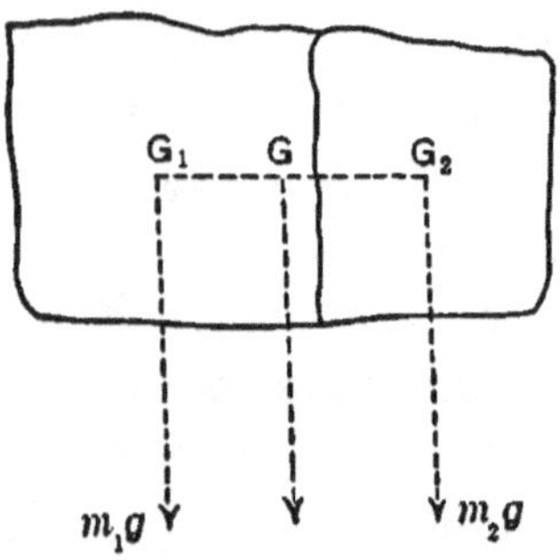

93. We pass at once to the centre of gravity of a *system* of bodies rigidly connected, by considering that each body may be conceived concentrated into a particle of equal mass acting at the centre of gravity of the body. Thus, reasoning as in Art. 89, if $m_1, m_2, \ldots$ represent the masses of two bodies, the centre of gravity G of the system will be found from

$$m_1 \times G_1 G = m_2 \times G_2 G.$$

Similarly, if G, G_1 are given, G_2 may be found.

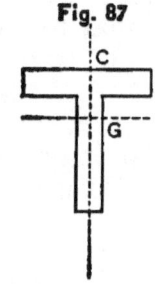

Fig. 87

Ex. 1. Weights of 1, 2, 3, 4, 5 pounds are strung on a uniform rod AB, whose weight is 3 pounds, at distances of 4 in. from each other: find the point at which the rod will balance.

Ans. $AG = 10\frac{2}{3}$ in.

2. Find the C. of G. of a T-iron, depth $= d$; depth of web $= d_1$; breadth of flange $= b$; breadth of web $= b_1$.

Ans. $CG\{bd - d_1(b - b_1)\} = bd \times \dfrac{d}{2} - d_1(b - b_1)\left(d - \dfrac{d_1}{2}\right).$

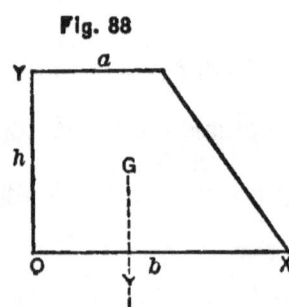

Fig. 88

3. A common form of cross-section of a reservoir wall or embankment wall is a trapezoid whose top and bottom sides are parallel. If top side $= a$, bottom $= b$, and height $= h$, show that

$$\bar{x} = \tfrac{1}{3}\left(a + b - \dfrac{ab}{a+b}\right);$$

$$\bar{y} = \dfrac{h}{3}\left(\dfrac{2a+b}{a+b}\right).$$

CENTRE OF PARALLEL FORCES.

4. Hence show, and also show independently, that if one-fourth part of a triangle is cut off by a line parallel to the base, the C. of G. of the remainder is at 2/9 of the line joining the vertex to the middle point of the base.

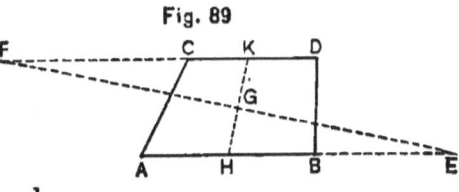

Fig. 89

5. From a circular disc another circular disc described on its radius as diameter is cut: show that the C. of G. is distant 1/6 radius from the centre.

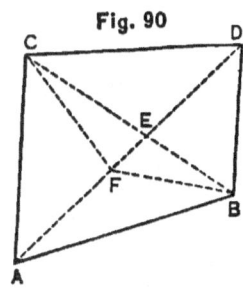

Fig. 90

6. Prove the following construction for finding the C. of G. of a trapezoid $ABCD$. (Fig. 89.) Prolong AB, making $BE = CD$; prolong DC, making $CF = AB$. The point of intersection of EF and HK, the line joining the middle points of AB, CD, is the C. of G.

7. Prove the following rule for finding the C. of G. of a quadrilateral: (Fig. 90.) Draw the diagonals. Make $AF = DE$. The C. of G. of the triangle CFB is also that of the quadrilateral.

94. The application of the general formula of Art. 90 to finding the C. of G. of bodies may be further illustrated by the following examples:

Ex. 1. To find the C. of G. of a circular arc AB.

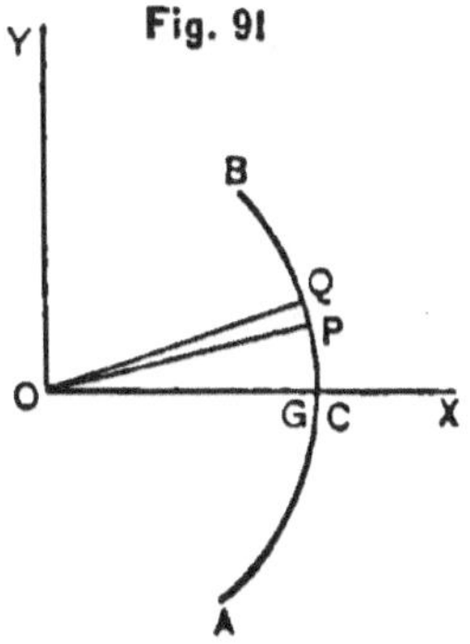

[The C. of G. must lie on a line OCX joining the centre O to the middle point C of the arc. Let ds denote the length of the indefinitely small part PQ of the arc, k its cross-section, ρ its density. The mass of $PQ = k\rho ds$. The coördinates of the C. of G. of PQ are the same as those of P, or x, y. Hence

$$\overline{x}\,(=OG) = \int k\rho ds \times x / \int k\rho ds$$
$$= \int x\,ds / \int ds.$$

If $COP = \theta$ and $OP = r$, then

$$x = r\cos\theta,\ ds = rd\theta,\ \text{and}\ \overline{x} = \int r\cos\theta\,d\theta / \int d\theta.$$

Fig. 91

If angle $AOB = 2\beta$, then, integrating between the limits $+\beta, -\beta$,

$$\bar{x} = r \sin \beta/\beta.]$$

2. To find the C. of G. of a semicircle. Ans. $\bar{x} = 2r/\pi$.
3. To find C. of G. of a circular sector AOB if angle $AOB = 2\beta$. (See last figure.)
[Divide the sector into triangular pieces as OPQ. Area $OPQ = \tfrac{1}{2}rd\theta \times r = \tfrac{1}{2}r^2 d\theta$. If G_1 is C. of G. of OPQ, then

$$x = OM = OG_1 \cos \theta = \tfrac{2}{3} r \cos \theta.$$

$$\therefore \bar{x} = \int_{-\beta}^{+\beta} \tfrac{2}{3} r \cos \theta \times \tfrac{1}{2} r^2 d\theta / \int_{-\beta}^{+\beta} \tfrac{1}{2} r^2 d\theta = \tfrac{2}{3} r \sin \beta/\beta.]$$

4. Find the C. of G. of a circular ring, radius $OA = r_1$, $OC = r_2$, angle $AOB = 2\beta$.

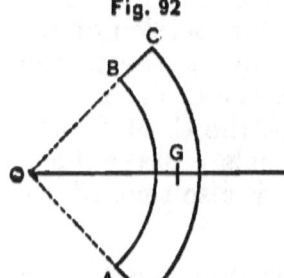
Fig. 92

[A practical application would be the front surface of a circular arch of which r_1 is the radius of intrados and r_2 radius of extrados.]
Ans. $\bar{x} = \tfrac{2}{3}(r_2^3 - r_1^3) \sin \beta / (r_2^2 - r_1^2)\beta$.

5. For a semicircle, $\bar{x} = 4r/3\pi$; for a quadrant of a circle, $\bar{x} = 4\sqrt{2}r/3\pi$.

95. Stability.—If a body suspended from a point O be slightly displaced from its position of equilibrium and let go, it will turn about the point of support. If the centre of gravity G is *below* the point of support, the tendency is for the body to return to its original position. This may perhaps be made more evident by resolving the weight W into F_1 along GO and F_2 at right angles to F_1. The force F_1 gives the pressure on the support, and F_2 the turning force which tends to swing the body to its former position. In this case the body in its original position is said to be in stable equilibrium.

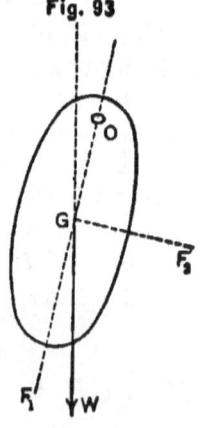
Fig. 93

STABILITY.

In Fig. 94 the centre of gravity is *above* the point of support, and the tendency for the body when disturbed is to move farther from its original position. In this case the equilibrium is *unstable*. If, however, the point of support is *at* the centre of gravity G, the body will remain at rest in any position, and the equilibrium is *neutral*.

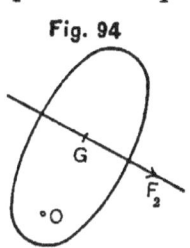

Fig. 94

Similarly, if the body, instead of being suspended from a point, rests at a point on a fixed support the equilibrium may be stable, unstable, or neutral, according as the forces acting on the body in its displaced position tend to restore it to its original position or make it move farther from that position, or are in equilibrium.

When one point O of a body is fixed the resultant of the external forces tending to cause translation is balanced by the reaction of the constraint at O. Also, if there is equilibrium the tendency to turn about O in one direction must be balanced by the tendency to turn in the opposite direction, or the sum of the moments about O must be zero. This, therefore, is the condition of equilibrium of a system of forces acting on a body with one point fixed.

Ex. 1. In suburban passenger traffic the train must stop and start quickly. The engine is built with a large wheel base. Why?

2. A circular table weighing w lbs. has three equal legs at equidistant points on its circumference. The table is placed on a level floor. Neglecting the weight of the legs, find the smallest weight which, when placed on the table, will upset it. *Ans.* w lbs.

3. If the table has four legs at equidistant points, find the least weight that will upset it.

4. Suppose $ABCD$ (Fig. 95) to be the cross-section of a wall built to withstand the pressure of earth or water on one side: for example, the wall of a reservoir or of a railroad embankment. Such a wall is called a *retaining-wall*.

STATICS OF A RIGID BODY.

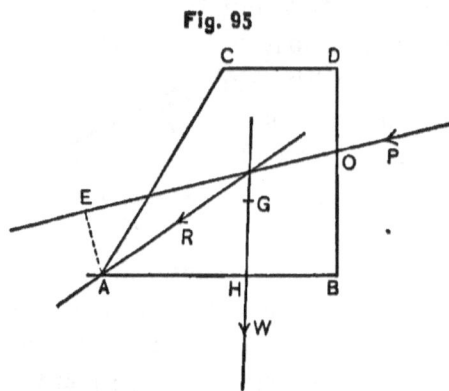

Fig. 95

[We assume that the wall is built so that it cannot give way except in one mass, and by being overturned about the edge A. Let P be the resultant of the forces pressing on the side BD, and let O be its point of application. The weight W acts vertically downward through the centre of gravity G. The stability depends on the difference of $P \times AE$ and $W \times AH$, the first tending to overturn, the second to restore. Hence, when the wall is just on the point of turning, we have the relation

$$W \times AH = P \times AE.]$$

5. The centre of gravity of a ladder weighing 50 lbs. is 12 ft. from one end, which is fixed. What force must a man apply at a distance of 6 ft. from this end to raise the ladder to a vertical position?   *Ans.* 100 pounds.

6. Find the proper elevation BE of the outer rail on a railroad track for a given velocity v of engine weighing m lbs., and on a curve of radius r, in order that there may be no flange or lateral pressure on the rails.

[The forces acting are the weight mg of the engine, the centrifugal force $C(=mv^2/r)$ and the reactions N_1, N_2 of the rails. Since there is no flange pressure the reactions are perpendicular to the track AB. Let θ be the inclination of AB to the horizon.

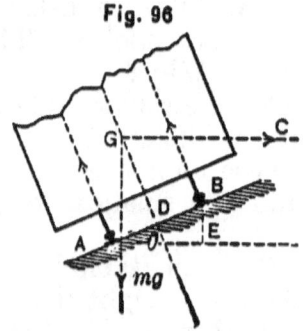

Fig. 96

Resolving the forces along AB, we have

$$C \cos \theta = mg \sin \theta, \quad \text{or} \quad \tan \theta = C/mg = v^2/gr.$$

But if θ is small, $\tan \theta = BE/AB =$ elevation/gauge;

∴ elevation of rail = gauge × v^2/gr.

For standard gauge of 4 ft. 8½ in., this gives

elevation of rail = $7v^2/4r$ inches, nearly,

v being expressed in feet per second, and r in feet.]

7. If in (6) the velocity V is expressed in miles per hour, show that

elevation of rail = $15 V^2/4r$ inches, nearly,

the radius r being, as before, expressed in feet.

8. Find the greatest velocity v a locomotive can have to be just on the point of overturning on a curved level track of radius r ft., the centre of gravity of the locomotive being 6 ft. above the rails, and the gauge of the track 4 ft. 8½ in.

Ans. 3.55 $\sqrt{r}$ ft. per sec. nearly.

96. Beam Supported at One Point.—Suppose a beam of wood or metal of length $2a$ suspended at a point O. The pressure on the support being equal to the weight W of the beam, the centre of gravity G of the beam will lie in the vertical OG. A weight P placed on the beam or suspended

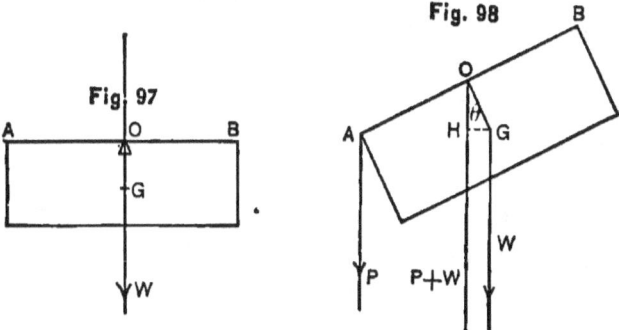

from it anywhere except in the line OG will cause the beam to take an inclined position, as in Fig. 98. Suppose P suspended at A, where $AO = a$. The forces P and W are parallel, and therefore their resultant must be equal to their sum. Being balanced by the reaction of the support

112 STATICS OF A RIGID BODY.

O, this resultant must pass through O. Hence the moment of W about O is equal to that of P about O, or

$$P \times OC = W \times GH,$$

or
$$P \times a \cos \theta = W \times h \sin \theta,$$

or
$$P = \frac{Wh}{a} \tan \theta.$$

By attaching a pointer to the beam free to move over a graduated arc we have a means of comparing weights. An example is afforded by the common letter-scale (Fig. 99).

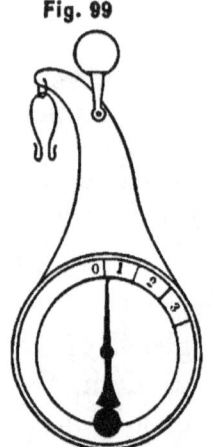
Fig. 99

97. Balance.—If in the beam represented in Fig. 97 we place two equal weights P, P at the same distance A from O, equilibrium will not be disturbed. For the moment about O is the same, being $= Pa$ in both cases. Hence the beam may be used for comparing equal weights. Attaching pans to A, B, the weights for comparison may be placed in these pans and the operation facilitated. Such an arrangement is the common **Balance**.

The parts of a balance should be arranged so as to secure the greatest accuracy in making the comparisons, and with the least loss of time. How can this be done?

Suppose the weights P, Q to be unequal, and that the points of support A, B are equidistant from O and in the

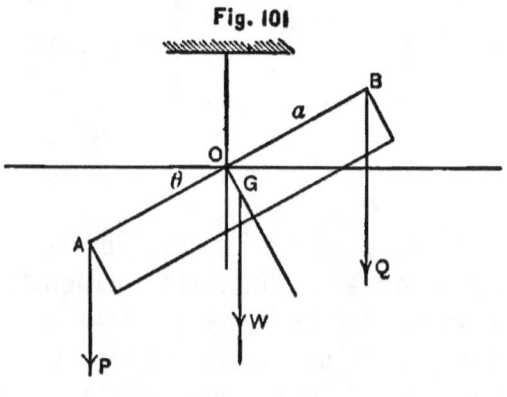
Fig. 101

same straight line with it. Let $AB = 2a$ and $OG = h$. Take moments about O, and

$$P \times a \cos \theta - Wh \sin \theta - Qa \cos \theta = 0,$$

or $\qquad \tan \theta = (P - Q)a/Wh.$

Now the balance will indicate small differences $P - Q$ the more clearly the greater the angle θ through which it swings for these differences. But $\tan \theta$ or θ is greatest when a/Wh is greatest, that is, when a is large or the beam has long arms, when W is small or the beam light, when h is small or the centre of gravity is just below the point of suspension. Such a balance has great *sensibility*, and is suitable for delicate investigations in Chemistry, Physics, Assaying, etc.

In scales for weighing large masses *stability* rather than sensibility is wanted; that is, for small differences of P and Q the angle of deviation of the beam from the horizontal as shown by $\tan \theta$ should be small. This requires Wh to be large or the beam to be heavy, with a long distance between the centre of gravity G and the point of suspension O. By making the arms long, a balance may be constructed which shall possess in a measure both sensibility and stability. As the two conditions are at variance, the amount of compromise must be decided by the use to which the balance is to be put.

Ex. 1. If the centre of gravity coincides with the point of suspension, the balance is in equilibrium in all positions.

2. The arms of a balance are equal, but the scale pans are not of the same weight. If a body weighs P lbs. in one and Q lbs. in the other, find the true weight.

$\qquad\qquad\qquad\qquad\qquad$ *Ans.* $\frac{1}{2}(P + Q)$ lbs.

3. A body placed in one scale pan appears to weigh P lbs. and in the other Q lbs. If the pans are of equal weight but the arms are not of equal length, show that its true weight $= \sqrt{PQ}$ lbs.

98. *Steelyard.*—Suppose (Fig. 102) a beam suspended

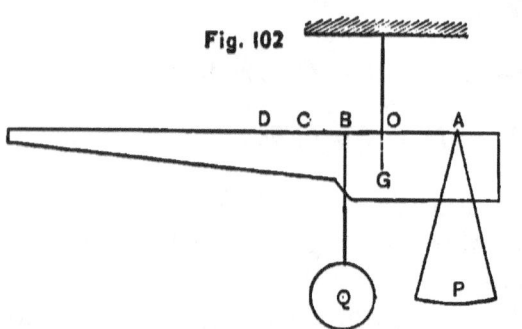

Fig. 102

from a point O directly above its centre of gravity G. The upper edge ABC being straight and at right angles to OG will be horizontal. If from the beam we suspend two bodies of unequal weights P, Q, it will still remain horizontal if the moments of P and Q about O are equal, or
$$P \times AO = Q \times BO.$$
Let the weight P suspended from A be a scale pan. If to P we add an unknown weight W, we shall still have equilibrium, provided Q is suspended from a point C such that
$$(P + W)AO = Q \times CO.$$
Subtract these equations, and
$$W \times AO = Q \times BC,$$
which gives the unknown W as soon as BC is measured.

To save measurements of BC at every weighing of a body, it is convenient to graduate the beam in the first place. Thus suppose $P = 1$ lb., $Q = 2$ lbs., and $AO = 4$ in. Then $OB = 2$ in., and a notch can be made at B, which, as the weight Q then balances the pan P only, would be marked 0. Let now $W = 1$ lb.; then $BC = \dfrac{W}{Q} \times AO = 2$ in., and C would be the position of the 1 lb. mark. Make $W = 2$ lbs. and $BD = 4$ in., giving D the 2 lb. mark, and so on. Hence in weighing a body it is only necessary to place it in the pan and move the weight Q until the notch is found where the beam will remain horizontal. The number at the notch indicates the weight. This instrument is called a **Steelyard**.

Ex. 1. Graduate a steelyard to weigh half-pounds.

BEAM SUPPORTED AT TWO POINTS. 115

2. If the point of suspension O be not over the centre of gravity and the movable weight Q placed at a point H

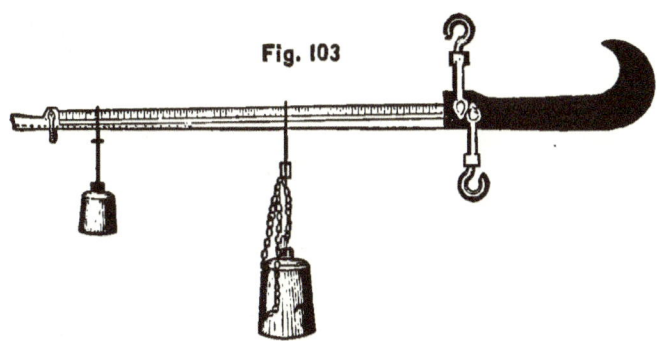

Fig. 103

holds the steelyard in a horizontal position, show that $HB = W \times AO/Q$, and hence show how to graduate the steelyard.

3. A steelyard beam weighs 3 lbs., the wt. Q is 4 lbs., and the distance of the centre of gravity from O is 3 in., and of the point of suspension of the scale A from O 5 in.: show that the 1 lb. graduation marks are at intervals of $\frac{3}{4}$ in.

4. A steelyard weighs W lbs. and is correctly graduated for a movable weight Q: prove that a weight $2Q$ may be used provided a fixed weight W is suspended at the centre of gravity of the steelyard.

5. A piece is broken off the longer arm of a steelyard: show that the customer is defrauded.

99. Beam Supported at Two Points.

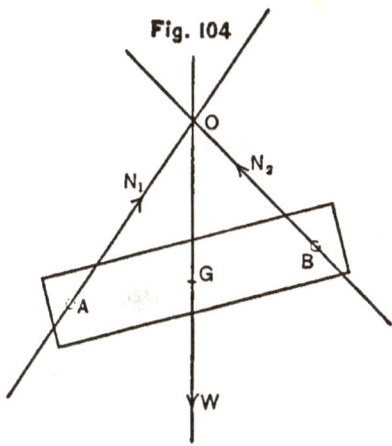

Fig. 104

—We naturally pass from a body supported at a single point to one in which two points A and B are supported, as for example a beam supported by two smooth horizontal pins A and B. The forces acting are the weight W vertically downwards through G and the reactions N_1, N_2 of the supports A, B in directions which are unknown. If we assume that they are in the same plane, the forces being three in number must meet in some point O in the vertical through G. Until we are able to fix the directions of N_1 or N_2, the problem is indeterminate, as there is an indefinitely great number of points in this line.

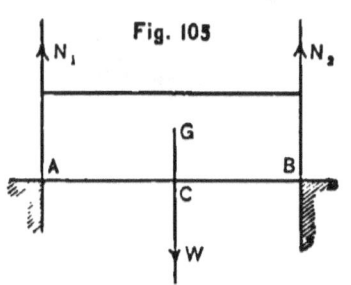

Fig. 105

100. If, for example, the beam rests on two props A, B in the same horizontal plane, the reactions of the props are vertical. Hence, resolving vertically, and taking moments about G,

$$N_1 + N_2 - W = 0,$$
$$N_1 \times AC - N_2 \times BC = 0,$$

from which N_1, N_2 are found.

Or take moments about A and B in succession, and

$$N_1 \times AB - W \times BC = 0,$$
$$N_2 \times AB - W \times AC = 0,$$

from which the same values result as before.

The pressures N_1, N_2 on the supports may also be determined *graphically* by the method of Art. 81.

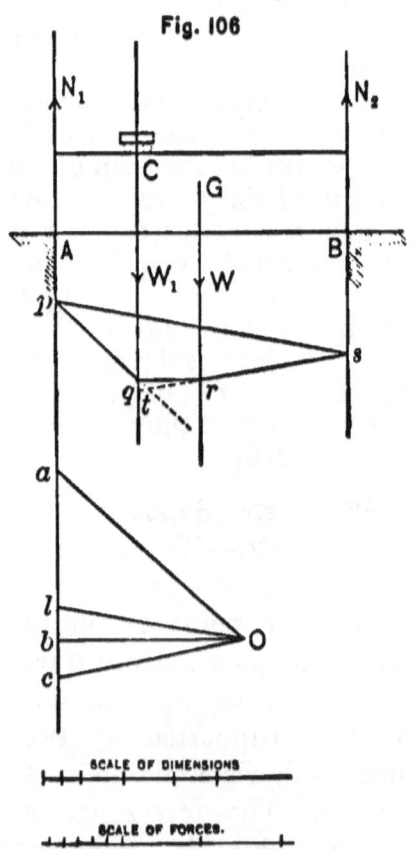

Fig. 106

Suppose the beam AB to carry besides its own weight W a load W_1 at C. Draw ab, bc to scale to represent W_1, W, and parallel to their directions. The force R

BEAM SUPPORTED AT TWO POINTS.   117

represented by the line cba which closes the polygon will hold W_1, W in equilibrium.

Take any pole O and join Oa, Ob, Oc. From any point p in the direction of N_1 draw pq parallel to aO; draw qr parallel to bO and rs parallel to cO. The intersection t of pq and sr gives the position of the resultant R. Its direction is parallel to cba, and is therefore vertical.

Join sp and draw Ol parallel to sp. Now cba (or R) may be resolved into Oa along pq and cO along sr. Also Oa may be resolved into Ol along sp and la along pA. And cO may be resolved into cl along sB and lO along ps. But the forces Ol, lO being equal and in opposite directions, must be in equilibrium. Hence cba (or R) is equivalent to la at A and cl at B. But cba holds W_1, W in equilibrium. Hence la, cl hold W_1, W in equilibrium, and are the reactions N_1, N_2 at A and B.

Hence the rule,

(a) Form the force polygon by laying off the forces to scale.

(b) Select a convenient pole O and form the polygon $pqrs$.

(c) Draw Ol parallel to the closing line sp dividing ca into parts la, cl, which will represent the reactions N_1, N_2 at A and B.

Ex. 1. A beam of 20 ft. span carries a weight of 10 tons 8 ft. from one end: find the pressures on the end supports.

2. A highway bridge 25 ft. long weighs 6 tons: find the pressures on the abutments when a $2\frac{1}{4}$-ton wagon is $\frac{1}{3}$ of the distance across.   *Ans.* 5 tons; 3.5 tons.

3. A beam of 40 ft. span weighs 1 ton per running foot. One half of it carries a uniform load (as a train of coal cars) of 2 tons and the other of 3 tons per running foot: find the pressures on the end supports. *Ans.* 65 tons; 75 tons.

4. A truss of 60 ft. span and weighing 100 tons carries an Erie consolidation engine as in the figure: find the pressures on the supports.

Fig. 107

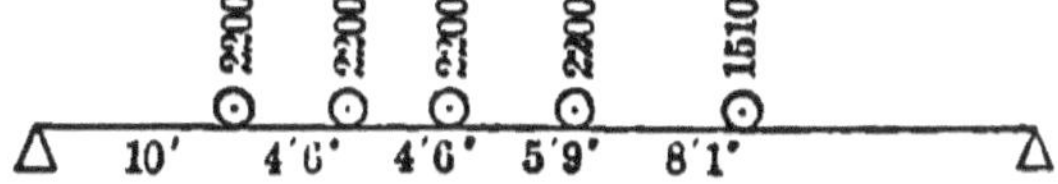

22000   22000   22000   22000   15100

10'   4'6"   4'6"   5'9"   8'1"

Ans. 66.6 tons; 84.9 tons.

101. Two Beams Hinged.—Again, suppose to the beam AB an equal beam BC attached at B by a hinge or pin, and the two beams to be supported by two pins at A, C in the same horizontal plane. The pin B being in equilibrium, the reaction N of AB on it is equal and opposite to that of BC on it. Since the beams are equal the direction of N must be horizontal. The weight W of the beam AB acts vertically through the middle point G. Hence the reaction N_1 of the pin A must pass through H, the intersection of the directions of N and W. Similarly for the beam BC.

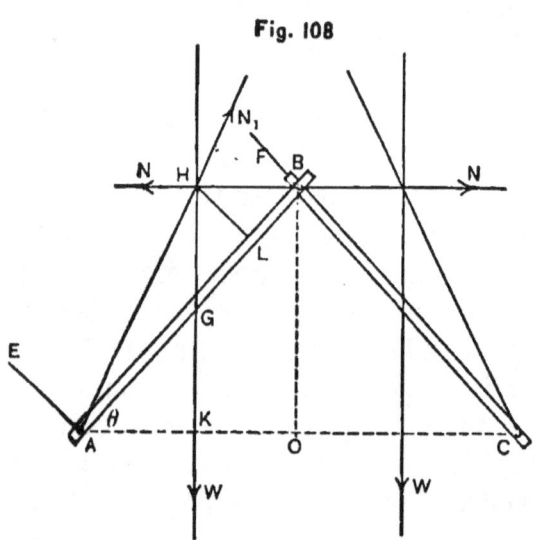

Fig. 108

The forces acting on the beam AB are parallel to the sides of the triangle AHK, and N, N_1 may be scaled off directly if HK be taken to represent the weight W.

Put the length $AB = l$, the height $BO = h$, the span $AC = 2a$, and we have

$$N = W \times AK/KH = Wa/2h,$$

$$N_1 = W \times AH/KH = W\sqrt{a^2 + 4h^2}/2h,$$

which give the algebraic values of the reactions.

These values may also be found by taking moments about

A and B in succession. Thus taking moments about A.

$$N \times HK = W \times AK,$$

giving N as before. Similarly for the value of N_1.

The reaction N_1 may also be found by resolving it into two components, X horizontal and Y vertical. Then

$$Y = W, \qquad X = N = Wa/2h,$$

and $\quad N_1 = \sqrt{X^2 + Y^2} = W\sqrt{a^2 + 4h^2}/2h,$

as before.

102. The reaction N_1 at A may be resolved into two components—a longitudinal force AL along the beam AB and a transverse force AE perpendicular to it; also N at B into a longitudinal force BL and a transverse force BF. The longitudinal force diminishes from AL at A to BL at B. The transverse forces AE, BF being each equal to HL, are equal to one another. Also $HL = HG \cos\theta = \dfrac{W}{2}\cos\theta$, so that the transverse forces are equal to half the component of W at right angles to the beam.

The values of the transverse forces are the greater the smaller the angle θ is, or the more nearly the beam is horizontal. When the beam is horizontal and the external forces are vertical, the longitudinal forces disappear and the transverse forces alone enter. In the study of structures it is necessary to consider the effect of both of these classes of forces.

103. The computation of the longitudinal and transverse forces, even in the simple case given, is tedious. It can readily be understood that in a complicated framework it would become intolerably so. Accordingly among architects and engineers a method of greater simplicity is followed, leading to results practically close enough. This is done by considering the loads carried by the frame, including its weight, to be concentrated at the joints of the frame, and applying the conditions of equilibrium to each joint in succession. Thence the stresses along each piece, meeting at a joint, are found by the triangle of forces.

The method belongs to a special branch of mechanics known as **Graphical Statics**. We add a short sketch of its application to the determination of the longitudinal stresses in simple trusses, forming as it does a good illustration of the triangle of forces.

104. Jointed Frames.—As the simplest possible example of a jointed frame, let us consider three beams hinged by pins at A, B, C, and resting on supports at A, C in the same horizontal plane. This is known as a **Triangular Truss**. Suppose the beams all alike, and of weight W each. The reactions of the supports balance these weights and act vertically upwards, the supports being horizontal. Hence the external forces acting and keeping the truss in equilibrium are as in Fig. 109.

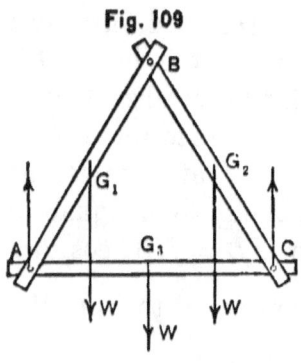
Fig. 109

Next transfer the weights to the pins. Thus
W at $G_1 = \frac{1}{2} W$ at $A + \frac{1}{2} W$ at B,
W at $G_2 = \frac{1}{2} W$ at $B + \frac{1}{2} W$ at C,
W at $G_3 = \frac{1}{2} W$ at $A + \frac{1}{2} W$ at C;
∴ sum =
W at $A + W$ at $B + W$ at C;
and each reaction being equal to half the total weight $3W$, we have the forces as in Fig. 110.

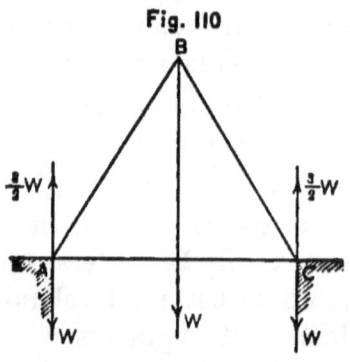
Fig. 110

Combining forces and reactions at A and C, we have finally the forces as in Fig. 111.

JOINTED FRAMES.

We have thus transferred the weights of the beams to the joints, and can now consider the beams as without weight, and indicating direction only. The resulting stresses in the pieces we next find.

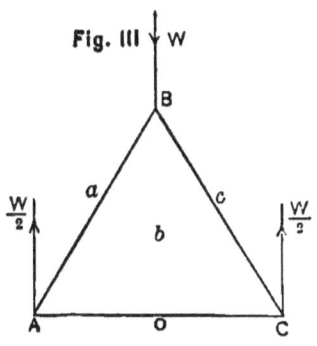

Fig. 111

Since the weights on *each* pin are in equilibrium with the stresses produced in the pieces meeting at the pin, we consider the pins one at a time.

(*a*) Pin A. The forces acting are $W/2$ vertically upwards, and the unknown stresses in AB, AC. Draw (Fig. 112) Oa to scale to represent $W/2$. From a draw ab parallel to BA and bO parallel to AC. Then ab, bO represent on the

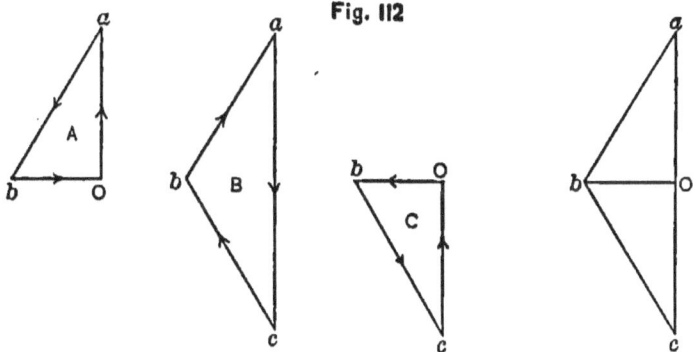

Fig. 112

same scale the stresses in AB, AC. Their directions are indicated by the arrow-heads.

(*b*) Pin B. The forces acting are the stress in AB and W which are known, and the stress in BC which is unknown. Draw ba to represent the stress in AB, ac to represent W; then cb will represent the stress in BC. Notice that the arrows on ab point in opposite directions in Figs. A and B. This is because the stress on the pin A is opposite to that on the pin B.

(c) Pin C. The forces are the stress in BC, $W/2$, and stress in AC, all of which are known. For check the diagram may be drawn as in Fig. C.

105. It is evident that we should have saved labor by adding the second figure to the first and the third to the sum as in the fourth figure, which is the complete **Stress Diagram**.

In practice it is convenient to consider the stress diagram as in two parts. Thus the line ac is the polygon of external forces, ac being the downward force at B balanced by the upward forces cO at C and Oa at A, and is complete in itself. The closing of this polygon shows that the reaction forces have been properly estimated. On this polygon as base the stress diagram is added step by step until complete.

In case the truss is symmetrical, as in our example, it is only *necessary* to consider the first half of the pins. But it is *safer* to consider all of them, as the symmetry of the drawing will furnish a test of its accuracy.

106. In Fig. A we see that in the beam AB the stress acts towards the pin A and also towards the pin B. The beam is thus *compressed* between the pins, and is called a **Strut**. Similarly for BC. In AC the stress is from the pin A and also from C, and the beam is in a state of *tension*. It is called a **Tie**, and in practice a rod would be used. Hence in designing a structure to carry an assigned load a study of the stress diagram will show not only the *amount* of stress but the *kind* of stress, and therefore whether a strut or tie should be employed.

107. For tracing the connection between the pieces themselves and the stresses in them as shown by the stress diagram, an exceedingly convenient system of notation has been devised.*

---

* Due to Prof. Henrici, London, but usually known as Bow's notation,

JOINTED FRAMES. 123

A beam or a stress is named by letters placed on either side of it. Thus (Fig. 111) Ob is the tie AC, Oa the reaction $W/2$ at the left support, ab the strut AB, ac the load W at B, and so on. These letters carried into the stress diagram (Fig. 112) give us ab the stress in the piece ab, cb the stress in cb, Ob the stress in the rod Ob. The letters A, B, C at the pins do not enter the stress diagram.

108. In the following examples first draw the truss to scale (inches to the foot) from the dimensions given, next compute the pin loads, next the reactions of the supports, next draw the force polygon (pounds to the inch), and finally the stress diagram. Scale off the stresses, and tabulate under the heads Compression and Tension.

Ex. 1. In a triangular roof truss the rafters are $2\frac{1}{2}$ ft. apart and the roofing material weighs 20 lbs. per sq. ft. The span is 24 ft. and height 5 ft. : find the stresses on the rafters. *Ans.* 590 pounds.

2a. Show that the stress diagram for the truss repre-

Fig. 113

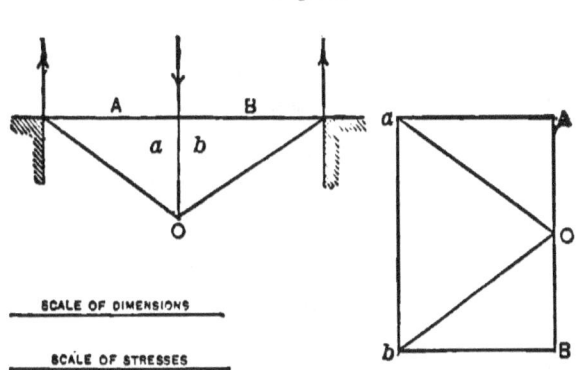

sented in the figure, loaded at the centre over the vertical piece ab, known as the king-post, is as in the margin.

2b. A foot-bridge (Fig. 113) 18 ft. span and 6 ft. breadth has a crowd of people on it equal to 100 lbs. per sq. ft. of floor surface. The king-posts of the two trusses are 3 ft. in depth: find the stresses.

Ans. Stress on post $ab = 2700$ pounds.

3. In (2a) the span is $2l$, depth d: show that the compres-

sion in Aa is $Wl/2d$, and find the tension in Oa and the stress in the vertical ab.

4. In a roof of 30 ft. span and height 10 ft. the trusses

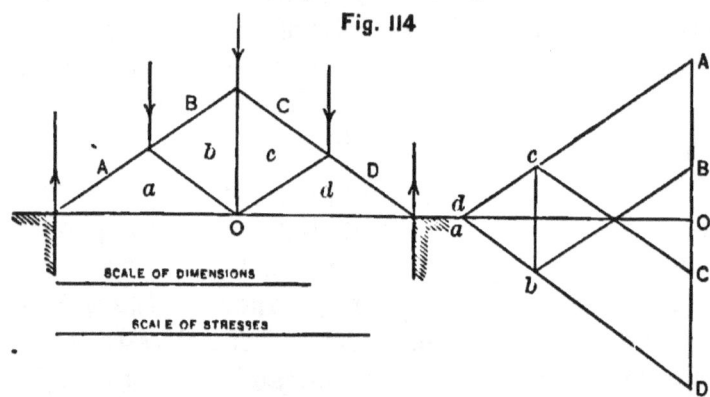

Fig. 114

are 10 ft. apart, and the pieces ab, cd come to the middle points of the rafters. If the weight of the roof covering is 25 lbs. per sq. ft. surface, draw the stress diagram and scale off the stresses.

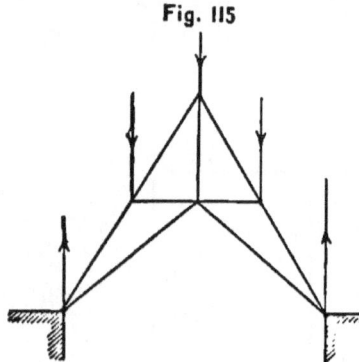

Fig. 115

5. Draw the stress diagram for a German truss loaded as in Fig. 115.

6a. Draw a stress diagram for a queen-post truss (Fig. 116). The queen-posts ab, bc divide the span into three equal parts, and the truss is loaded at the joints with weights W.

6b. A foot-bridge (queen-post) of span 25 ft., breadth 7 ft., length of queen-posts 3 ft., carries a load of 150 lbs. per sq. ft. of floor: find the stresses developed, the queen-posts dividing the span into three equal parts.

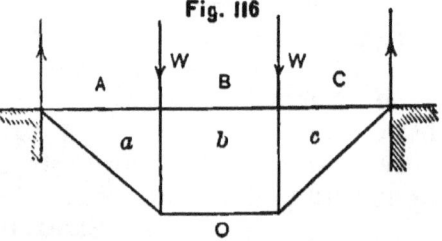

Fig. 116

7. Draw stress diagrams for the roof trusses represented; the first being that of the Rock Island Arsenal and the second the Masonic Temple, Philadelphia (Figs. 117, 118).

JOINTED FRAMES. 125

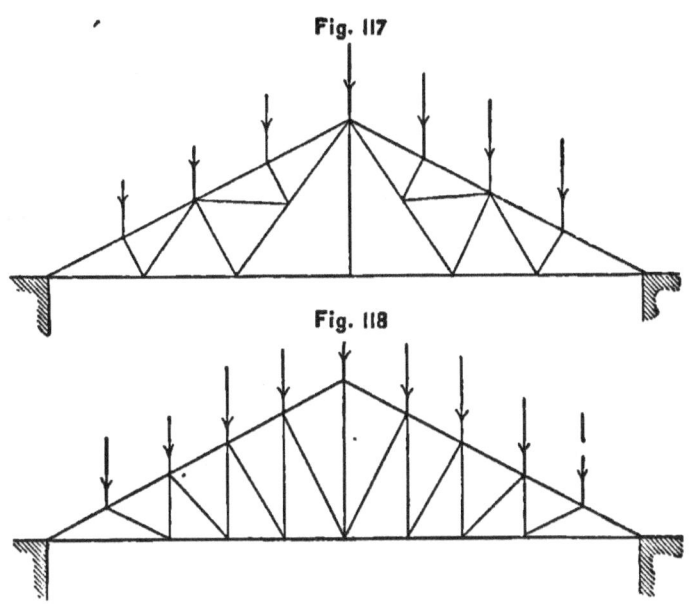

Fig. 117

Fig. 118

109. The graphical method may be conveniently applied to finding the stresses in a mechanism. Take, for example, the steam-engine. Let P be the pressure exerted by the piston on the pin A (Fig. 120) of the cross-head. It is transmitted by the connecting-rod to the crank-pin B, and

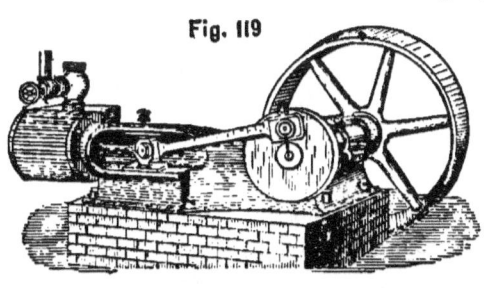

Fig. 119

thence to the crank axis C. If now the machinery is driven by a wheel CG on the axis C working in another wheel at G, the resistance R would be tangent to the pitch circles of these wheels. [This includes the case of a locomotive when the traction is exerted by adhesion to the rail XY. The amount of this adhesion corresponds to R.]

Consider the pin A. It is in equilibrium under the pressure P along the axis of the piston-rod, the thrust Q

along the connecting-rod, and the reaction N of the guide-bar of the cross-head. Hence plot P to scale, and complete the triangle of forces, from which scale off Q and N.

Again, the wheel CG is in equilibrium under the action of Q, R and the reaction S of the crank axis C. All three must meet in the point D, where Q and R meet. Hence plot the triangle of forces, and scale off S and R. The

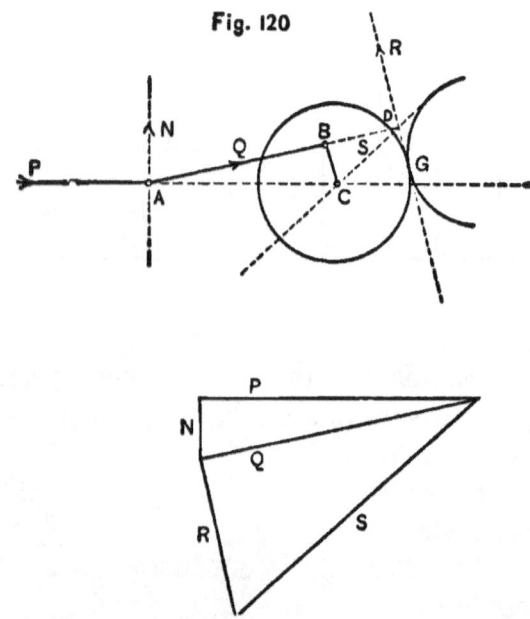

Fig. 120

relation between P the piston pressure and R the force transmitted to the mechanism is therefore determined.

We have neglected the weights of the pieces. The only one important to consider is the weight resting on the crank axis C. Call it W. It acts vertically. Combine Q and W into one resultant R_1. The reaction S will now pass through the intersection of R_1 and R. Hence complete the triangle of forces for R, S, R_1, and scale off S and R. Thus the relation between P and R is found.

Similarly, the weights of all of the pieces may be taken into account if desired.

110. Attraction.—In astronomy and mathematical electricity an important application of the composition of forces is to find the resultant attractive force between a finite body and a particle, the law of force being that known as the "law of inverse squares." This law may be stated as follows: *Every particle of matter in the universe attracts every other particle with a force whose direction is in the line joining them, and whose magnitude varies directly as the mass of each particle and inversely as the square of the distance between them.* Thus if the masses are m, m_1, and r the distance between them, the mutual attraction F is given by

$$F = cmm_1/r^2,$$

when c is a constant.

The attraction of one particle on another being an independent attraction, the total attraction of a number of particles (or body) on a particle is a problem of summation which is most readily solved by means of the integral calculus. We shall develop one problem to illustrate the method.

Ex. 1. To find the attraction of a uniform thin circular disc, radius a, thickness h, and density δ, on a particle O of unit mass situated on a line OC through the centre of the disc and perpendicular to its plane.

Let the distance $OC = b$. Conceive the disc divided into an indefinitely great number of concentric rings, centre C, and let x be the radius of any one of the rings and dx its width. Then mass of ring $= 2\pi x dx h \delta$, and distance of all points of the ring from $O = \sqrt{b^2 + x^2}$. Hence

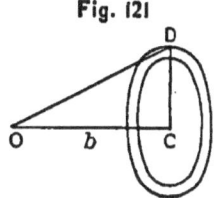

Fig. 121

attr. of ring along $OC = c \times 2\pi \delta h x dx \cos COD/(b^2 + x^2)$,

and result. attr. of disc $= 2\pi \delta c b h \int_0^r x dx/(b^2 + x^2)^{\frac{3}{2}}$

$$= 2\pi \delta c h \{1 - (b/b^2 + r^2)^{\frac{1}{2}}\},$$

an important result in mathematical electricity.

2. If the disc is of indefinitely great extent, show that the attraction $= 2\pi\delta c h$.

3. If the particle is indefinitely near to the disc, show that the attraction $= 2\pi\delta c h$. (See Thompson's *Electricity and Magnetism*.)

4. Hence show that all parallel discs of the same thickness, forming the bases of cones having the same vertical angle, exert the same force on a particle at the vertex.

5. Hence show from (4) that the resultant attraction of a thin spherical shell of uniform density on a particle situated within it is *nil*.

CHAPTER V.

FRICTION.

111. As already stated, greater simplicity and clearness are secured by considering the properties of bodies one at a time, and thus leading up to the actual state of the case—which is quite complicated, since bodies in nature possess many properties. Thus far the surface of a body has been assumed to be perfectly smooth, that is (Art. 63), to exert a pressure in a normal direction only, or what is the same thing, to offer no resistance to the motion of a body pressing against it. But in reality we know that if one body be moved along another (as a book along a table) a certain resistance will be offered to the motion. The resistance arises from irregularities in the surfaces in contact, from elevations and depressions which fit more or less closely into one another. To it the name **Friction** is given.

Suppose a body of weight W to rest on a horizontal table, and to be pressed by a vertical force Q (as of a load resting upon it). The total pressure $P\,(= Q + W)$ is balanced by the vertical reaction N of the table. If now a force is applied parallel to the table, and gradually increased, a magnitude F will be reached when the body is just on the point of moving. The body is held in equilibrium by the force P, the force F, and the reaction R, which can be no longer vertical. Let R be resolved into vertical and horizontal components. The vertical component must

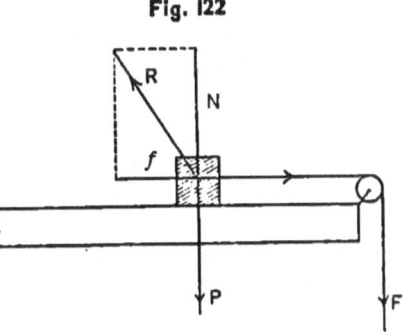

Fig. 122

be equal to P, and is therefore equal to the reaction N. The horizontal component f must be equal to the horizontal force F. This horizontal component arises from the frictional resistance, so that we may treat friction as if it were a force precisely similar to the acting force F, but of the contrary sense. The body being just on the point of moving, the friction resulting is named **Static Friction.**

From experiments carried out with this form of apparatus it is found that between surfaces with little or no lubrication, under moderate loads, and just beginning to slide on one another, the amount of static friction is—

(1) *Proportional to the normal pressure between the surfaces in contact.*

(2) *Independent of the areas in contact.*

(3) *Dependent on the material of which the bodies are composed.*

These are known as the laws of static friction. They are roughly true, not only when the motion is on the point of occurring, but also when the velocity of motion is small. Hence the friction f corresponding to the normal pressure N may be found from

$$f = \mu N,$$

where μ is a constant. It is called the **Coefficient of Friction,** and its value must be determined by experiment.

112. The above "laws" of friction were deduced from experiments made with surfaces having little or no lubrication, and moving with low velocities; and for such conditions only are they to be depended on. In machines, however, surfaces without lubrication and moving with low velocities are the exception, and we there have an entirely different set of conditions. The friction is now **Kinetic.***

---

* The distinction between static and kinetic friction was first pointed out by Coulomb (1736–1806). The laws of static friction were enunciated by Coulomb, and confirmed by the later experiments of Morin at Metz in 1837–1838.

Recent experiments show that even with surfaces of the same material, the character of the lubrication, the load, the velocity, the form of the surfaces, whether flat or curved, the areas as in contact, and the temperature of the surfaces have each great influence on the friction produced. No general relation between the friction (f) and the pressure (N) producing it has yet been deduced depending on these conditions. Special experiments are necessary in all cases where the conditions differ in any of the points mentioned from those entering into experiments already made.

We may, however, in general, write

$$f = \mu N,$$

when the value of μ is determined by the conditions of the problem. These conditions will show whether we may assume the so-called laws of statical friction or have recourse to special experiment.

Roughly, the coefficient of friction μ for *well-lubricated* surfaces is from $\frac{1}{6}$ to $\frac{1}{10}$ that for dry surfaces; and if the pressure and velocity are not very large, it varies inversely as the pressure, directly as the area in contact, and inversely as the temperature.

Ex. In a locomotive the engineer applies the brakes sufficiently to prevent slipping of the drivers in order to obtain the maximum brake retardation. Explain.

113. When one surface rolls on another, the resistance encountered is termed **Rolling Friction**. In mechanisms it is in general small, and need only be considered in very special cases. In a locomotive the rolling friction between the wheels and the rails, like the journal friction of the wheels, tends to diminish the adhesion of the engine on the rails.

114. The following coefficients of friction may be regarded as average values, to be used when no special experiments covering the cases under consideration are possible. The circumstances may be such that the tabular values are very far from the truth in these cases. Indeed, at present we may be said to be acquainted with no quantitative laws of friction of much value.

Metal on metal,	0.10 to 0.30
Metal on wood,	0.10 to 0.60
Wood on wood,	0.10 to 0.70
Wood on stone,	0.30 to 0.60
Stone on stone,	0.40 to 0.75

115. In the experiment of Art. 111, suppose the friction f and the reaction N combined into a single resultant R. Let ϕ denote the angle which R makes with the normal to the table. Draw to scale and complete the triangle of forces F, P, R. Then

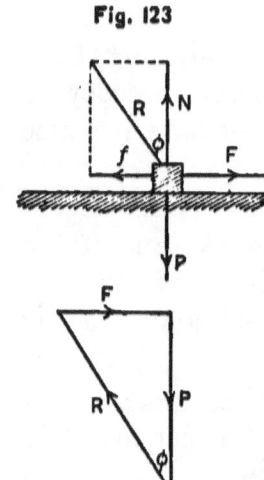

Fig. 123

$$\tan \phi = F/P = f/N = \mu.$$

Hence ϕ has always the same value so long as the substances in contact are the same and under the same conditions. It is called the **Angle of Friction**.

The fact that the reaction force R, which holds the applied forces F and P in equilibrium, makes with the normal to the surfaces in contact an angle equal to the angle of friction, gives a key to the application of the graphical method of the polygon of forces to problems involving friction. The method is especially valuable in cases where the forces are interlaced as in mechanisms.

Ex. 1. The weight on the driving-wheels of a locomotive is twenty tons, and the coefficient of friction is 0.2: find the greatest pull the engine is capable of. *Ans.* 4 tons.

2. A train moving at 40 miles an hour is brought to rest

by friction in half a minute. Prove that the coefficient of friction is 11/180.

116. If the reaction N is constant the direction of R will depend on the value of f, that is, of F. Hence, if F is such that the inclination of R to the normal exceeds the angle of friction, motion will take place. This gives us the clue to an experimental method of determining ϕ.

Suppose a body of weight W to rest on a table, and that the table is tilted through an angle θ about the edge A. We have now the body resting on an inclined plane. Continue tilting until the body is just on the point of moving down the plane. At this point the forces holding it in equilibrium are W, N, and f, which act as shown by the arrows. Draw the triangle of forces, and

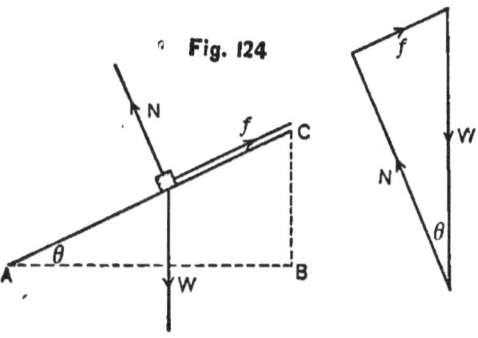
Fig. 124

$$f/N = \tan \theta.$$
But $$f/N = \tan \phi.$$

Hence, $\theta = \phi$, or the angle of inclination of the plane, is equal to ϕ, the angle of friction. For this reason the angle of friction is called the **Angle of Repose.**

Ex. 1. Deduce the relation between θ and ϕ by resolving the forces vertically and horizontally.

2. A boy's sled weighs 10 lbs. To pull it over a horizontal stretch of snow requires a force of 1 pound: find the coeff. of friction. *Ans.* 0.1.

3. Is it correct to say that between smooth surfaces the pressure is normal, but when friction occurs the pressure is inclined to the normal at the angle of friction?

[No. Pressure between surfaces is *always* normal. The

resultant of the pressure and friction makes an angle ϕ with the normal.]

4. To find the angle β which a given force F must make with the normal that a body of weight W may just be on the point of sliding on a horizontal surface.

Ans. $F \sin (\beta + \phi) = W \sin \phi$.

5. In Ex. 4 find for what value of β the force F is the least possible. *Ans.* $\beta = 90° - \phi$.

6. Find the force necessary to drag a body of weight W up the incline AC, the inclination θ of the plane and the direction β of the force being given.

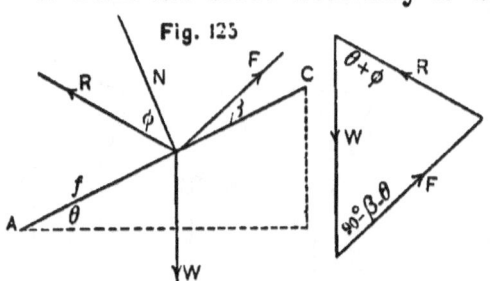

Fig. 125

[The force f will act down the plane. The forces acting are F, W, R. Form triangle of forces, and scale off F and R. Or compute from $F \cos (\beta - \phi) = W \sin (\theta + \phi)$. Get the same answer by resolution of forces.]

7. If the force is horizontal, prove
$$F = W \tan (\theta + \phi).$$

8. If the force is parallel to the plane, prove
$$F = W (\sin \theta \pm \mu \cos \theta)$$
as the body is on the point of moving up or down the plane.

9. In Ex. 6 find the force necessary to push the weight down the plane. *Ans.* $P \cos (\beta + \phi) = W \sin (\theta - \phi)$.

10. The force necessary to haul a train at uniform speed on a 1% grade is 3.5 times that on the level. Show that the coefficient of friction is 1/250.

11. The angle of a wooden incline is 68°. Show that it is impossible to drag a wooden block up the plane by a horizontal force, the coefficient of friction being 0.4.

12. The foot of a ladder of length l rests on the ground at A and the top at B against a rough vertical wall: find its inclination θ when on the point of sliding, the coefficient of friction in each case being 0.5.

Ans. $\tan \theta = \frac{3}{4}$.

117. Motion on a Rough Surface.

—Suppose a particle of mass m to slide on a rough horizontal plane of which the coefficient of friction is μ; then the normal pressure being mg and the friction μmg, we have for the acceleration of motion

$$a = -\mu mg/m = -\mu g.$$

If u is the initial velocity, we have, by substituting in the equations of Art. 13,

$$v = u - \mu gt,$$
$$v^2 = u^2 - 2\mu gs,$$
$$s = ut - \tfrac{1}{2}\mu gt^2,$$

and the motion is completely determined.

If the plane is inclined at an angle θ, then resolving mg into its components $mg \sin \theta$ along the plane, and $mg \cos \theta$ at right angles to it, the latter represents the pressure on the plane. Hence the friction is $\mu mg \cos \theta$, and the force causing motion down the plane is $mg \sin \theta - \mu mg \cos \theta$. Therefore the acceleration down the plane is found from

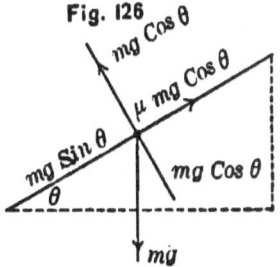

Fig. 126

$$a = (mg \sin \theta - \mu mg \cos \theta)/m$$
$$= g (\sin \theta - \mu \cos \theta)$$
$$= g \sin (\theta - \phi)/ \cos \phi,$$

if ϕ is the limiting angle of friction.

Ex. 1. A body with initial velocity u slides along a rough horizontal plane on which the coefficient of friction is μ: show that it will come to rest in $u/\mu g$ seconds after passing over a distance $u^2/2\mu g$.

2. If a body is projected up a plane whose inclination is θ, show that $a = -g \sin (\theta + \phi)/ \cos \phi$.

3. A train of w lbs. is hauled along a horizontal track by a constant pull of p pounds. If the resistance of friction

is f pounds, find the velocity of the train in t seconds after starting from rest, and the distance passed over in that time. *Ans.* $s = \frac{1}{2}(p-f)gt^2/w$.

4. A train of 100 tons (excluding engine) runs up a 1% grade with an acceleration of 1 ft. per sec. If the friction is 10 pounds per ton, find the pull on the drawbar between engine and train. *Ans.* $4\frac{5}{8}$ tons.

We now pass to various practical applications of the principles laid down.

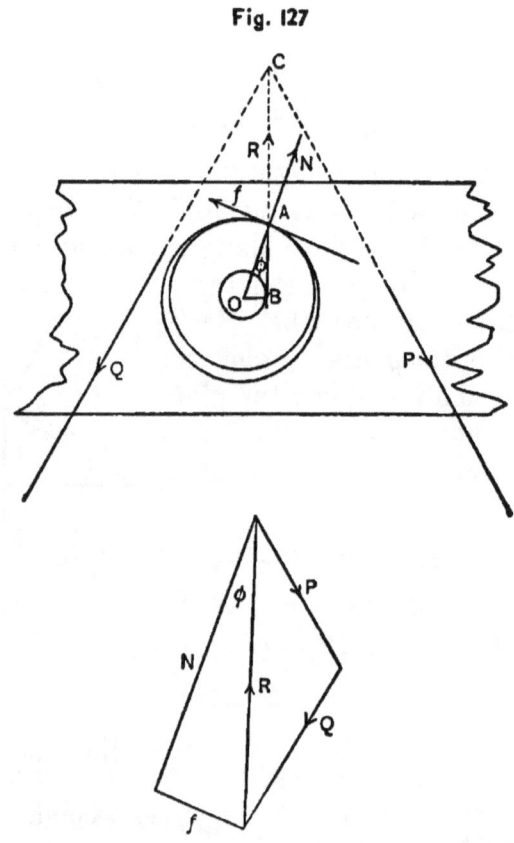

Fig. 127

118. Axle, Journal, or Pin Friction.—A beam AB is pierced by a shaft O, about which as an axis it is acted on by two forces P, Q, of which P is the driving force and Q the resistance.

Suppose P to be on the point of overcoming Q. The pressure N between the two surfaces being normal, passes through the centre O. The resultant R of N and the friction f must pass through C, the intersection of P and Q, and at the same time be inclined to the direction of N at an angle ϕ. Hence plot P to scale, construct the triangle of forces, and scale off Q and R. The point A, through which the resultant R passes, is the point where the pressures on the axles are concentrated. The reaction N and friction f at A may be found by completing the triangle of forces to the left.

Notice that if we drop a perpendicular OB on R and describe a circle with radius OB, the direction of R is a tangent to this circle. But $OB = r \sin \phi$, a known quantity. Hence, to plot R describe a circle of radius $= r \sin \phi = \mu r$ nearly, and a tangent from C, the intersection of P and Q, to this circle will give the direction of R. This circle is known as the **Friction Circle.***

From C two tangents may be drawn to the friction circle. The one to be chosen can always be found by considering the direction of the driving force and the consequent direction of the friction (and therefore of R) between the journal and bearing to oppose it.

If the axle rotates *uniformly*, the solution is the same. For when it is just on the point of motion the condition of equilibrium is that the moment of the driving force is equal to that of the resistance. If now the axle revolves uniformly, the force acting must be a centripetal force, and the moment of this force about the axis being *nil*, the condition of equilibrium remains unaltered.

Ex. 1. If P and Q are parallel, show that
$$f = \mu(P + Q), \text{ nearly.}$$

2. Show that the pull on the drawbar of a train due to journal friction is per ton weight of the train

* The friction circle was first given by Rankine (1820–1872).

$= 2000 \mu r_1/r_2$ pounds, when r_1 is the radius of the journal, r_2 the radius of the wheel, and μ the coefficient of friction.

119. A good illustration of sliding and axle friction in a mechanism is afforded by the reciprocating parts of a steam-engine. (See Figs. 119, 123.)

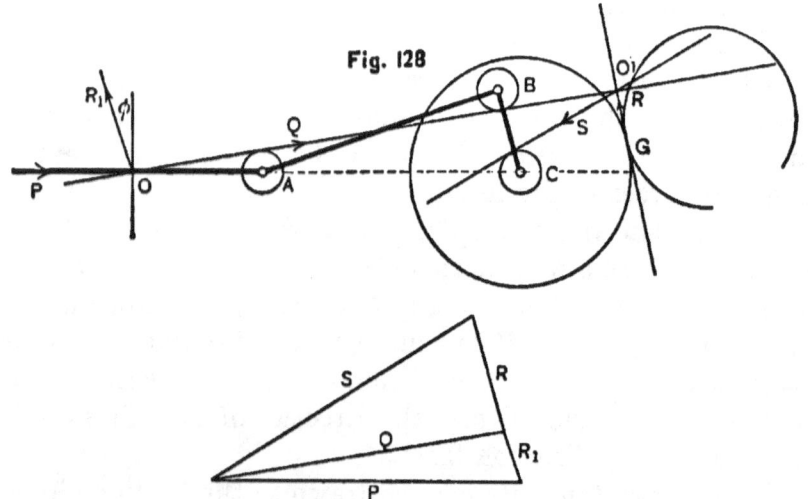

Fig. 128

Draw the friction circles at the pins A, B, C. The thrust Q along the connecting-rod lies in the common tangent to the friction circles at A and B (Art. 118).

Consider the pin A. It is in equilibrium under the piston pressure P along the axis of the piston-rod, the thrust Q of the connecting-rod, the sliding friction f, and the reaction N at the cross-head guides. The resultant R_1 of f and N makes the angle of friction ϕ with the normal to the sliding surface. Its direction must pass through O, the intersection of P and Q. Hence plot P to scale, complete the triangle of forces, and scale off Q and R_1.

Again: the wheel CG is in equilibrium under Q, R, and the reaction S of the crank axis C. All three must meet in the point O_1, where Q and R meet. Hence plot the triangle of forces for Q, S, R, and scale off the values of S and R.

BELT FRICTION.

The relation between P and R is therefore determined.

Ex. Draw the stress diagram if the weight W of the wheel CG is taken into account.

120. We have already found the ratio of R to P when friction was neglected (Art. 109). This was a purely theoretical value. The actual case in which friction occurs is that just considered. The ratio of R to P is here less than in the former case. The ratio of the latter or actual value to the theoretical value is known as the *efficiency* of the mechanism. (See Art. 139.)

121. Belt Friction.—Consider a belt or rope passing over (or around) a cylindrical block securely fastened, and let P_1, Q_1 denote the forces at the ends of the belt. Suppose P_1 to be just on the point of overcoming Q_1, or that the belt is moving with uniform velocity. The forces acting on the belt are P_1, Q_1, the reaction of the cylinder and the friction of the cylinder. In order to find the relation between them, conceive the arc of contact θ of the belt cut into elements of indefinitely small length ds, find the relation for one element, and then sum up for the whole arc. Consider now a single element ab of the belt, and let P, $P + dP$ be the tensions at the points a, b; p the normal pressure per unit of length of arc, and therefore pds the pressure on ab, which may be taken to act at a, and $\mu p ds$ the frictional resistance on ab. Call $aOb = d\theta$.

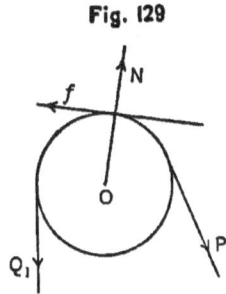

Fig. 129

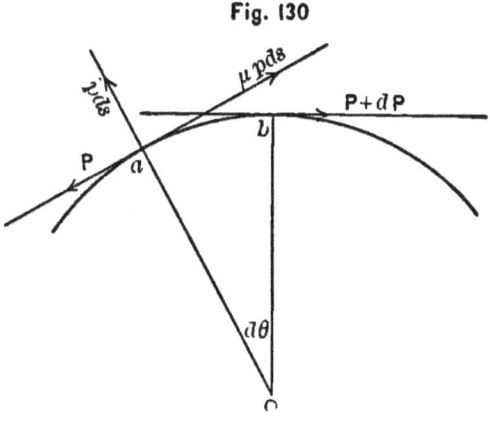

Fig. 130

Then, neglecting the weight of the belt,
$\mu p ds = (P + dP) \cos d\theta - P = dP$, ultimately;
$p ds = (P + dP) \sin d\theta = P d\theta$, since $d\theta$ is small.

Eliminating pds, we have
$$dP = \mu P d\theta.$$
Summing up all of the elements of the rope in contact with the cylinder,
$$\int_{Q_1}^{P_1} dP/P = \int_0^\theta \mu d\theta,$$
or $\quad \log_e P_1/Q_1 = \mu\theta,$

or $\quad P_1 = Q_1 e^{\mu\theta},$

when e is the base of the natural system of logarithms ($= 2.718$) and θ is the angle subtended by the arc of contact between the rope and the cylinder expressed in circular measure.

Transferring to the common system of logarithms, as more convenient for computation,
$$\log_{10} P_1/Q_1 = 0.434 \mu\theta.$$

If the weight Q_1 is on the point of slipping down instead of being drawn up, the action is the same as if P_1 and Q_1 changed places, and therefore $Q_1 = P_1 e^{\mu\theta}$.

The conditions are the same and the relation between P_1 and Q_1 is the same if the cylinder instead of being fixed is capable of turning about O, and no slipping occurs, axle friction being neglected.

122. Suppose, for example, the pulley B drives the pulley A of radius r by means of a belt passing round them. Let P, Q denote the tensions of the belt on the two sides of A. The effective driving force is $P - Q$, the difference of the tensions. This may

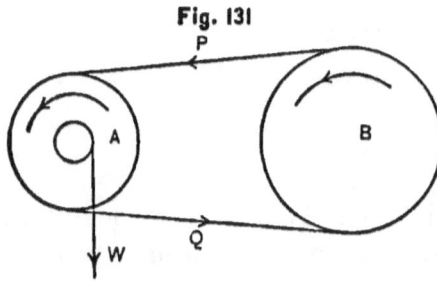

Fig. 131

BELT FRICTION. 141

be balanced by the raising of a weight W on a concentric pulley of radius s. Just at the point of motion we have

$$Ws = (P - Q)r,$$

from which equation, along with $P = Qe^{\mu\theta}$, P and Q may be found. (See Art. 138.)

Ex. 1. A rope passing over a wooden cylinder supports a barrel of flour weighing 196 lbs., find the force which will just raise the barrel, the coefficient of friction being 0.4.
Ans. 689 pounds.

2. In Ex. 1 find the force that will just keep the barrel from slipping down. *Ans.* 56 lbs.

3. Find the number n of turns of rope round a snubbing-post that a man pulling P pounds may just be able to hold a canal-boat pulling Q pounds. *Ans.* $2\pi\mu n = \log_e P/Q$.

4. A chain is wrapped twice round an iron drum: find the coefficient of friction if a pull of 100 pounds just supports 50 tons. *Ans.* 0.55.

5. If $\mu = 0.25$, and a rope passes twice round a post, prove that any force will balance another more than twenty times as great.

6. In the St. Louis cable road the contact is two wraps of the cable on the driving drum, which is 10 ft. diameter: compare the tension of the taut side of the cable with the tension of the slack side.

123. *Effect of Centrifugal Force.*—The relation between the tension and pressure at any point results from the second equation on p. 140. For

$$P = pds/d\theta = pr.$$

When a belt is run at a high rate of speed, the effect of the centrifugal force of the belt is to lessen the normal pressure on the pulley. If w is the weight of 1 unit length of belt, and v the velocity, the centrifugal force per unit length is wv^2/gr where r is the radius of the pulley. Hence the normal pressure p per unit on the pulley is $P/r - wv^2/gr$, and

$$P = pr + wv^2/g,$$

or the tension is increased by wv^2/g. Hence the greatest tension instead of being P_1 is $P_1 + wv^2/g$, when centrifugal force is taken into account.

This value, substituted for the greatest tension in the preceding formulas, will enable us to find the belt dimensions.

124. Pulley Tackle.—We may discuss the friction of pulley tackle as a special case of axle friction. The resistance arises mainly from the friction of the axles of the sheaves.

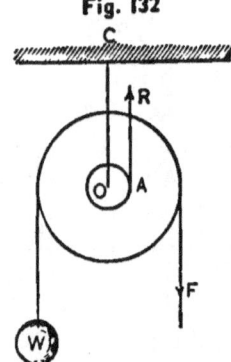

Fig. 132

Consider the simple case of the fixed pulley. Let F be the driving force, W the weight of the body to be raised, r radius of pulley axle and a radius of pulley sheaf.

Describe the friction circle of radius μr and centre O. The resultant pressure is tangent to this circle and parallel to F and W. If F is on the point of moving down, its position is as in the figure. Take moments about A,

$$F(a - \mu r) = W(a + \mu r),$$

or
$$F = W(a + \mu r)/(a - \mu r)$$

$$= (1 + 2\mu r/a) W, \text{ nearly,}$$

$$= \lambda W, \text{ suppose,}$$

where the coefficient λ is introduced for convenience of writing. It gives the relation between F and W.

Ex. 1. If the axle were smooth, then $F = W$.
2. The efficiency $= 1/\lambda$.
3. The effect of the friction is the same as the raising of an additional weight $(\lambda - 1) W$ if the axle were smooth.
4. Find the tension of the cord supporting the pulley.

DIFFERENTIAL PULLEY.

In the derrick represented in Fig. 133, where the rope passes under the movable pulley and over the fixed, we have the tensions as follows: F the driver, F/λ the first driver, F/λ^2 the second driver. Hence, considering the cords parallel,
$$W = F(\lambda + 1)/\lambda^2.$$

Fig. 133

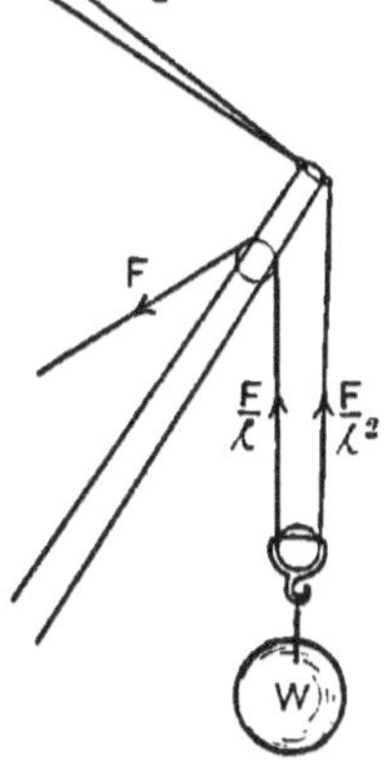

Ex. 1. If friction is neglected, show that $W = 2F$.
2. The efficiency $= (\lambda + 1)/2\lambda^2$.
3. Solve the problem by a graphical construction.
4. With two double sheave blocks
$$W = F(\lambda^6 - 1)/(\lambda^5 - \lambda^4).$$
5. With two double sheave blocks, neglecting friction, $W = 5F$. Hence find the loss due to friction.
6. In a double sheave tackle the under block is fixed and the upper movable: find the pull on the support A, and the loss due to friction.

125. The **Differential Pulley** consists in the upper block of two sheaves, radii a, b, fastened together, and in the lower block of a single sheaf of diameter $a + b$. An endless chain passes round the sheaves as in the figure. Notches are cut or teeth set in the upper block sheaves which fit the links of the chain.

Let F be the force applied, and W the weight which is on the point of being raised. Consider the lower pulley. One chain is driver the other is driven. If F_1 denotes the tension of the driver, the tension of the driven is λF_1, from Art. 124. Hence
$$W = F_1 + \lambda F_1. \quad \ldots \ldots \quad (1)$$

On the upper block F and F_1 drive and λF_1 is driven: F and λF_1 act on the larger sheaf, and F_1 when reduced to this sheaf is $F_1 b/a$. Hence
$$F + F_1 b/a = \lambda \times \lambda F_1 = \lambda^2 F_1.$$

144 FRICTION.

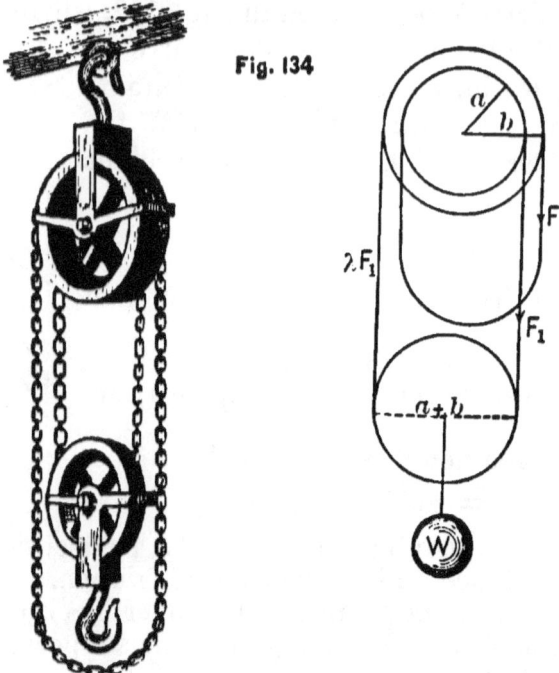

Fig. 134

Substitute for F_1 its value from (1) and

$$F = W(\lambda^2 a - b)/a(1 + \lambda),$$

which gives the relation between F and W.

If the driving force F is removed, that is, if $F = 0$, then, whatever be the weight, we must have for equilibrium

$$\lambda^2 a - b = 0,$$

which gives the relation between the radii, that this may be possible. If $\lambda = 1.1$ then $b/a = 1.2$, and the diameters of the pulleys are roughly as 6 to 5. For these dimensions the chain will not slip, whatever weight is being raised. The practical value of the pulley lies largely in this circumstance.

THE SCREW. 145

Ex. 1. Examine a pulley of this kind in a machine-shop.
2. In a differential pulley the diameters of the pulleys of the compound sheave are a, b in.: find how many revolutions are required to raise the weight c inches.
Ans. $2c/\pi(a+b)$.

126. The Screw.—In the cases of axle friction considered, the motion has been simply a motion of rotation,—either the bearing rotating about the axis as in the pulley, or the axle rotating in the bearing as in shafting. We may conceive, however, the axle not only to revolve, but to *advance* in the bearing, or the bearing to revolve and advance along the axis. The combination of the two motions gives rise to **Screw Motion**.

Thus suppose H to be any point on the circumference of a cylinder AB which revolves in a bearing, or *nut* and at the same time advances uniformly along the axis.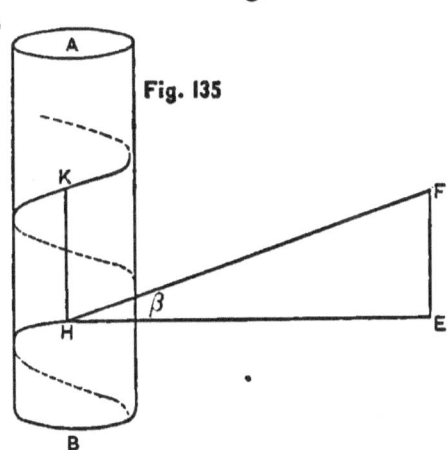
AB. By the motion of rotation alone, while the cylinder makes a revolution, H would describe a path equal to the circumference. Develop this in the line HE. But the motion of translation carries it a distance equal to EF. Hence it is found at K, and the path HK would be traced by wrapping the triangle HEF about the cylinder. The path of the point H is called the **Thread** of the screw, and the distance HK or EF between consecutive threads the **Pitch**.

The inclination of the thread to the axis is given by the angle $EHF(=\beta)$. Now

$$\tan \beta = EF/HE$$
$$= \text{pitch/circum. of cylr.},$$

Fig. 135

a constant quantity. Hence the inclination of the thread to the axis is always the same.

Consider a screw-jack with a force F applied at the end of a lever l, and that a weight W is on the point of being raised.

The force F with lever arm l is equivalent to Fl/r with lever arm r, or acting along the thread. The screw is in

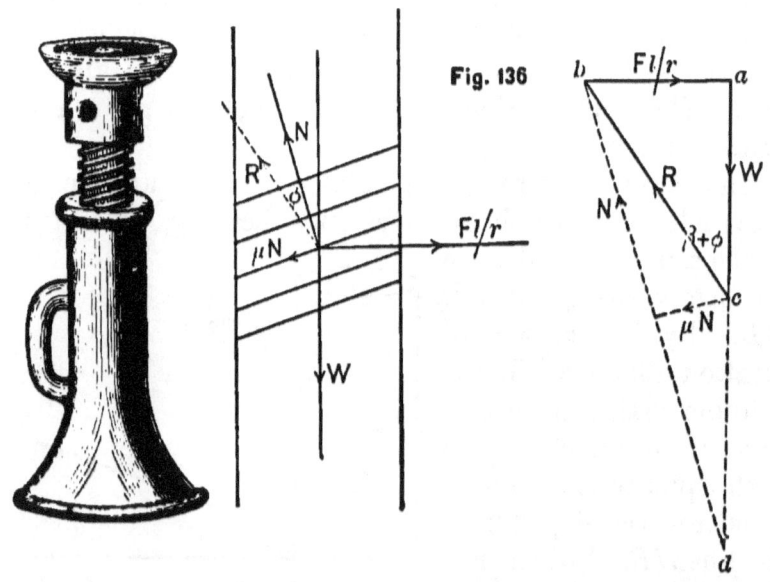

Fig. 136

equilibrium under the action of W vertical, Fl/r horizontal, the reaction N inclined at the pitch angle β to the axis, and the friction μN along the thread. The resultant R of N and μN makes an angle ϕ with the normal. Hence lay off W to scale, complete the triangle of forces, and scale off Fl/r and R. Or from the triangle we have at once

$$\frac{Fl}{r} \Big/ W = \tan(\beta + \phi),$$

or
$$Fl = Wr \tan(\beta + \phi).$$

THE SCREW.   147

Without friction, equilibrium exists between Fl/r, N, and W. Hence abd would represent the triangle of forces, and

$$\text{efficiency} = \frac{ac}{ad} = \frac{ac}{ab} \Big/ \frac{ad}{ab} = \tan \beta / \tan (\beta + \phi)$$

Ex. 1. Deduce the relation between F and W by resolution of forces.

2. If $\beta = 0$, the efficiency is null. Explain.

3. In what other case is the efficiency null?

4. Show that the efficiency of a screw is greatest when the pitch angle is 45°, nearly.

5. In a screw the pitch angle is 45° and the coefficient of friction 0.16: find the efficiency.   *Ans.* 0.72.

6. If $\tan \beta = 0.1$, $\tan \phi = 0.01$, prove efficiency $= 0.9$;
      $\tan \beta = 0.1$, $\tan \phi = 0.1$,   "   " $= 0.5$;
      $\tan \beta = 0.1$, $\tan \phi = 0.2$,   "   " $= 0.3$.

Hence show the importance of lubrication.

CHAPTER VI.

WORK AND ENERGY.

127. When an agent exerts force on a body the effects produced are change of position and change of form. The first of these has been considered in the preceding chapters, the effect of force being measured by the acceleration produced. All of the results found depend on the experimental principles assumed, the laws of inertia, mass-acceleration, and stress.

We now proceed to study the effects of force from another point of view, and to lay down a method of treating these effects more general than that stated hitherto, in that it applies to change of form as well as to change of position. The comparison of results reached by the two methods affords a test of the truth of the new method just as already pointed out, that the truth of the laws of motion is not capable of direct demonstration, but must be tested by consequences arising from assuming their truth.

In order that change of position or change of form may occur by the action of a force, the body must yield to the force, or, in other words, the point of application of the force must be displaced. When this displacement occurs, **Work** is said to be done *by* the force and *on* the resistance offered. Thus when a body is falling freely, work is done by the force of gravity on the body; while a spring is being bent, work is done by the acting force on the spring; and so on. If a body is lifted vertically upwards, work is being done by the lifting force and against the force of gravity.

If, then, we take work in the direction of a force as +, that done against a force must be taken as —.

In lifting a weight W (that is, in overcoming the gravity force of W) through a height h, the work done depends on the values of W and h, and is measured by the product Wh. In general, *the work K of a force F is measured by the product of the force and the displacement s of its point of application in the direction of the force*, or

$$K = Fs.$$

This is the case whether the displacement is actually made or is only conceived to be made. In the latter case the work is said to be *virtual* (= hypothetical).

128. In the definition nothing is said about the *path* of the point of application of the force. If, then, the point of application A of a force F acting along the line OA be displaced to B in any path, and BC be let fall perpendicular to OA, the distance AB is the total displacement, and the distance AC is the displacement s of A in the direction of the force. Hence by the definition

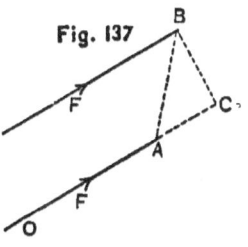

Fig. 137

$$\begin{aligned} K &= F \times AC \\ &= F \times AB \cos \theta \\ &= F \cos \theta \times AB; \end{aligned}$$

or, *the work done by a force acting obliquely to the path of a body is measured by the product of the force and the projection on its direction of the total displacement, or by the product of the component of the force along the total displacement by that displacement.*

When $\theta = 90°$, then $\cos \theta = 0$ and $K = 0$. Hence when the displacement is at right angles to the direction of the force, the work of the force is *nil*.

Ex. In a pendulum find the work done by the pull of the rod on the bob as it swings to and fro.   *Ans. nil.*

129. In the general formula for work

$$K = Fs;$$

taking $F = 1$, $s = 1$, we have $K = 1$; and therefore the *unit of work* is taken to be the work done by unit force acting through unit distance. Two forms are in common use—the scientific or laboratory unit, and the engineering unit or unit of every-day life.

The scientific unit of work in the F. P. S. system is the work done by a force of one poundal acting through a distance of one foot, and is called the **Foot-poundal**; in the C. G. S. system it is the work done by a force of one dyne acting through one centimeter, and is called the **Erg**. Thus a force of 10 poundals acting through 2 ft. will do a work of 20 ft.-poundals, and 10 dynes through 1 meter a work of 1000 ergs. To avoid inconveniently large numbers, an enlarged unit, the **Joule**, equal to 10^7 ergs, is often used in the C. G. S. system.

The engineering unit of work is based on the gravitation measure of force, and is the work done by a force of one pound acting through a distance of one foot. This is usually called a **Foot-pound**. Thus the work done in raising 100 lbs. vertically through 6 feet is the work done in overcoming a weight (= gravity force) of 100 pounds through 6 feet, and is 600 foot-pounds. In the metric system the engineering unit is the kilogrammeter (kgm.), which is the work done by a force of one kilogram acting through a distance of one meter.

130. The dimensions of the unit of work will be the dimensions of $F \times s$. The dimensions of F are ML/T^2 (Art. 41) and of s, L. Hence the dimensions of K are ML^2/T^2.

CONDITION OF EQUILIBRIUM. 151

This is the same result as that obtained for the dimensions of the moment of a force* (p. 95).

Ex. 1. Prove 1 kilogrammeter = 7.23 foot-pounds.
2. Prove 1 foot-pound = 13.56 × 10^6 ergs, approx.
3. Prove 1 foot-poundal = 0.42 × 10^6 ergs, nearly.
4. The tractive force of a consolidation engine is 10 tons. Find the work done in hauling a train one mile.
Ans. 105600000 ft.-pounds.

131. When the direction of displacement of the point of application is not in the line of action of the force considered, the body must be acted on by other forces, and the work done estimated for each separately. Thus consider a particle of weight W to rest against a smooth vertical wall, and to be raised vertically by a force F acting at an angle θ to the vertical. Let AB be the displacement. The work done against gravity is $W \times AB$. The work done by the reaction N is *nil*. The work done by F is $F \times BC$.

Fig. 138

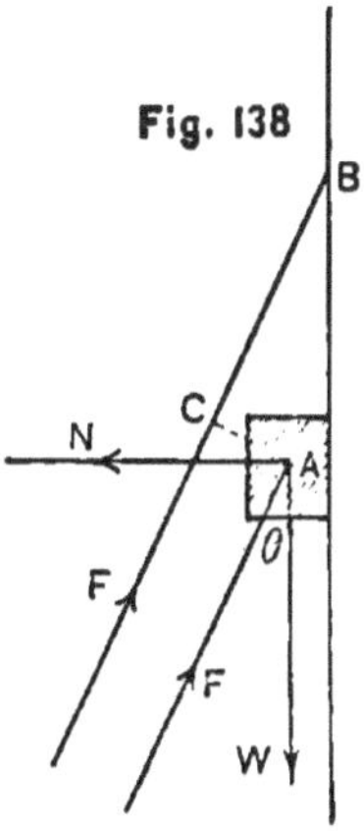

If the motion is uniform, that is, if the forces acting are in equilibrium, we have, by resolving vertically,

$$F \cos \theta - W = 0.$$

Multiply each member by AB, and

$$F \cos \theta \times AB - W \times AB = 0,$$
or
$$F \times BC - W \times AB = 0;$$

or, *when equilibrium exists, the sum of the works of the forces acting at the point is zero.*

---

* There is really a difference between the dimensions of the two, as unit work is the product of a force into a displacement in the direction of the force, and unit moment is the product of a force into a distance perpendicular to the direction of the force, so that the latter is strictly $\sqrt{-1} ML^2/T^2$.

132. More generally, let several forces F_1, F_2, ... act at a point causing a displacement OA. Let R be the resultant of the forces.

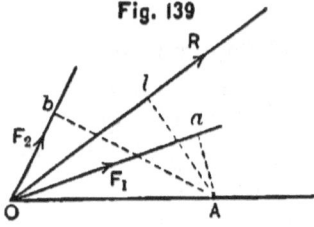
Fig. 139

From A let fall perpendiculars on the directions of the forces, and let θ_1, θ_2, ... be the inclinations of these directions to OA, and θ the inclination of the resultant R. Then (Art. 50)

$$R \cos \theta = F_1 \cos \theta_1 + F_2 \cos \theta_2 + \ldots,$$

or $\quad R \times Oa/OA = F_1 \times Ob/OA + F_2 \times Oc/OA + \ldots,$

or $\quad R \times Oa = F_1 \times Ob + F_2 \times Oc + \ldots;$

or the work done by the forces is equal to that done by their resultant.

The equation may be written

$$0 = -R \times Oa + F_1 \times Ob + F_2 \times Oc + \ldots,$$

which shows that *the algebraic sum of the works done by a system of forces acting at a point and in equilibrium is equal to zero.*

Conversely, if any number of forces act at a point, the condition of equilibrium is that the sum of the works done for every displacement shall be equal to zero. For the sum of the works is equal to the work of the resultant, and for equilibrium the work done by the resultant must be equal to zero for each and every displacement. This is the **Principle of Work** as applied to forces acting at a point, or to forces acting on a particle.

133. The principle of work may be regarded as included in the law of stress (Art. 27), the work done by the forces F_1, F_2, ... corresponding to the action, and the work done by $-R$, or rather the work done against R, to the reaction. In this sense we have merely the law in another form, the action of the agent being measured by the work done by it, and the reaction of the resistance by the work done against it. Looked at in this light, the principle of work falls within our old lines, and is therefore consistent with them.

134. It follows by summing up from particle to particle of a rigid body, that the condition of equilibrium is that the sum of the works done by the forces acting is for every displacement equal to zero. For, the body being rigid, no work is done as the forces are transferred from particle to particle, since there is no yielding. Hence it is necessary to take into account the external forces only.

The same principle will evidently apply to a *system* of bodies rigidly connected, or so connected that the geometrical relations existing among the parts are not disturbed by the displacement, and hence to what we call a **Machine**. A machine is so constructed that the configuration of the parts is not disturbed when it is in operation.

The external forces, that is, the driving force and the resisting force, form a system in equilibrium; and hence the relation between them follows at once by equating to zero the sum of the works done. The work done by the driving and resisting forces being contrary in character, will be denoted by opposite signs.

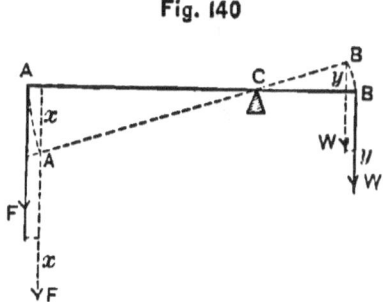

Fig. 140

Ex. 1. In the straight lever to find the relation between F and W.

[Let the point of application A of the force F descend a distance x, and B consequently ascend a distance y. Then
$$Fx - Wy = 0.$$
But from similar triangles
$$x : y = AC : BC.$$
$$\therefore F \times AC = W \times BC,$$
which is the "principle of the lever" (Art. 88).]

2. In a pulley tackle the driving force descends 1 ft., while the weight to be raised ascends 1 in. What force will raise 1 ton? *Ans.* $166\frac{2}{3}$ pounds.

3. In a bell-bottom jack-screw (Fig. 136) with force F applied at the end of a lever arm l a body of weight W is being raised with uniform velocity. Prove
$$F \times 2\pi l = W \times \text{pitch of screw}.$$
[Notice that while the lever arm makes one turn, the weight is raised a distance equal to the pitch of the screw.]

4. Find the relation between F and W in the copying-press (Fig. 72), $2l$ being the length of the handle.

Ans. $F = W \times \text{pitch of screw}/4\pi l$.

5. In a telescopic jack-screw a smaller screw C works in

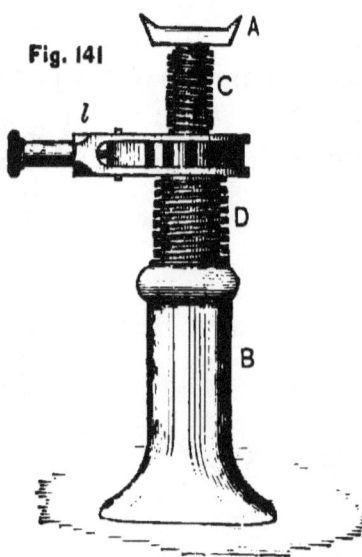

Fig. 141

a companion nut cut in the larger screw D, which latter works in a nut in the fixed block B. The block A being fixed, the upper screw does not rotate. If l is the length of the lever arm, find the relation between F and W.

Ans. $F \times 2\pi l = W \times $ diff. of pitch of screws.

6. In a hoisting machine (Fig. 142) the gears are 36 to 36 teeth, the drum 21 in. diameter, and the load for one horse $1\frac{1}{2}$ ton. Find the pull exerted by the horse at the end of a 7 ft. horizontal lever.

Ans. 375 pounds.

WORK AGAINST FRICTION. 155

7. In a derrick winch (Fig. 80) the crank is l in. leverage,

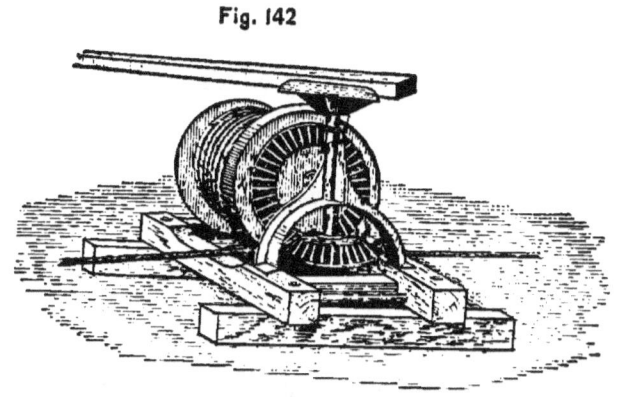
Fig. 142

the gears n to 1, and the drum d in. diameter. Find the two-man-power capacity, each man exerting a force of p pounds.

Ans. $4pln/d$ pounds.

8. In a combination of single-threaded worm and wheel used in hoists, the worm wheel has n teeth, the lever handle is l in. long, and the radius of the drum around which the lifting rope winds is r in. Find the relation between F and W. *Ans.* $Fln = Wr$.

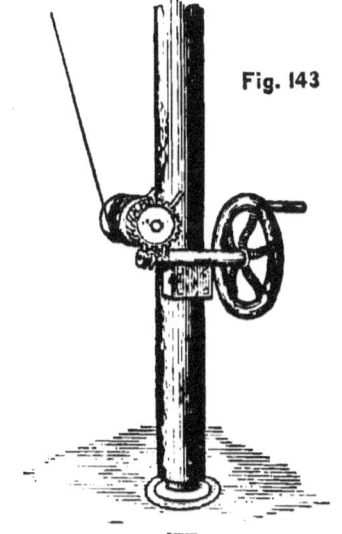
Fig. 143

135. To overcome friction, as to overcome any resistance, a certain driving force or *effort* is necessary. In a machine, therefore, work must be done to balance the friction that arises. Part of the effort communicated is taken up in doing this work, which is, as it were, *absorbed*. This work may serve no useful purpose, and is therefore said to be wasted. This does not mean that the work is lost, as we shall see presently.

The work absorbed by friction is measured as the work

done by any other resistance. We have

Work against fric. = fric. × dist. desc. = $P\mu s$,

where P is the normal pressure on the journal, μ the coefficient of friction, and s the distance described.

Thus the work done in overcoming the frictional resistance in one revolution of a journal of diameter d and carrying a load of W lbs. is $W\mu \times \pi d$ ft.-pounds. In case the journal revolves n times per minute the work absorbed is $W\mu \times \pi d \times n$ ft.-pounds per minute.

Ex. 1. Find the work done in hauling a sled weighing 500 lbs. half a mile, the coefficient of friction being 0.2.

Ans. 264,000 ft.-pounds.

2. Show that the work done in hauling a body of weight W up a rough incline AC is equal to that done in hauling it along the level AB, the coefficient of friction being the same, and in raising it through the height BC.

Fig. 144

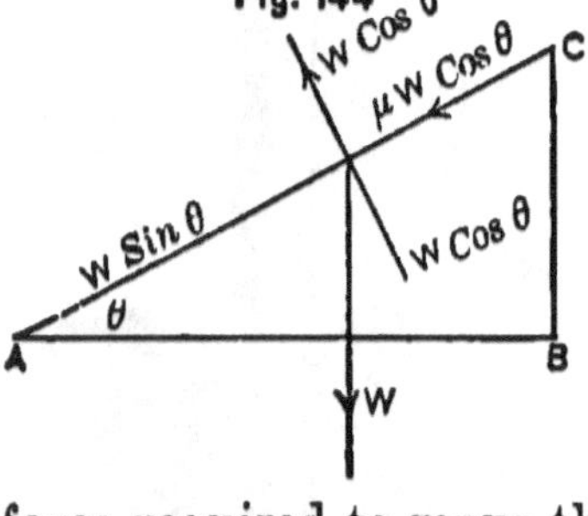

[For W is equivalent to $W \sin\theta$ along the plane, and $W \cos\theta$ at right angles to it. Hence the force of friction along the plane is $\mu W \cos\theta$. The total effective force required to move the body up the plane is

$$W \sin\theta + \mu W \cos\theta.$$

Work done in moving from A to C

$$= (W \sin\theta + \mu W \cos\theta)AC$$
$$= W \times BC + \mu W \times AB,$$

which proves the proposition.

For moderate inclines the work done may be taken equal to $W \times BC + \mu W \times AC$.]

3. Find the work done in hauling a train of 100 tons one mile up a 1% grade, the resistance being 8 pounds per ton.

Ans. 2800 × 5280 ft.-pounds, nearly.

WORK OF A VARIABLE FORCE.

136. We have considered the force acting and the resistance to be overcome as uniform in their action. It more frequently happens that they are *variable*. For example, the pressure of a compressed spring, the pressure on the piston of a steam-engine before and after the steam is cut off, etc. In cases of varying resistance, the work done is the same as would be done by a force acting uniformly, and which is equal to the *average* of the varying forces. This average as in the case of velocities is most conveniently estimated graphically (Art. 8).

Thus let AL plotted to scale represent the distance passed over by the point of application of the force, and let Aa plotted to scale represent the force at A. If the force is uniform throughout, the work done $(= AL \times Aa)$ is represented by the area of the rectangle Al.

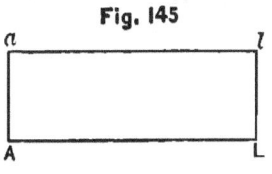

Fig. 145

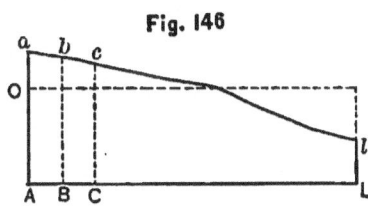

Fig. 146

If the force is variable, let the distance AL be divided into a large number, n, of equal parts $AB, BC, \ldots$ and let $Aa, Bb, \ldots$ represent the corresponding forces. The average force acting through the distance AB may be taken to be $\tfrac{1}{2}(Aa + Bb)$, through BC to be $\tfrac{1}{2}(Bb + Cc)$, etc. Hence, by addition,

$$\text{Work done} = \frac{1}{2}\frac{AL}{n}(Aa + 2Bb + 2Cc + \ldots + Ll).$$

If $AB, BC, \ldots$ are indefinitely small, the curve $abc \ldots l$ becomes continuous, and represents the varying action of the force. It is called the **Curve of Resistance**. The total work done would be represented by the area $AalL$.

By means of certain contrivances the curve of resistance may be plotted mechanically by the resistance itself, as, for example, in the steam-engine by the **Indicator**. Having the curve, the mean resistance AO may be found by stretching a string so as to have equal areas above and below it. Or the area may be read off at once by an Amsler polar planimeter, and the work done found directly. Or the indicator drawing or "card" may be divided up by drawing equidistant ordinates, the lengths of these ordinates scaled off, and the formula above applied. All of these methods are at times useful.

137. Power.—It is important to notice that the term work, as defined above, is not in all respects the same as what is called work in ordinary language. Ordinarily the idea of time enters, and the idea of motion is not essential. A man merely supporting a load does not come under the mechanical definition, no matter how long he may support it, though he is doing work in the ordinary sense of the term.

The definition is somewhat arbitrary, which is quite allowable so long as we use the term consistently with the definition. It is plain from the definition that any small force can do work of any magnitude provided sufficient time is given. Hence, in order to compare *agents* which do work, it is necessary to take the time employed into consideration.

To indicate the amount of work performed in a given time, the term **Power** is used. By the unit of power we mean the power of an agent which can do unit work in one second. This is expressed as foot-poundals per second, or ergs per second, or foot-pounds per second, according to the system of units employed. Thus to raise 1 ton of coal through 100 feet in 10 min. would require an expenditure of 2000×100 ft.-pounds of work in 10 min., or of 20,000 ft.-pounds per minute, which would be the expression of the power of the agent.

When the power of an agent doing work is great, no very definite idea is conveyed by the large numbers of the above units that indicate this, and accordingly multiples of the units are used. In engineering work the multiple unit employed is called a *horse-power*. The term horsepower was introduced by James Watt. As horses formerly did the work done by steam-engines, it was natural to institute a comparison. Watt found that a Clydesdale horse could walk $2\frac{1}{2}$ miles an hour, and at the same time raise a weight of 150 lbs. This is equivalent to $2\frac{1}{2} \times 5280 \times 150/60 = 33000$ foot-pounds per minute. The agent, therefore, which could do a work of 33000 ft.-pounds per minute, or 550 ft.-pounds per second, was named a *horse-power*.

The enlarged unit used in electrical work is the *watt*. It is the power of an agent which can do a work of one joule ($= 10^7$ ergs) per second.

The relations between these units will be seen in the examples.

Ex. 1. Show that one H. P. = 550 ft.-pounds per sec.
   = 396,000 inch-pounds per min.
   = 198 inch-tons per min.
2. Show that one H. P. = $550g$ ft.-poundals. per sec.
3. Show that one H. P. = 746 watts.
4. Show that one joule = $\frac{3}{4}$ ft.-pound, approx.
5. The French H. P. is 75 kilogrammeters per sec.; show that it is about $\frac{1}{70}$ less than the British H. P., and that it is equal to $735\frac{3}{4}$ watts.
6. Show that one watt = $\frac{3}{4}$ ft.-pound per sec., approx.
7. 22 tons of coal are to be hoisted through 50 yards in 10 min.: find the H. P. of engine necessary. *Ans.* 20 H. P.
8. How many gallons of water would be raised per minute from a mine 600 ft. deep by an engine of 175 H. P.? *Ans.* 1152 gals.

9. A belt passing round two pulleys moves with a velocity of 10 ft. per sec.: find the H. P. transmitted if the difference of tension of the belt above and below the pulleys is 1100 pounds. *Ans.* 20 H. P.

10. Show that the dimensions of power or rate of doing work, that is, of Fs/t, are ML^2/T^3.

11. A shaft 14 ft. in diameter is to be sunk in gravel in 10 days of 10 hours each. Taking the weight of the gravel at 100 lbs. per cubic ft., find the H. P. required.

138. For determining the power developed by a steam-engine or other machine, the **Prony Brake** is used. The idea is to balance the work done by the machine by a frictional resistance, compute this resistance, and thence find the power of the machine. The brake *absorbs* the work to be measured.

Let O be a shaft of radius r, to which the brake AB is fastened. By means of the screws a, b, the friction of the

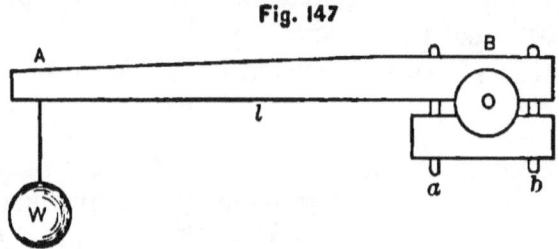

Fig. 147

brake on the shaft may be regulated. Suppose it adjusted so that the engine develops a friction f, just sufficient to balance a body of weight W placed at the end A of the beam. Then the moments of f and W about O must be equal, or

$$fr = Wl.$$

Suppose the shaft to revolve uniformly n times per minute. Then, assuming that the friction for uniform motion of the shaft is the same as at the point of just beginning to move, we have

Work done in one min. = friction developed in n revs.

$$= f \times 2\pi r \times n$$

$$= 2\pi n Wl.$$

If W is expressed in pounds and l in feet, then the

$$\text{H. P.} = 2\pi n W l/33000$$
$$= 0.00019 n W l.$$

Similarly, in the mechanism shown in Fig. 131, Art. 122, if the H. P. transmitted by the belt and the velocity v of the belt per second were given, then the tensions P, Q of the belt would be found from

$$\text{H. P.} = (P - Q)v/550; \quad P = Q e^{\mu\theta}$$

or, if the H. P. and the number of revolutions per minute n of the driving pulley were given, the tensions would be found from

$$\text{H. P.} = (P - Q)\pi d n/33000, \quad P = Q e^{\mu\theta}$$

when d is the diameter of the pulley.

A common case is when $\mu = 0.3$, and from 0.4 to 0.5 of the smaller pulley is embraced by the belt. Then θ varies from 0.8π to π, and $P = 2Q$, nearly. Also, the

$$\text{H. P.} = 0.00005 P d n,$$

P being the tension of the belt on the taut side.

139. In a machine, owing to friction between the pieces, part of the work done by the driving force is wasted, so that the resulting useful work done is less than the total work done by the effort in the first place. We have, in fact,

Total work = useful work + useless work.

The ratio of the useful work to the total work is known as the **Efficiency** of the machine. Or, since the total work is given by the indicated horse-power (Art. 136) and the useful work by the braked horse-power (Art. 138) we may define efficiency to be the ratio of the B. H. P. to the I. H. P., or

Efficiency = B. H. P. / I. H. P.

WORK AND ENERGY.

Ex. 1. In testing a Corliss engine running at 100 revolutions per minute, the lever arm was 10½ ft., and the weight at A 2000 lbs.: find the H. P. developed. *Ans.* 400 H. P.

2. "A C. and C. electric motor shows on a Prony brake a pull of 5 ounces on a one-ft. lever, that is, 2 ft.-pounds per revolution, or about $\frac{1}{10}$ H. P. at 1500 revolutions per minute." Check the conclusions in this statement.

3. In a Corliss engine running at 100 pounds pressure and 100 revolutions per minute, the diameter of the cylinder is 18 in., and length of stroke 42 in. If the brake was used on a pulley 6 ft. in diameter, and keyed to the engine shaft, find the friction on the face of the pulley.
Ans. $f = 9450$ pounds.

4. A 6-ton fly-wheel on a 14-in. axle makes 90 revolutions per minute. Find the H. P. absorbed in friction, the coefficient of friction being 0.1. *Ans.* 12 H. P.

5. A steam hoist of 3 H. P. is found to raise a weight of 10 tons to a height of 50 ft. in 20 min. How many ft.-pounds of work are wasted by friction in a day of 10 hours?
Ans. 29,400,000 foot-pounds.

6. The tractive force of a consolidation engine is 10 tons: find the H. P. exerted in hauling a train one mile in 2 min.
Ans. 1600 H. P.

7. A pumping engine of piston area 100 sq. in., steam-pressure 60 pounds per sq. in., length of stroke 3 ft., and number of revolutions per min. 25, raises 500 gallons of water per minute a height of 50 ft.: find the efficiency.
Ans. 0.25, nearly.

8. A traction engine weighing 5 tons hauls a load of 10 tons at 8 miles an hour, the resistance being 20 pounds per ton: find the H. P. exerted. *Ans.* 6.4 H. P.

9. A train weighing 100 tons runs at 42 miles an hour on a level track, the resistance being 8 pounds per ton: find its speed up a 1% grade (1 ft. rise in 100 ft.) if the engine power is unchanged.

[Total resist. $= 8 + 2000/100 = 28$ pounds per ton. $\therefore 8 \times 42 = 28 \times x$, and $x = 12$ miles an hour.]

10. A traction engine weighing 5 tons can haul 15 tons on a level, the coefficient of friction being 0.02: find the net load it can haul up a 1% grade. *Ans.* 8⅓ tons.

POWER.

11. A train of 100 tons is hauled by an engine of 150 H. P. The resistance is 14 pounds per ton: find the greatest velocity that the engine can attain.

Ans. 60 miles an hour, nearly.

12. Check this statement : "55 pounds mean effective pressure at 600 ft. piston speed gives 1 H. P. for each sq. in. of piston area."

13. Prove H. P. of an engine $= SNAP/33000$, where $S =$ stroke in ft., $N =$ number of strokes per min., $A =$ area of piston in sq.in., $P =$ mean steam pressure in pounds per sq. in. of piston area.

14. Find the work done per hour at the crank-pin of an engine revolving 40 times a minute and acting against a resistance of 7000 lbs., the radius of the crank being 18 inches. (See Fig. 119.)

Ans. $2\pi \times 1\frac{1}{2} \times 7000 \times 40 \times 60$ ft.-pounds.

14*a*. In the Strong locomotive 444, built for the L. V. R. R., the cylinders are 20 in. in diameter, the stroke is 24 in., and the diameter of the driving wheels 62 in. At 160 lbs. steam-pressure per sq. in. find the work done at each stroke.

Ans. $\frac{\pi}{4} \times 20^2 \times 2 \times 160$ foot-pounds.

14*b*. Find the tractive force P of the engine.

[In each stroke of the piston the drivers make a half revolution. Hence, there being two cylinders,

$$\frac{\pi}{4} \times 20^2 \times 24 \times 160 = \frac{\pi}{2} \times 62 \times P, \text{and } P \text{ is found.}]$$

15. Show that the cylinder diameter of an engine that will produce n horse-power at a piston velocity of s ft. per minute under a mean effective pressure of p pounds per sq. in. is $210\sqrt{\frac{n}{ps}}$ inches, nearly.

16. The driving pulley (Fig. 131) runs at 100 revolutions per minute, and is 2 ft. in diameter. The engine is 3 H. P. Find the tensions of the belt if $\frac{1}{4}$ of the circumference of the driving pulley is covered, and the coefficient of friction is 0.3.

17. In the California Street cable road, San Francisco, the total H. P. required to haul the cable alone is 84, and the speed is six miles an hour: find the total pull transmitted by the driving drum.

140. Energy.—We have seen that when the forces acting on a body are in equilibrium, or the body moves with a uniform motion, the sum of the works done is zero, that is, the work done by the resultant force or *effort* is equal to that done on the resistance. Now the action of a force is to cause acceleration. If, then, the motion is uniform, the acceleration caused by the effort is balanced by the equal and opposite acceleration caused by the resistance. But if the acceleration caused by the effort exceeds that caused by the resistance, velocity is gained, and the motion is not uniform. We proceed to inquire as to the work necessary to be done in order to change the velocity of a body of mass m from say u ft. per sec. to v ft. per sec. Let F denote the effort or acting force, a the acceleration produced, and s the distance passed over in the line of action of the force; then (Art. 13)

$$as = \tfrac{1}{2}v^2 - \tfrac{1}{2}u^2.$$

But (Art. 34) $\qquad F = ma.$

Hence, eliminating a, $Fs = \tfrac{1}{2}mv^2 - \tfrac{1}{2}mu^2.$

Now Fs is the work done by F in passing over a distance s in its line of action, and therefore a mass m in having its velocity changed from u to v feet per second must have $\tfrac{1}{2}mv^2 - \tfrac{1}{2}mu^2$ units of work done on it.

If the force F does not act uniformly, we have, from Art. 34,

$$F = m d^2s/dt^2,$$

and

$$\therefore \int F ds = \int_u^v m \frac{d^2s}{dt^2} ds = \tfrac{1}{2}mv^2 - \tfrac{1}{2}mu^2\,;$$

or, *the work done depends on the initial and final velocities, and is independent of the intermediate velocities.*

If $u = 0$, or the body starts from rest,

$$Fs = \tfrac{1}{2}mv^2,$$

and therefore the work done in giving a body of mass m a velocity v is $\tfrac{1}{2}mv^2$ units of work. The force F which will generate a velocity v in acting through a distance s will destroy the same velocity if acting through the same distance in the opposite direction; in other words, the body by virtue of its velocity v can do a work Fs units in giving up that velocity and coming to rest. This capacity which the body possesses of doing work in consequence of its velocity known as its *vis-viva* or **Kinetic Energy**. Hence the measure of the kinetic energy possessed by a body of mass m and velocity v is $\tfrac{1}{2}mv^2$ units of work. In acquiring the velocity v by the work done on the body energy may be said to be *stored* in it, to be *restored* in doing work as it parts with this velocity and returns to its original condition. We may therefore state the general relation

$$Fs = \tfrac{1}{2}mv^2 - \tfrac{1}{2}mu^2$$

in the form: If a body or system of bodies with configuration remaining the same is in motion under the action of force, the work done in passing from one position to another is equal to the corresponding change of the kinetic energy. This is called the **Principle of Kinetic Energy.**

Ex. 1. Find the work done in stopping a 100-lb. shot moving with a velocity of 1000 ft. per sec.
Ans. 1,562,500 ft.-pounds.

2. Find the force exerted in stopping a train of 250 tons in 1000 ft. from a velocity of 30 miles an hour.
Ans. 15,125 pounds.

3. A shot pierces a target of a certain thickness h: show that to pierce one of 4 times the thickness twice the velocity is necessary. $[\tfrac{1}{2}mv_1^2 h = \tfrac{1}{2}mv_2^2 \times 4h. \ \therefore \ v_1 = 2v_2.]$

4. A blacksmith's helper using a 16-lb. sledge strikes 20 times a minute, and with a velocity of 30 ft. per sec.: find his rate of work. *Ans.* 3/22 H. P.

5. A stone is thrown with a horizontal velocity of 50 ft. per sec.: find the velocity with which it strikes the ground which is horizontal and 6 ft. below the point of projection.
Ans. 53.7 ft. per sec.

6. Show that to give a train a velocity of 20 miles an hour requires the same energy as to lift it vertically through a height of 13.3 feet.

7. A hoisting engine lifts an elevator weighing 1 ton through 50 ft. when it attains a velocity of 4 ft. per sec. If the steam is shut off, how much higher will it rise?

$$Ans. \quad \frac{2000 \times 4^2}{2} = 2000g \times \text{dist.}$$

8. In (7) find the time of rising 50 ft., supposing the motion uniformly accelerated, and also find the H. P. of the engine. *Ans.* 25 sec.; 7.3 H. P.

9. Show that the energy stored in a train of weight W lbs. and moving with a velocity of V miles per hour is $WV^2/30$ foot-pounds.

10. A train of 100 tons is running at 30 miles an hour up a 2% grade: find the H. P. required, the resistance on a level being 10 lbs. per ton, due to axle friction chiefly.
Ans. 400 H. P.

11a. In the Strong locomotive (L. V. R. R. 444) running on the level at 30 miles an hour the tractive force is 8 tons. Taking the resistance of friction as 10 lbs. per ton, find the number of 20-ton cars that can be hauled if engine and tender weigh 100 tons. *Ans.* 75 cars.

11b. Find the number that would be hauled up a 2% grade. *Ans.* 11 cars.

11c. Find the H. P. exerted in the former case.
Ans. 1280 H. P.

12a. An engine exerts on a car weighing 20,000 lbs. a net pull of 2 lbs. per ton: find the energy stored in the car after going 2½ miles. *Ans.* 264,000 ft.-lbs.

12b. If shunted to a level side-track when the frictional

ENERGY.

resistance is 10 lbs. per ton, find how far it will run before coming to rest.   *Ans.* 264,000/10 × 10 ft. = ½ mile.

12c. If shunted on a side track with a 1% grade, how far will it run before coming to rest?

Ans. 264,000/(20 + 10) 10 ft. = ¼ mile.

12d. If there are brakes on half the wheels, and these are applied with a pressure of half a wheel load, how far will the car run up a 1% grade, the coefficient of friction between wheel and brake-shoe being 0.2.

[Total resist. = brake + grade + fric. = 130 lbs. per ton.
Ans. 203 ft., nearly.]

13. In the Westinghouse brake tests (Jan. 1887) at Weehawken a passenger train moving 22 miles an hour on a down grade of 1% was stopped in 91 ft. There was 94% of the train braked. Taking the frictional resistance as 8 lbs. per ton, find the net brake resistance per ton and the grade to which this is equivalent.

[The brake has to overcome the energy due to the velocity and the resistance due to the grade, but is aided by the resistance due to friction. Hence brake resist. per ton = 2000 × 22²/(30 × 91) + 20 − 8 = 367 pounds.

As only 94% was braked, we have the net brake resist. per ton = 367/0.94 = 390 pounds, which is equivalent to a grade of 390/20 (= 19.5) per cent.]

14. The tractive force of an engine is P tons. If the weight of engine and train is W tons and the frictional resistance n lbs. per ton, show that in going up an a% grade the velocity acquired in t seconds from rest will be Qgt ft. per sec. and the energy $0.5 WQ^2gt^2$ ft.-tons, where

$$Q = P/W - a/100 - n/2000.$$

141. The term energy arises from the consideration of muscular exertion in the first place. In doing what is called work in ordinary language we recognize that effort is needed, and that exhaustion follows after a time. It is necessary to store up work-capacity or energy by consuming food in order to be able to continue doing work.

The same idea is extended to machines where the force exerted by the expansion of steam, by water in motion, by air in motion, etc., produces effects which can also be obtained by muscular exertion directly applied. The machine is then said to be doing work, and from analogy the term *agent* is applied to it as well as to man. The agent thus forms, as it were, the converter of energy, whether of food, or of coal, etc., into work.* The energy existing in a stored-up condition is ready to be called on, and is hence known as **Potential Energy.**

Suppose we call on the potential energy of steam to give motion to operate a mechanism, as for example a locomotive. The energy of the steam has enabled the locomotive to overcome the resistance offered by the friction of the wheels, the resistance of the air, etc., and to attain besides a certain velocity. If the steam be shut off the locomotive will not at once come to rest, but will continue for a time to overcome resistance as before. The energy communicated in excess of that required to overcome the resistances is not lost, but is stored in the form of motion. The energy existing in virtue of the motion, which thus continues to do work until exhausted, is, as stated above, called **Kinetic Energy.**

It would thus seem that the energy of motion is produced at the expense of energy stored, and conversely the energy of motion may be made to do work of some kind to be stored in some form or other. The subject is a very large one, and we cannot go into it in detail. It is sufficient to

---

* "Now, Buckland," said Stephenson, "I have a poser for you. Can you tell me what is the power that is driving that train?" "Well," said the other, "I suppose it is one of your big engines." "But what drives the engine?" "Oh, very likely a canny Newcastle driver." "What do you say to the light of the sun?" "How can that be?" asked the doctor. "It is nothing else," said the engineer; "it is light bottled up in the earth for tens of thousands of years—light absorbed by plants and vegetables being necessary for the condensation of carbon during the process of their growth, if it be not carbon in another form; and now, after being buried in the earth for long ages in fields of coal, that latent light is again brought forth and liberated, made to work as in that locomotive, for great human purposes."—*Smiles.*

POTENTIAL. 169

state, that, as a result of observation and experiment, the conclusion is arrived at, that energy may be transferred from one form to another, but can neither be created nor destroyed. In a word, *energy is indestructible;* or, as it may be expressed: *The total energy of any body or system of bodies is a quantity which can neither be increased nor diminished by any mutual action of these bodies, though it may be transformed into any of the forms of which energy is susceptible.*

This principle, known as the **Conservation of Energy,** is the general principle premised at the beginning of this chapter. It involves the laws of motion and the principle of work as special cases, and consequently on it may be made to rest the whole subject of mechanics.

142. Potential.*—An important application of the prin-

---

* A graphical illustration of the fact that in the case of two electrified spheres the potential function is a measure of work, is given by Prof. A. M. Mayer as follows: Suppose an electrically charged sphere fixed in space with its centre at O, and that another sphere charged with a unit of similar electricity is pushed towards O from an infinite distance along the line OX, and that the electric strain on the moving sphere causes (without work) a vertical rod to slide out of its top in proportion as the stress between the spheres increases. As the sphere progresses along OX it will thus mark at each point of its progress the repulsive force existing between it and the fixed sphere. The end of the sliding-rod during the motion of the sphere from X towards O will have traced out the curve $DFCG$, whose ordinates are as the inverse squares of their distances from O.

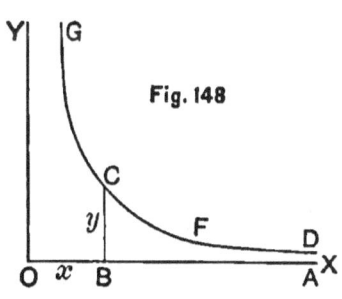

Fig. 148

The potential at any point reached in the progress of the charged body towards O = work done = resistance overcome in pushing body from infinite distance to that point; and this work done is measured by the sum of the resistances at each point of the path × length of path. But this product is equal to the *area* included between the

ciple of work is the determination of the work done during the passage of a body of given mass from one position to another under the action of a force of attraction or of repulsion on the body. The region in which the force acts is called the **Field of Force**. We shall confine ourselves to fields of force, in which the law of force is that of the inverse square of the distance (Art. 110), and the forces themselves are gravitational, electrical, or magnetic.

Thus suppose a particle of mass m placed at O to exert an attractive force on a unit mass in its motion from A to B, the law of force being that of the inverse square of the distance. The force F of attraction between the particles is cm/r^2, when they are at a distance r from one another, c being a constant. The work done by the force as the particle moves the indefinitely small distance CD in its path is $c\dfrac{m}{OD^2} \times DE$, when CE is perpendicular to OD. Or putting $OD = x$, $DE = dx$, and noting that the force

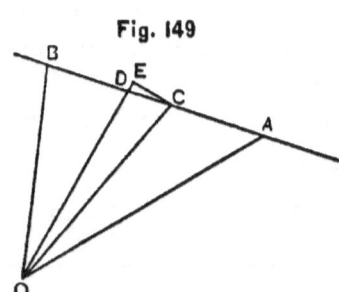

Fig. 149

ordinate (say B) of path, the axis of X, and the curve, both indefinitely extended; or say $CBAD$.

The equation of the curve is

$$y = a/x^2.$$

Area $ABCD$, indefinitely extended, =

$$\int_x^\infty y\,dx = \int_x^\infty a\,dx/x^2 = a/x.$$

Or area *indefinitely extended*, which represents the work, is inversely as the distance of y, the bounding ordinate of area, from O or $V = Q/d$, when $Q =$ quantity and $d =$ distance of the centres of the two charged spheres.

being attractive dx is negative, this may be written $-c\dfrac{m}{x^2}dx$. Hence the work done in bringing the particle from A to B is

$$-cm\int_a^r \frac{dx}{x^2} = cm\left(\frac{1}{r} - \frac{1}{a}\right),$$

when $OA = a$, $OB = r$.

If the starting-point A is at an indefinitely great distance from the source of attraction O, then $1/a =$ zero, and the work done is cm/r, a result independent of the form of the path AB.

The work necessary to bring a particle of unit mass from a position of zero attraction, that is, from an indefinitely great distance, to a position B, where the force of attraction is finite and the distance from the attracting particle r, is called the **Potential** at the point B. It is usually denoted by the letter V, so that

$$V = cm/r,$$

when r is the distance of B from O.

If the field at O consists of several particles of masses $m_1, m_2, \ldots$, with distances $r_1, r_2, \ldots$ from the unit mass B, the potential of B will be

$$c(m_1/r_1 + m_2/r_2 + \cdots).$$

It follows that if V_1 denote the potential at any other point C the work done in bringing the particle from C to B by any path is $V - V_1$.

143. Conceive a surface at every point of which the potential has the same value. Such a surface is called an **Equipotential Surface**. If a particle is moved from any one point to any other point on this surface no work is done. Thus, if a railroad track is located on a "level" no work is done against the force of gravity in hauling a train on this track.

An equipotential surface for the force of gravity could be determined by finding the places at which the same mass would compress a spring the same amount. Roughly, it would be a sphere concentric with the earth. The work done on any body by the force of gravity in falling to the earth from any point of this equipotential surface would be the same in amount. So also the work done in falling from one such surface to another would be constant in value. This suggests a method of finding the relation between the resultant force R and the potential V at any point. For suppose the potential at points A, B situated on two equipotential surfaces to be V_A, V_B, respectively. The resultant force R at A (as force of gravity on a falling body) will be in a line AC, normal to the surface at A. The work done in moving a particle of unit mass from A to B will be the same as from A to C, when C is the point in which the normal at A meets the second surface, and is equal to $R \times AC$. But this work is by definition equal to the difference of potential at A and B, or $V_A - V_B$. Hence

$$R \times AC = V_A - V_B.$$

If the distance between the surfaces is indefinitely small ($= dr$), this may be written

$$R = dV/dr,$$

or the resultant force is the rate of change of potential at the point in question, the direction of the force being normal to the equipotential surface through the point.

Potential being expressed in terms of work done, the *unit of potential* is the same as the unit of work, the foot-poundal or erg.

The theory of the potential is of great use in magnetic and electrical investigations.

Ex. 1. Show that the dimensions of potential are ML/T^2.

POTENTIAL.

2. Show that (theoretically) an equipotential surface could be determined by finding the points at which a pendulum beating seconds had the same length.

3. To find the potential of a particle O of unit mass on the line through the centre C and perpendicular to the plane of a uniform circular disc of radius a, thickness h, and density δ, the distance OC being $= b$.

[As in Art. 110,

$$\text{mass of ring} = 2\pi r \times dr \times h \times \delta.$$

Hence
$$V = \int_0^a c \times 2\pi h \delta r dr / OD$$

$$= \int_0^a c \times 2\pi h \delta r dr / \sqrt{b^2 + r^2}$$

$$= 2\pi c h \delta (\sqrt{b^2 + a^2} - b).]$$

4. In (3) find the potential at the centre of the plate.
Ans. $2\pi c h \delta a$.

5. Find the potential at the centre of a circular wire of density δ and indefinitely small thickness h. *Ans.* $2\pi c h \delta$.

6. Find the potential at any point within a spherical shell of mass m and radius a. *Ans.* cm/a.

7. Find the potential at a point without a spherical shell of mass m, radius a, and distant b from the centre.
Ans. cm/b.

8. Assuming the earth to be a sphere of 8000 miles diameter, prove that the potential of the unit mass 1 lb. situated on the earth's surface is $-21,120,000$ foot-pounds.

9a. In a series of concentric spherical equipotential surfaces the distance between any two is proportional to the square of the geometric mean of the distances from the centre.

9b. Hence show that at great distances from the earth's centre the pound mass must be moved over a long path in order to do a ft.-pound of work on it.

9c. For example, at the moon, 240,000 miles distant from the earth's centre, find the shortest path. *Ans.* 3600 feet.

CHAPTER VII.

KINETICS OF A RIGID BODY.

144. The term rigid body is used in the sense already defined of a body regarded as composed of particles so connected that no part of the body can be moved relatively to any other part.

As in the case of a single particle, we shall consider the nature of the motions of the particles of the body, without reference to the forces causing the motions. This forms a problem in kinematics.

A rigid body is fixed in position by fixing three points A, B, C, not in the same straight line. These points determine a plane ABC with reference to which the positions of all points in the body may be defined. Hence the displacement of any point in the body may be determined by noting the change in the positions of these three points, since the point in question must keep in a fixed position relative to the three points A, B, C during the motion.

If the two points A, B remain unchanged in position during the motion, the third point C must describe a circle about an axis through A, B, and the motion is one of rotation. If only one point A is fixed, the points B, C may be brought from their initial to their final positions B_1, C_1 by two rotations. For by one rotation AB may be brought into the position AB_1, and by revolving about AB_1 as an axis the plane AB_1C may be brought into the position AB_1C_1. If no point is fixed, the new position $A_1B_1C_1$ may be reached by a translation of A to A_1, and by two rotations bringing A_1BC successively into the positions A_1B_1C

and $A_1B_1C_1$. Hence every motion of a rigid body is either a motion of translation or of rotation, or some combination of the two.

The most important case is that in which the particles of the body move in parallel planes. Such a motion is called *plane motion*.

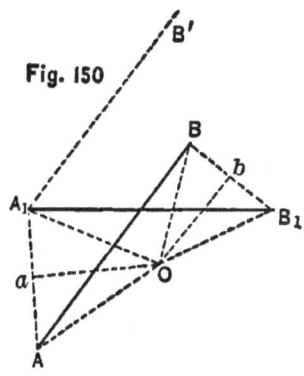

Fig. 150

Let us consider the motion of a line joining the points A, B in the plane of the paper. A translation AA_1 and a rotation through an angle $B'A_1B_1$ will displace AB into the position A_1B_1. So far as the displacement itself is concerned, it makes no difference whether the translation and rotation occurred simultaneously, or not.

But this displacement might have been produced by a rotation only. For bisect AA_1, BB_1 in a, b, and let the perpendiculars aO, bO intersect in O. Then evidently $OA = OA_1$, $OB = OB_1$, and angle $AOB = A_1OB_1$. Hence the displacement may be produced by rotation about the point O.

It follows therefore that any plane motion may be regarded as a motion of rotation about a centre in the plane of the motion, or, in other words, that a translation and a rotation about an axis perpendicular to the direction of rotation may be combined into a single rotation giving an equivalent motion.

145. In many cases the final displacement is difficult to arrive at. This is particularly the case in mechanisms where the connections of the parts are often very complicated. Besides, the final displacement may not define clearly the intermediate displacements. It is therefore necessary to study the displacement from instant to instant of the motion.

Suppose two points A, B of a body to have any motion in the plane of the paper. The points A, B will each trace out a path. Consider A. The line joining two consecutive positions of A will give the direction of motion in the path. This line is the direction of the tangent to the path at A. Since an indefin-

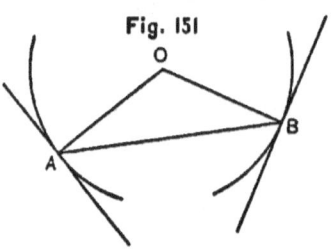

Fig. 151

itely great number of curves may have a common tangent at a point, it follows that this tangent is quite independent of the form of the path. Hence *for the instant* we may consider the path to be a circular arc. The perpendicular AO to the tangent will pass through the centre of the circle, and conversely, the direction of motion at A for the instant will be perpendicular to the radius of the circle. Hence the instantaneous motion of A is the same as if it took place in a circle with centre somewhere on AO. Similarly, the motion of B is the same as if in a circle with centre somewhere on BO. But O is common to AO and BO. Hence the instantaneous motion of A and B, and therefore of the line AB, is a motion of rotation about a point O, which is called the **Instantaneous Centre**. An axis through O perpendicular to the plane of the paper is the **Instantaneous Axis**.

The points A, B are any two points in the body. Hence, whatever the form of the body, and whatever its plane motion, it is always possible to find a point O such that for the instant the motion about it shall represent the actual motion, in other words, at any instant one point O is at rest, and the other points are moving in directions perpendicular to the lines joining them to this point.

If in Fig. 151 the radii AO, BO do not intersect, the tangents to the paths at A, B are parallel, and the motion is a motion of translation. The radii being parallel may be said to intersect at infinity, and hence a motion of translation may be regarded as a rotation about a centre at an infinite distance.

146. In general, the instantaneous centre O will vary in position from instant to instant. The locus or path described by it is called a **Centrode**.* But in case the radii AO, BO continue to intersect in the same point O, as the motion progresses the instantaneous centre becomes a permanent or fixed centre. For example, a wagon wheel revolves about the axle as a permanent centre, but with reference to the ground it revolves about the point of contact as an instantaneous centre. The path traced by the wheel on the ground is the centrode.

Ex. 1. A ladder BC slides between a vertical wall and the ground, which is horizontal: find the instantaneous centre and the centrode.

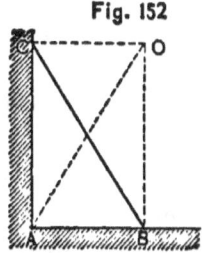

Fig. 152

[The paths are along AB, AC. Hence the instantaneous centre is at the intersection O of the perpendiculars BO, CO. It is evident that $AO = BC$, the length of the ladder, and $\therefore O$ is at a constant distance from A. Hence the centrode is a circle, with A as centre.]

2. A lever moves about a fulcrum: find the nature of the centre of motion.

147. In the case of moving bodies rigidly connected together, the determination of the velocity of one with respect to another may be based on the preceding. For illustration take the ordinary steam-engine. The mechanism itself has been already shown in Fig. 119. Suppose we wish to find the

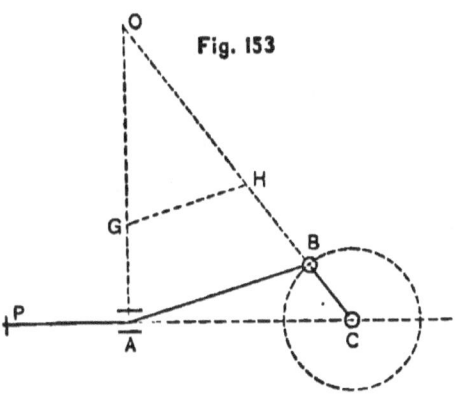

Fig. 153

---
* Term introduced by Clifford (1845-1879).

velocity of the piston P, relative to the crank-pin B. The velocity of the piston is the same as that of the extremity A of the connecting-rod AB. The velocity of the crank-pin B is the same as that of the extremity B of the connecting-rod. Hence the relation sought is the same as that between the velocities of the extremities A and B of the connecting-rod.

The bed-plate AC is fixed. The extremity A moves in a straight line PC, and the direction of motion being along PC, the instantaneous centre is in a line AO at right angles to PC. The extremity B moves in a circle of centre C, and therefore the instantaneous centre is in the line CB. Hence the connecting-rod is *for the instant* in the condition of a wheel turning about an axis through O, the intersection of OA and CB. Consequently,

$$\text{velocity } A : \text{velocity } B = OA : OB,$$

or the velocities are as the distances from the instantaneous centre.

If therefore the velocity of one of the two, piston or crank-pin, is given, that of the other follows at once. Thus, suppose the crank-pin to have a velocity 10 ft. per sec. Lay off to scale a distance $BH = 10$ ft., and draw HG parallel to BA. Then, since

$$HB : GA = OB : OA,$$

we scale off GA as the velocity of the piston.

By drawing the crank in different positions, and finding the corresponding positions of G, a curve will result, the ordinates of which will give the velocity of the piston through its stroke.

Ex. 1. In the above example draw the complete curve of piston velocity on a scale of velocity 5 ft. per sec. = 1 in. and of dimensions 1 ft. = 1 in.

2. Find the height above the track of a point on a 6-ft. locomotive wheel running on a straight track, that has half the velocity of the highest point of the wheel.

Ans. 1.5 ft.

148. Angular Velocity.—If the motion of the body is a motion of rotation about a fixed axis, each particle describes a circumference, whose centre is in the axis. Since each circumference is described in the same time, the velocities of the particles must be proportional to the distances of the particles from the axis, the greater the distance the greater the velocity. It is therefore clear that we can attach no meaning to the phrase "velocity of a body" as in the case of the motion of translation. In a word, we have a new kind of motion, and we must introduce new modes of measurement.

Thus suppose the body to revolve about an axis through O, and that it moves through an angle AOa in t sec. Then the angle described in one second, or the **Angular Velocity** ω, would be measured by AOa/t. This angle is described by every point in the body, so that one characteristic of rotation is that the angular velocity of every point is the same.

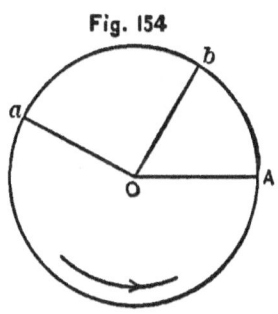

Fig. 154

The *unit of angular velocity* is naturally taken to be unit angle described in one second. The unit angle employed is the **radian** or the angle AOb, whose arc Ab is equal in length to the radius AO.

The angular velocity ω will therefore be denoted by the number of radians described per second. Thus if a body revolves 60 times per minute, or once per second, the number of radians described per second is 2π.

The relation between the angular velocity ω of the body and the linear velocity v of any particle A situated at a distance r from the axis of rotation follows at once. For the time of motion being t, we have

$$\omega = AOa/t, \qquad \text{arc } Aa = vt.$$

But

$$AOa : AOb = \text{arc } Aa : \text{arc } Ab,$$

or

$$\omega t : 1 \text{ radian} = vt : r,$$

and

$$\omega = v/r \text{ radians},$$

the relation sought.

Ex. 1. Show that the dimensions of angular velocity are $1/T$.

2. If ω is expressed in degrees, show that $v = 2\pi\omega r/360°$.

3. A body makes n revolutions per second: show that the linear velocity of a particle 1 ft. from the centre is $2\pi n$ ft. per sec. and the angular velocity $2\pi n$ radians per sec.

4. A belt passes over a pulley d ft. in diameter and making n revolutions per min. Find its velocity.

Ans. $\pi d n$ ft. per min.

5. A wheel 4 ft. in diameter revolves 420 times per min. Find the angular velocity and the linear velocity of a point 1.5 ft. from the centre.

Ans. 14π radians per sec. : 21π ft. per sec.

6. The crank of an engine makes n revolutions per min. Its radius is r ft. Find the linear velocity of the crank-pin.

Ans. $\pi r n/30$ ft. per sec.

7. In the driving wheel of a locomotive show that for an instant one point is moving twice as fast as the locomotive and in the same direction.

8. Find the ratio of the angular velocities of the hour and second hands of a watch. *Ans.* $1/720$.

9. A locomotive is running at 45 miles an hour. The driving wheels are 6 ft. in diameter, and the stroke is 2 ft. Find the piston velocity. *Ans.* $44/\pi$ ft. per sec.

149. Angular Acceleration.—Angular velocity, like linear velocity, may be uniform or variable. If variable, the rate of change is called the **Angular Acceleration.** The unit of angular velocity being one radian per second, the *unit of angular acceleration* is one radian-per-second per second.

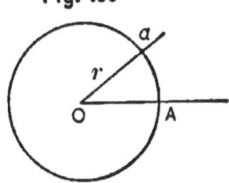
Fig. 155

If the body rotates with a uniform angular acceleration α, the gain of circumferential velocity per second (or the linear acceleration) of a particle A at a distance r from the axis is measured by an arc Aa equal to αr. Hence we may write

linear accel. = ang. accel. × rad.

The direction of the acceleration at A for an indefinitely small arc is normal to AO, that is, along the tangent at A, so that we have

tang. accel. = ang. accel. × rad.

Hence, if m denotes the mass of the particle A,

tang. force = mass × tang. accel. (Art. 34)
= $mr\alpha$.

Ex. When steam is shut off, the fly-wheel of an engine is making 90 rev. per min. If the coefficient of friction is 0.1, find the time in which the wheel will come to rest. *Ans.* 30π sec.

Thus far we have considered the kinematics of a rigid body. We now proceed to discuss its kinetics.

150. Equations of Motion.—The result of the action of a force on a particle of a rigid body is different from that on the particle if free. For besides this force other forces act on the particle resulting from the action of the adjacent particles of the body on one another. The real acting force is therefore the resultant of the external and internal forces, and the motion is the same as if we considered the particle free, but subject to the action of a force equal to the resultant of all external and internal forces. To this resultant the name of **Effective Force** is given.

Thus, suppose P to be a particle of a body of mass m_1, F_1 the component in a certain direction of the external force impressed on it, and F_1' the component of the resultant internal forces in the same direction. If a_1 is the component of the acceleration in this direction due to the resultant of the forces F_1, F_1', the effective force acting on the particle must be equivalent to $m_1 a_1$. Hence

$$F_1 + F_1' = m_1 a_1.$$

Similarly, $\quad F_2 + F_2' = m_2 a_2.$

. . . . . .

By addition,

$$\Sigma F + \Sigma F' = \Sigma m a.$$

But from the law of stress the internal forces occur as pairs of forces equal in magnitude and opposite in sense, or $\Sigma F' = 0$, and therefore

$$\Sigma F = \Sigma m a,$$

or the system of impressed forces is in equilibrium with the system of effective forces reversed.

Now if $\bar{a}$ is the acceleration of the centre of gravity of the body, then (Art. 90)

$$\bar{a} = \Sigma m a / \Sigma m,$$

and $\quad \therefore \Sigma F = \Sigma m a;$

or the linear acceleration of the centre of gravity is the same as that of a particle of mass Σm acted on by a force ΣF.

EQUATIONS OF MOTION. 183

Consider now the rotation of a rigid body about a fixed axis under the action of external forces.

Let the axis through O be perpendicular to the plane of the paper, and let at an assigned instant $F_1, F_2, \ldots$ be the components of the external forces on the particles $A, B, \ldots$ acting at distances $r_1, r_2, \ldots$ from the axis, and parallel to the plane of the paper. Also, let $F_1', F_2', \ldots$ be the components in their respective planes of the internal forces on the particles $A, B, \ldots$, and denote by $R_1, R_2, \ldots$ the resultant forces at $A, B, \ldots$. These resultant forces may be resolved into components along the tangent and radius to the paths of $A, B, \ldots$. The tangential acceleration is due to the tangential component. If, therefore, α denotes the angular acceleration of the body, the linear tangential acceleration at A is $r_1\alpha$, and the tangential force (or *inertia-resistance*) $m_1 r_1 \alpha$. Denote the normal component at A by N_1. Similarly, we have $m_2 r_2 \alpha$ and N_2 at B, and so on for the other points. These are the effective forces. Taking moments about O, we have, if $p_1, p_2, \ldots$; $p_1', p_2', \ldots$; $\ldots$ denote the perpendiculars let fall from O on $F_1, F_2, \ldots$; F_1', F_2'; $\ldots$; $\ldots$ respectively,

$$m_1 r_1 \alpha \times r_1 + m_2 r_2 \alpha \times r_2 + \ldots$$
$$= F_1 p_1 + F_2 p_2 + \ldots + F_1' p_1' + F_2' p_2' + \ldots$$

or $\quad \Sigma m r^2 \alpha = \Sigma F p + \Sigma F' p'$.

But the internal forces consisting of pairs of equal and opposite forces, we must have $\Sigma F' p' = 0$. Also, since α is the same for all the particles, $\Sigma m r^2 \alpha = \alpha \Sigma m r^2$; and we have, finally,

$$\alpha \Sigma m r^2 = \Sigma F p.$$

The right-hand member of this equation is the ordinary expression for statical moment. The left-hand member is the sum of the moments of the inertia-resistances $m_1 r_1 \alpha$,

$m_2 r_2 \alpha$, ... about the axis, and may therefore be appropriately called the **Moment of Inertia*** of the body about the axis. But the term moment of inertia is more usually applied to the factor Σmr^2, which is constant for the body considered and independent of the varying acceleration α. This factor is denoted by the letter I, so that

$$I = \Sigma mr^2.$$

We may therefore write the equation

ang. accel. = mom. of ext. forces/mom. inertia.

The relations

$$\Sigma F = \bar{a} \Sigma m,$$
$$\Sigma Fp = \alpha \Sigma mr^2,$$

the first giving the acceleration of the centre of gravity in terms of the external forces and the mass, the second the angular acceleration about a fixed axis, are called the **Equations of Motion** of a rigid body.

Having found the accelerations from these equations, and being given the initial velocities, the velocities at the end of any given time and the distances passed over may be determined.

151. The conditions of equilibrium of a rigid body already found in Art. 88 follow at once. For for equilibrium the acceleration of the centre of gravity must be zero and the angular acceleration must be zero. Hence, since $\bar{a} = 0$, $\alpha = 0$, we have

$$\Sigma F = 0, \quad \Sigma Fp = 0,$$

or, *the sum of the components of the external forces in any direction is zero, and the sum of the moments of the external forces about any point is zero.*

In fact all static problems may be regarded as limiting cases of kinetic problems, and may be treated accordingly.

---

* The term was introduced by Euler (1707–1783).

MOMENT OF INERTIA. 185

152. *Moment of Inertia*.—It will be convenient in this place to give some examples of moments of inertia that are of frequent occurrence. We shall for simplicity and convenience make use of the integral calculus. Indeed, the finding of moments of inertia is a problem of *summation* or integration, and is to be regarded as such, and not a mechanical question at all. This summation may, however, sometimes be effected without the calculus, and as an illustration Ex. 1 is solved in both ways.

First take the axis through the centre of gravity of the body.

Ex. 1. To find the moment of inertia I of a thin uniform rod, mass M, length l, about an axis OY through its centre O, and at right angles to the rod.

Fig. 156

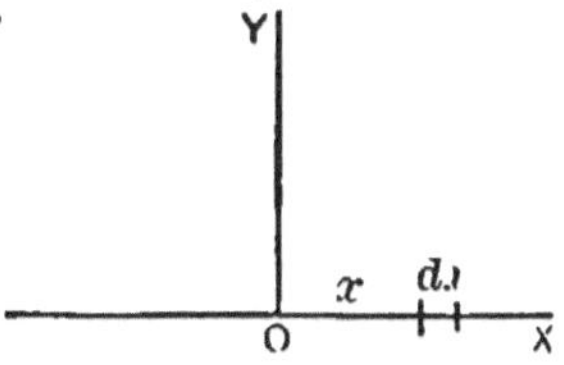

[Conceive the rod cut into elements of indefinitely small length dx, and let x be the distance of any one of these elements from O. Then moment of inertia of element $= \delta dx \times x^2$ when δ is the linear density, and $\therefore \delta dx$ the mass of length dx. Hence

$$I = \int_{-\frac{l}{2}}^{+\frac{l}{2}} \delta x^2 dx = \delta l^3/12 = M l^2/12.$$

Or thus: Suppose the rod divided into a large number $2n$ of equal parts $l/2n$. The distances of these parts from O may be taken to be the distances of their centres of gravity from O, that is, $l/4n$, $3l/4n$, ... Hence, taking half the rod,

$$\tfrac{1}{2}I = \delta \frac{l}{2n}\left(\frac{l}{4n}\right)^2 + \delta \frac{l}{2n}\left(\frac{3l}{4n}\right)^2 + \ldots \text{ to } n \text{ terms}$$

$$= \frac{\delta l^3}{32n^3}(1^2 + 3^2 + \ldots \text{ to } n \text{ terms})$$

$$= \frac{\delta l^3}{24}\left(1 - \frac{1}{4n^2}\right)$$

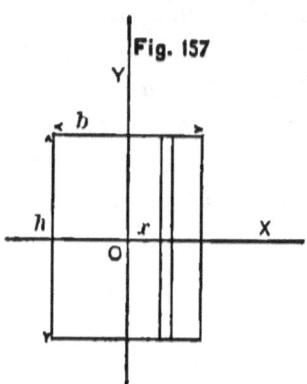

Fig. 157

$$= \frac{\delta l^3}{24}, \text{ when } n \text{ is indefinitely great,}$$

and $I = Ml^2/12$, as before.]

2. A thin rectangular lamina or plate of breadth b and depth h, about an axis through its centre of gravity O and parallel to h.

[Conceive the lamina cut into strips parallel to the axis, and of breadth dx. Let x denote the distance of one of these strips from the axis, δ its density; its mass is $\delta h \times dx$. Hence

$$I = \int_{-\frac{b}{2}}^{+\frac{b}{2}} \delta h \times dx \times x^2 = \tfrac{1}{12}\delta h b^3 = \tfrac{1}{12}Mb^2.]$$

3. If in (2) the axis is parallel to the side b, show that $I = Mh^2/12$.

4. A thin circular plate, radius r, about a diameter YOY' as axis.

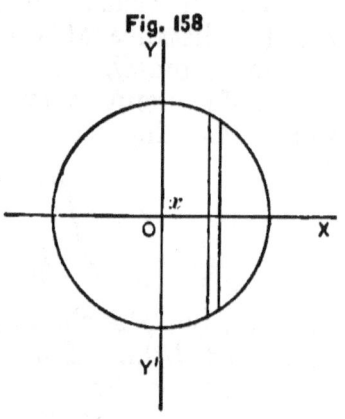

Fig. 158

[Conceive the plate cut into strips parallel to the axis, and of breadth dx. Then the equation to the circle being $x^2 + y^2 = r^2$, the length of a strip at a distance x from O is $2\sqrt{r^2 - x^2}$, and mass of strip $= \delta \times 2\sqrt{r^2 - x^2}dx$. Hence

$$I = \int_{-r}^{+r} 2\delta x^2 \sqrt{r^2 - x^2}dx = \delta \pi r^4/4 = Mr^2/4.$$

5. A square plate of side a about a diagonal.
   Ans. $I = Ma^2/12$.

6. A hexagon of side a about a diagonal.
   Ans. $I = 5Ma^2/4$.

7. A triangle of base b, height h, about an axis through its centre of gravity and parallel to the base.
$$Ans. \ I = bh^3/36.$$

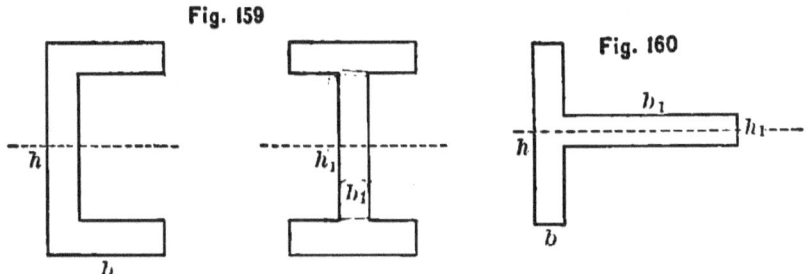

Fig. 159

Fig. 160

8. A channel iron or I-iron, base b, depth h, thickness of web b_1, depth of web h_1, about axis h through C. of G.
$$Ans. \ I = \{bh^3 - (b - b_1)h_1^3\}/12.$$

9. A T-iron with dimensions as in Fig. 160 about axis through C. of G.
$$Ans. \ I = (bh^3 + b_1 h_1^3)/12.$$

153. The form of the expression for the moment of inertia about a fixed axis or a fixed point, Σmr^2, shows that we may define it as the sum of the products of the masses of the particles of a rigid body into the squares of their distances r from the fixed axis or from the fixed point.* If the body consist of an indefinitely thin plane lamina, and be referred to rectangular axes OX, OY in its plane, we may write $r^2 = x^2 + y^2$ and
$$I = \Sigma m(x^2 + y^2)$$
for the moment relative to O or to an axis through O perpendicular to the plane of the lamina. But Σmx^2, Σmy^2 are the moments of inertia relative to the axes OY, OX, respectively. Hence, for a body in the form of an indefinitely thin lamina, if I_1, I_2 denote the moments of inertia relative to two rectangular axes OX, OY, in the plane, and I the moment relative to an axis through O perpendicular to the plane, we have
$$I = I_1 + I_2.$$

---

* This is the usual definition. It fails to show the significance of the term moment of inertia. (See Art. 150.)

Ex. 1. A rectangular lamina, breadth b, depth h, about an axis through its centre of gravity and perpendicular to its plane. *Ans.* $I = M(b^2 + h^2)/12$.

2. A circular plate, radius r, about an axis through its centre and perpendicular to the plate. *Ans.* $I = Mr^2/2$.

3. A ring of radii r_1, r_2 about an axis through its centre and perpendicular to its plane. *Ans.* $I = M(r_1^2 + r_2^2)/2$.

4. A sphere, radius r, about a diameter as axis.

[Conceive the sphere divided into plates of width dx by planes perpendicular to the axis. Let the distance of any plate from the centre O be x. Then radius of plate $= \sqrt{r^2 - x^2}$, and mass of plate $= \delta\pi(r^2 - x^2)dx$. Hence, from Ex. 2,

$$I = \int_{-r}^{+r} \tfrac{1}{2}\delta\pi(r^2 - x^2)dx \times (r^2 - x^2),$$

$$= \tfrac{8}{15}\delta\pi r^5 = \tfrac{2}{5}Mr^2.]$$

5. Show, by differentiating the result of Ex. 2, that the moment of inertia of an indefinitely thin ring of radius r about an axis through its centre and perpendicular to its plane is Mr^2.

6. Show by differentiating the result of Ex. 4 that the moment of inertia of an indefinitely thin spherical shell about a diameter is $2Mr^2/3$.

154. The moment of inertia of a body about an axis *not* passing through the centre of gravity may be readily referred to a parallel axis through that point. For suppose the two parallel axes through a point O and the centre of gravity G to lie in a plane perpendicular to the plane of the paper. Take G as origin, the plane of the paper the plane of X, Y, and OGX the axis of X. Let x, y denote the coördinates of any particle P of mass m. Call the distance

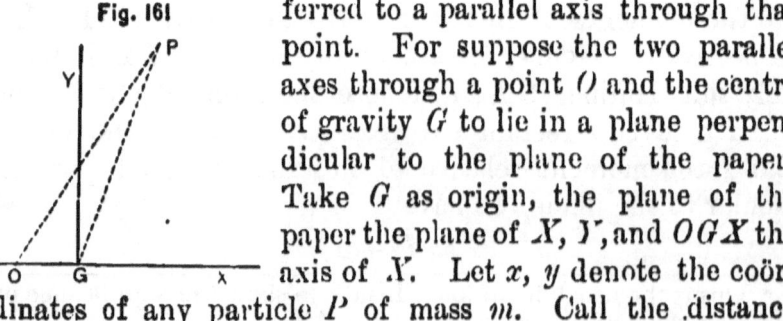

Fig. 161

MOMENT OF INERTIA.

$GO = d$. Then if I denote the moment of inertia about an axis through O, we have

$$I = \Sigma m\{y^2 + (x+d)^2\}$$
$$= \Sigma m(y^2 + x^2) + 2d\Sigma mx + d^2\Sigma m,$$

since the distance d is constant.

Of the three expressions in the right-hand member, the first is equal to I_1, the moment of inertia about G; the second is equal to zero, since G is the centre of gravity (Art. 90); and the third is equal to Md^2, where M is the total mass. Hence

$$I = I_1 + Md^2,$$

or *the moment of inertia about any axis is equal to the moment of inertia about a parallel axis through the centre of gravity, together with the product of the mass into the square of the distance between the two axes.*

Ex. 1. Given that the I of a rod of length l about an axis through its centre is $Ml^2/12$ (Ex. 1, p. 185), show that about one end it is $Ml^2/3$.

2. A rectangular lamina about AGB has $I = Mh^2/12$ (Ex. 3, p. 186): show that about CD it is $= Mh^2/3$.

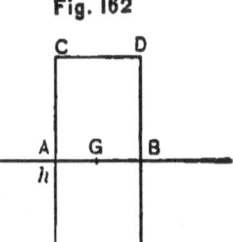
Fig. 162

3. A circular lamina, radius r, about its centre O has $I = Mr^2/2$ (Ex. 2, p. 188): show that about any point in the circumference $I = 3Mr^2/2$.

4. A triangular lamina of base b, height h, about an axis (1) coincident with the base, (2) through the apex and parallel to the base.

Ans. $bh^3/12$; $bh^3/4$.

5. Prove that I is the same for all parallel axes situated at equal distances from the centre of gravity.

6. Of all parallel axes the I of that which passes through the centre of gravity is the least.

155. *Radius of Gyration.*—The general expression for the moment of inertia of a body relative to an axis is

Σmr^2, the sum of the products of the mass of each particle into the square of its distance from the axis. Now instead of the particles being distributed in this way, we may conceive them concentrated into a single particle of mass M equal to the whole mass, and at such a distance k from the axis that the product $Mk^2 = \Sigma mr^2$. To this distance k the name **Radius of Gyration*** is given.

If the axis passes through the centre of gravity, we write $Mk_1^2 = \Sigma mr_1^2$ where k_1 is called the *principal radius of gyration*.

The relation between k and k_1 follows at once from the preceding article. For

$$\Sigma mr^2 = \Sigma mr_1^2 + Ma^2,$$
or $\quad Mk^2 = Mk_1^2 + Ma^2,$
or $\quad k^2 = k_1^2 + a^2,$

the relation sought.

Also, since $I_1 = Mk_1^2$, the value of k_1 is at once found.

Ex. 1. Show that the principal radius of gyration is a minimum radius for parallel axes.

2. For a straight line of length l with reference to its centre, show that $k_1^2 = l^2/12$.

3. For a rectangle of breadth b, depth h, with reference to its centre of gravity, show that $k_1^2 = (b^2 + h^2)/12$.

4. For a circle of diameter d with reference to its centre show that $k_1^2 = d^2/16$.

5. For a triangle of base b, height h, about an axis through its centre of gravity parallel to the base, show that $k_1^2 = h^2/18$.

6. Find k_1^2 for a right cylinder about its axis, r being the radius of cross-section.

[Since the cylinder may be conceived to consist of an infinite number of plates, each of which has the same radius of gyration with respect to an axis through the centre and perpendicular to their planes, the radius of gyration of the cylinder is the same as that of any plate, and $\therefore k_1^2 = r^2/2$.]

---

* Called also *radius of inertia*.

7. For a right cylinder about an edge $k_1^2 = 3r^2/2$.

8. For a hollow cylinder, inner radius r_1, outer radius r_2, relative to its axis, $k_1^2 = (r_1^2 + r_2^2)/2$.

9. For a vertical cylinder, radius r, length l, about a horizontal axis through its centre of gravity show that $k_1^2 = r^2/4 + l^2/12$.

10. For a rectangular prism of dimensions a, b, c about the edge a, show that $k_1^2 = (b^2 + c^2)/12$.

156. We shall now give some applications of the general equations of motion to special cases in which the axes of rotation are fixed, and in which they are instantaneous.

(*a*) **The Physical Pendulum.**—In Art. 73 was considered the problem of the time of oscillation of a heavy particle P suspended from a fixed point by a weightless rod, and acted on by the force of gravity. This problem is purely hypothetical, as no such apparatus can be constructed.

But just as a rigid body is regarded as built up of particles joined together, so an actual or physical pendulum may be regarded as composed of simple pendulums whose oscillations so act on one another as to result in a common oscillation. The duration of this oscillation will give the length of a simple pendulum which fulfils exactly the same conditions of motion.

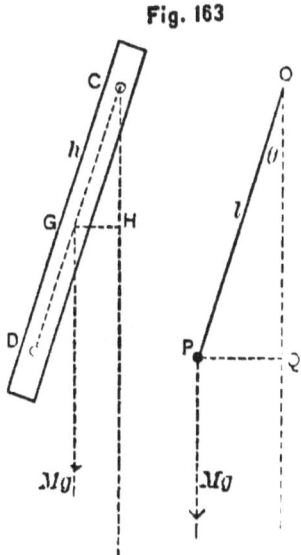

Fig. 163

Suppose the physical pendulum to be a body of any form, and let the two be placed side by side, and both swung through an angle θ. The external forces on the physical pendulum are the weight Mg acting at the centre of gravity G, and the reaction R at the point of support C. Hence, since the moment of

R about C is *nil*, we have

$$\text{ang. accel.} = Mg \times GH/I$$
$$= Mgh \sin \theta/I,$$

where I is the moment of inertia with respect to the axis through C, and h is the distance CG.

For the simple pendulum, Mg being the weight of the particle at P,

$$\text{ang. accel.} = Mg \times PQ/\text{mom. inertia}$$
$$= Mgl \sin \theta / Ml^2$$
$$= g \sin \theta / l.$$

But the angular acceleration being the same in the two cases,

$$Mgh \sin \theta / I = g \sin \theta / l,$$
or $$l = I/Mh,$$

which gives the length of a simple pendulum with the same motion as the compound.

Hence the time of oscillation t of the compound pendulum is (Art. 73)

$$t = \pi \sqrt{l/g} = \pi \sqrt{I/Mgh}.$$

A point D at a distance l from C, the point of suspension, is called the **Centre of Oscillation**,* for the reason that the time of oscillation of the whole pendulum is the same as that of a simple pendulum of length l and swinging about C. Denote the distance DG by k, so that $h + k = l$.

Suppose now the pendulum inverted, and suspended at D instead of at C. The time of an oscillation is

$$\pi \sqrt{I'/Mgk},$$

---

* First determined by Huygens.

where I' is the moment of inertia about D. To find the centre of oscillation if the time of oscillation is the same as if suspended at C, we must find the length l_1 of the simple equivalent pendulum. We have

$$I = I_1 + Mh^2,$$

$$I' = I_1 + Mk^2,$$

where I_1 is the moment of inertia about G (Art. 154).

But $\quad I = Mhl, \quad I' = Mkl_1,$

and $\therefore$ by an easy reduction

$$l = l_1,$$

or the centre of oscillation in the latter case is the centre of suspension in the former.

Hence the points of suspension and of oscillation can be interchanged without changing the time of oscillation, and appropriately therefore a pendulum with points of suspension situated as C, D is known as a **Reversion Pendulum**.

The principle of reversion is employed to determine the length l of the simple equivalent pendulum experimentally. Theoretically, l can be found from $I = Mhl$, but practically it is difficult to make the measurements required by that equation. Hence the experimental method is generally employed: A pendulum of given form is suspended from a point C (on a knife edge) and caused to oscillate. By trial another point D is found, from which if it is suspended it will oscillate in the same time. The distance between C and D is carefully measured, thus giving the length l.

Again, the value of l being known, and the position of the centre of gravity found as by balancing on a knife edge, we have at once the moment of inertia of the pendulum from

$$I = Mhl.$$

This method of finding moments of inertia is particularly useful with solids of irregular figure, or if not perfectly homogeneous throughout. The solid is mounted as a pendulum.

Still further: The length l being known and the time of oscillation being observed, we have from the relation $t = \pi \sqrt{l/g}$ the value of g, the acceleration due to gravity.

The length of the seconds pendulum was used in England for a time as the standard of length, but was afterward abandoned for a certain brass rod called the *standard bar*, for the reason that several of the elements of reduction of pendulum experiments are doubtful.

Ex. 1. A rod of length l is suspended at one end, and caused to oscillate: find the length of the equivalent simple pendulum. *Ans.* $2l/3$.

2. If the rod in Ex. 1 is suspended at $\frac{1}{3}$ of its length from one end, find the time of an oscillation.

3. If a pendulum is suspended at the principal centre of gyration, prove that the time of oscillation is a minimum. [For $t = \pi \sqrt{(h^2 + k_1^2)/gh}$, and t is a min. when $h = k_1$.]

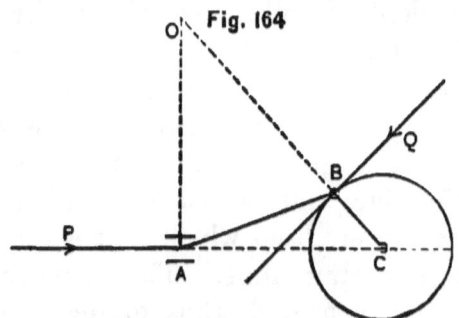

Fig. 164

(*b*) **The Steam Engine.**—To illustrate motion about an instantaneous axis, we shall confine ourselves to the steam engine, and the still more simple case of the rolling disc or sphere.

The relation between the piston pressure P and the crank-pin resistance Q, when the connecting-rod is inclined at any angle, has already been solved in Art. 109, but may be solved more simply by aid of the instantaneous centre.

For the velocity v_1 of the cross-head is to the velocity v_2 of the crank-pin as the instantaneous radii OA, OB, *directly* (Art. 147). But by the principle of work, $P \times v_1 = Q \times v_2$. Hence

$$P \times OA = Q \times OB;$$

or, P is to Q as the instantaneous radii *inversely*.

The value of Q for a given piston pressure will thus vary according to the position of the connecting-rod. It may be represented graphically, as in the case of the indicator diagram (Art. 136).

The *average* of the values of Q for a complete revolution of the crank corresponding to a given piston pressure P will be found by equating the work done by each of the two forces. We have, if r is the radius of the crank arm and S the length of the stroke,

$$Q \times 2\pi r = P \times 2S.$$

But $$S = 2r;$$

$$\therefore \pi Q = 2P,$$

the relation required.

Ex. 1. In a Norris engine the diameter of the cylinder is 14 in., and the steam-pressure 75 pounds per sq. in.: find the average value of the force acting on the crank-pin.

Ans. $2 \times 7^2 \times 75$ pounds.

2. In (1) find the force acting when the crank stands at 60°, and the ratio of the connecting-rod to the crank is $5\frac{1}{4}$.

3. In a steam riveting machine the piston pressure P is applied at the joint a, and the rivet squeezed between the jaws c, d. Find the relation between P and the force Q exerted on the rivet. [The instantaneous centre is at O,

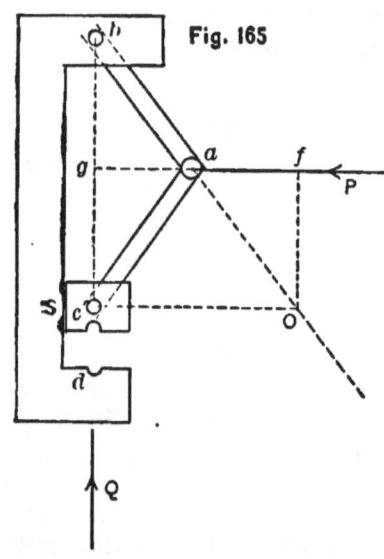

Fig. 165

where ba and the perpendicular through c to the sliding surface S intersect. Hence

$$P \times aO = Q \times cO.$$

As a approaches g, cO diminishes; and when a reaches g, Q becomes indefinitely great. Hence the advantage of the apparatus in that an enormous pressure may be produced by a moderate force acting through a small distance.

This is an example of the **Toggle Joint**, a mechanism of very considerable importance. It is applied, for example, in the Westinghouse air brake on locomotive drivers, in cider, oil, and other presses, etc., etc. In Fig. 166 is shown part of a power screw oil press.

Fig. 166

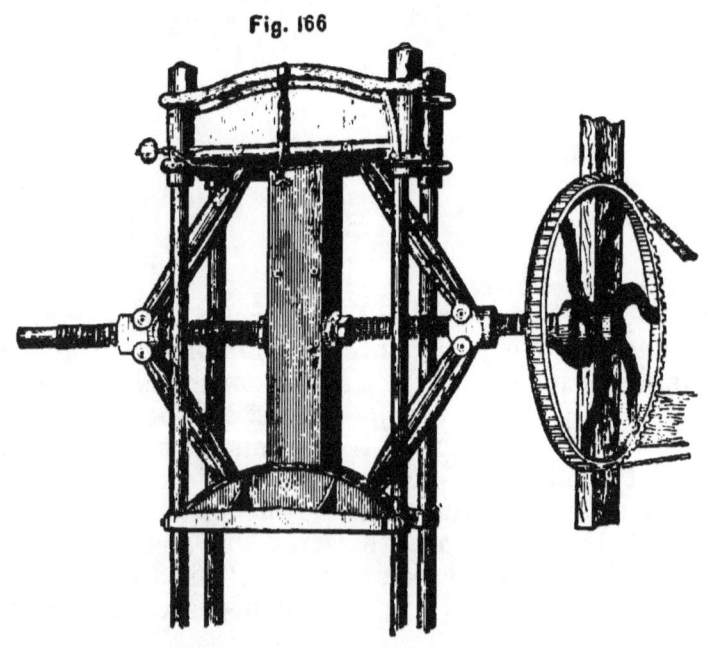

4. A cylinder rolls down an inclined plane of height h from rest: find its velocity v at the bottom.

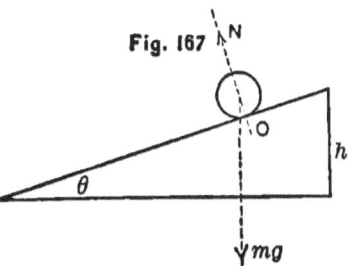

Fig. 167

[O is the instan. centre; r the radius of the cylinder. The forces acting are the wt. Mg and the reaction N.

∴ ang. accel. $\alpha = Mgr \sin \theta / \tfrac{3}{2} Mr^2 = \tfrac{2}{3} g \sin \theta / r$;

∴ linear accel. of centre $= r\alpha = \tfrac{2}{3} g \sin \theta$,

and $v^2 = 2as = 2 \times \tfrac{2}{3} g \sin \theta \times \dfrac{h}{\sin \theta} = \tfrac{4}{3} gh$.]

5. A spherical shot rolls down a plane 70 ft. long and inclined at 30° to the horizon: find its velocity at the bottom. *Ans.* 40 ft. per sec.

6. A sphere will roll and not slide down an inclined plane if the coefficient of friction is greater than $\tfrac{2}{7} \tan \alpha$ where α is the inclination of the plane.

7. The kinetic energy acquired by a sphere in moving from rest down a smooth plane is to that acquired by an equal sphere rolling down a rough plane of the same inclination and length as 7 to 5.

157. Energy of Rotation.—The energy stored in a body rotating with a given angular velocity ω will be found by adding together the energy of each particle. If v is the linear velocity of a particle and r its distance from the axis of rotation, we have $v = \omega r$, and the energy stored $= \tfrac{1}{2} m v^2 = \tfrac{1}{2} m \omega^2 r^2$. Hence the energy stored in the body is $\Sigma \tfrac{1}{2} m \omega^2 r^2$ where Σ is the symbol of summation. If n is the number of revolutions made per minute, $\omega = 2\pi n/60$, and we have finally energy of rotation $= \Sigma \tfrac{1}{2} m \omega^2 r^2 = \tfrac{1}{2} I \omega^2 = I n^2 / 180$, nearly.

We shall confine ourselves to the cases of a circular disc and of a ring rotating about axes through their centres, perpendicular to their planes. Common examples are a car-wheel and a fly-wheel.

For a uniform disc of radius r, $I = \tfrac{1}{2}Mr^2$, and for a ring with r_1, r_2 the inner and outer radii $I = \tfrac{1}{2}M(r_1^2 + r_2^2)$, or if r_1, r_2 are nearly equal, $I = Mr_m^2$, where r_m is the mean radius of the ring.

It is seldom that a wheel is in the form of a simple uniform disc. In general the greater part of the weight is contained in a ring next to the rim of the wheel. This is more the case in a locomotive-wheel than in a car-wheel, and more in the fly-wheel of a stationary engine than in a locomotive-wheel. The two extremes are the uniform disc and the ring.

In order to find readily the mass M of a fly-wheel, we notice that since 1 cub. in. cast-iron weighs 0.261 lb., we have, if A is the area of the cross-section of the rim in square inches, and d the diameter in inches,

$$M = \pi d \times A \times 0.261 = 0.82 dA \text{ lb., nearly};$$

and $\therefore I = 0.205 A d^3$, nearly.

158. In a stationary engine the fly-wheel is introduced to give steadiness. It does this by giving up when called on part of the energy stored in it.* To compute the dimensions of a wheel, we must decide on the greatest amount of energy that should be demanded of it, and also on the maximum range of velocity that can be allowed. Suppose

---

* "The proprietor was showing to a friend the method of punching holes in iron plates. He held in his hand a piece of iron ⅜ in. thick, which he placed under the punch. Observing after several holes had been made that the punch made its perforations more and more slowly, he called to the engine-man to know what made the engine work so sluggishly, when it was found that the fly-wheel and punching apparatus had been detached from the steam-engine just at the commencement of his experiment."—*Babbage*.

ENERGY OF ROTATION. 199

we wish to call on it for 36000 ft.-pounds, and that the velocity may change from 48 to 52 revolutions per minute.

Then $\quad I(52^2 - 48^2)/180 = 36000g$

and $\quad I = 16200g.$

If we decide to make the wheel 14 ft. in diameter,

$$Mr^2 = 16200g$$

and $\quad M = 5 +$ tons,

whence the cross-section of the rim may be computed from the formula given above.

159. In many cases a body possesses both an energy of translation and an energy of rotation, and their comparative amounts or their sum may be required. Take, for example, a railroad car in motion. Each wheel of the car acts as a fly-wheel in which energy is stored to be given out before the car comes to rest. If v is the velocity of the train, the tangential velocity ωr of the wheel is equal to the velocity of translation v. Hence the energy stored in the wheel considered as a disc $= \frac{1}{2}I\omega^2 = \frac{1}{2} \times \frac{1}{2}Mr^2 \times v^2/r^2 = \frac{1}{4}Mv^2$, being one half that due to the forward motion of the wheels. Suppose the total (loaded) weight of the car to be 40000 lbs., and that the eight wheels weigh 4500 lbs., and the velocity is 30 miles an hour. Then the total energy stored in the car is

$\frac{1}{2} \times 40000 \times 44^2 + \frac{1}{4} \times 4500 \times 44^2$ foot-poundals,

which may be reduced to foot-pounds by dividing by 32.2.

Ex. 1. In a disc revolving about its axis the radius of gyration is nearly 0.7 of the actual radius.

2. The rim of the fly-wheel of a Norris engine is 14 ft. in diameter, and weighs 11400 lbs.: find its I about the centre.

3. The rim of a fly-wheel weighs 15 tons, and its diameter is 20 ft.; the wheel makes 60 revolutions per minute : find the energy stored.   *Ans.* 1,875,000 ft.-pounds.

4. A fly-wheel of a tons wt. and b ft. diameter makes c revolutions per minute : find the energy accumulated.
Ans. $0.087ab^2c^2$ ft.-pounds, nearly.

5. The weight of a fly-wheel is W lbs., and its diameter d_1 inches. If it is making n revolutions per minute, find in how many revolutions it will be stopped by the friction of the axle if its diameter is d_2 inches and the coefficient of friction μ.   *Ans.* $\pi n^2 d_1^2 / 7200 \mu g d_2$.

6. Examine the following statement: "Every engineer knows that a thing so balanced as to stand in any position is not necessarily balanced for running: that a 4-lb. weight at 3 in. from the axis of rotation though balanced statically by a 1 lb. weight at 12 inches from the axis is not balanced by it dynamically. On the contrary, a 4-lb. weight at 5 in. is balanced by a 1-lb. weight at 10 in. from the axis."

CHAPTER VIII.

ELASTIC SOLIDS.

160. In laying down the foundations of the subject it was stated as the result of observation and experiment that forces acting on a body might change its motion or its form, or that both changes might take place. The effect of the force depends on the nature of the body acted on. As most simple, we have considered first of all changes of motion only. The action of the external forces was conceived to be resisted by the internal reactions of the particles on one another in such a way that the particles retained their original distances from one another so that change of form did not take place, or the body acted on was rigid. The conditions of equilibrium and of change of motion on this hypothesis have been developed in the preceding chapters.

Experience shows that no perfectly rigid body exists in nature. The internal reactions do not prevent changes of form, the body yields to the external forces and changes its form or its size. If it returns towards its original configuration on the removal of the forces, it is said to be **Elastic**—a body possessing elasticity of form being called a *solid*, and one altogether devoid of elasticity of form a *fluid*.

Conceive an elastic body (as a bent spring) in equilibrium under the action of given forces. When in this condition, nothing will be changed by supposing it to become rigid. The conditions of equilibrium of a rigid body may therefore be applied to it in its distorted form, and the problem solved as for a rigid body. So that just as we use the particle as a stepping-stone to the rigid body, we use the rigid body as a stepping-stone to the elastic body.

202 ELASTIC SOLIDS.

161. The form of the body when in the position of equilibrium being distorted, differs from the original form. Hence, before we apply the conditions of equilibrium we must first of all inquire into the changes of form capable of being produced by the external forces. To do this it is necessary to appeal to experiment.

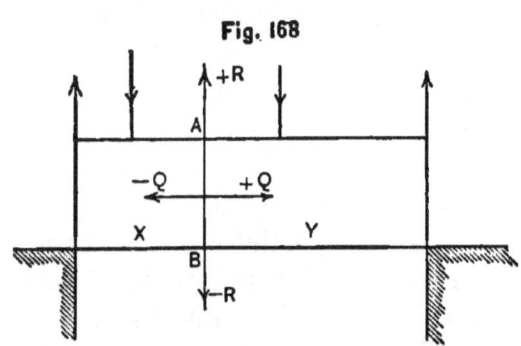

Fig. 168

Conceive a uniform beam with horizontal axis and resting on two supports under the action of external forces. These forces are transferred from particle to particle of the beam, and give rise to internal forces or reactions.

Let Fig. 168 represent a vertical section through the axis of the beam. For simplicity consider first the external forces to be parallel to this plane and let them be resolved into components along and at right angles to the axis. Conceive the beam divided, by a plane AB perpendicular to the axis, into two parts X and Y. The equilibrium will remain as before, provided forces equal and opposite to the internal forces at the section are applied. Let these forces be resolved into vertical and horizontal components, and let these be combined into single resultants, Q, Q; R, R. The forces of which Q, R are the resultants being distributed over the surfaces of the section and forming pairs in equilibrium, are known as **Internal Stresses**.

The part X is in equilibrium under the action of the external forces and the stresses $+ R$, $- Q$ representing the action of Y upon X, and the part Y under the external forces and the stresses $- R$, $+ Q$ representing the action of X upon Y. In finding the relation between the external forces and the internal stresses the equilibrium of either X or Y may be considered. We shall take X, the section to the left of the cutting plane.

162. To the stresses various names are given. Thus the stresses along the beam may tend to pull the pieces apart or to push them together. To the pull the name of tensile stress or **Tension** is given, and to the push the name of compressive stress or **Compression**.

The transverse stress (consisting of equal and opposite forces $+R$, $-R$, considered acting indefinitely near the plane of section, but on opposite sides) causes the pieces to slide along the plane, and forms the shearing stress or **Shear**. The transverse stress may cause X, Y to turn about an axis in the plane AB, and forms the **Bending Stress**.

If the external forces are not in the same plane, the bending stress may take place about an axis perpendicular to the plane AB, and forms the twisting or **Torsion Stress**. This generally occurs in machine shafting.

These are the simple forms of stress. Usually stresses are compound, but may be resolved into two or more of the simple forms.

163. When a beam is subjected to the action of a stress it yields. The change of dimension is known as a **Strain**. Remove the stress, and the beam returns to its original dimensions. This is observed to be true for stresses up to a certain amount. When that amount is exceeded, the beam will not return to its original form on removing the stress, but will assume another form between the two, or take a **Permanent Set**, as it is called. Increase the stress still further, and the beam will be finally ruptured.

The discussion of stresses and strains forms the **Mechanics of Materials**, and will be found in special treatises.

164. Impact.—Suppose a sphere of mass m to come in contact with another of mass m_1, a collision or **Impact** takes place. This impact is said to be *direct* if the bodies are moving in the same straight line, and the common tangent plane at the point of meeting is perpendicular to the direction of motion: if not, the impact is said to be *oblique*.

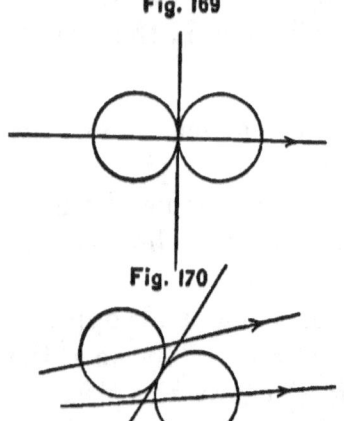

Fig. 169

Fig. 170

165. *Direct Impact*.—In consequence of the impact there is a mutual pressure produced, which increases the velocity of one of the bodies and diminishes that of the other. The velocity u of m is changed to v say, and the velocity u_1 of m_1 to v_1. The impact action requires a certain time, which may be conceived divided into small intervals. Let P be the pressure developed in any one of these intervals, and a, a_1 the accelerations produced in the masses m, m_1, respectively. Then (Art. 34) $P = ma$, $P = m_1 a_1$, and

$$\therefore a : a_1 = m_1 : m.$$

Similarly for all of the intervals. Hence, by addition,

total accel. of m : total accel. of $m_1 = m_1 : m$,

or $\quad v - u : u_1 - v_1 = m_1 : m$,

or $\quad mu + m_1 u_1 = mv + m_1 v_1$; . . . (1)

that is, the sum of the momenta before impact is equal to the sum of the momenta after impact,—a statement indeed implied in the law of stress.

This equation contains two unknowns, v and v_1. We must therefore have another relation between them, as two equations are necessary to determine two unknowns. Now it is found by experiment that when two bodies impinge directly their relative velocity after impact bears a constant ratio to their relative velocity before impact so long as the material of the bodies is the same, but is in the opposite direction. This constant ratio is called the **Coefficient of Restitution** of the two bodies, and is denoted by the letter e. We have therefore

$$v - v_1 = -e(u - u_1) \quad \ldots \quad (2)$$

as the second relation between v and v_1. Solving (1) and (2), we find the values of v and v_1.

The value of e depends on the material composing the bodies. From its definition it follows that the extreme values of e are 0 and 1. If $e = 0$, or the bodies are **Inelastic**, then

$$v = (mu + m_1 u_1)/(m + m_1) = v_1, \quad \ldots \quad (3)$$

or the bodies move together with a common velocity after impact. If $e = 1$, then

$$v - v_1 = -(u - u_1),$$

or the velocity of one body relative to the other after impact is the same as it was before impact, but in the opposite direction. In this case the bodies are **Elastic**.

No examples of either perfectly inelastic or of perfectly elastic bodies occur in nature. But some bodies with very little elasticity, as clay for example, may be regarded as belonging to the first class, and others, as glass, to the second class.

Ex. 1. Two inelastic balls are brought to rest by the impact: prove that they must have been moving in opposite directions, with velocities inversely proportional to their masses.

2. Two balls of equal mass are perfectly elastic: prove that after impact they will exchange velocities.

3. A row of equal elastic balls are placed in contact in a

straight line. An equal ball impinges directly on them. Show that all will remain at rest but the last, which will fly off. Verify experimentally.

4. Find the elasticity of two balls of masses m and M in order that if M impinges on m at rest it will itself be brought to rest. *Ans.* M/m.

166. *Oblique Impact of a Sphere against a Fixed Smooth Plane AB.*—Let u be the velocity before impact, and v the velocity after impact; θ the inclination of u to the normal, and β the inclination of v.

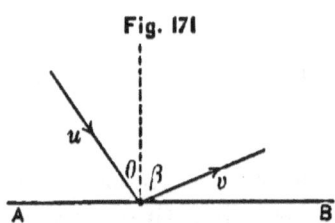

Fig. 171

Resolve the velocities along and normal to the plane. The plane being smooth, it exerts a normal pressure only. Hence the impact may be considered direct, with velocity $u \cos \theta$ before and $v \cos \beta$ after impact; and

$$\therefore v \cos \beta = -eu \cos \theta.$$

Also, since the pressure is normal, the action along the plane is unchanged by the impact. Hence

$$v \sin \beta = u \sin \theta,$$

and v and β are found.

Ex. 1. What are the values of v and β above?

2. If the elasticity be perfect, show that the angle of incidence θ is equal to the angle of reflection β.

3. To hit a ball Q by a ball P after reflection from the edge CA of a billiard table. "Aim at a point B as far behind the edge CA as Q is in front of it." Prove this.

4. Deduce a rule for reflection at two edges of the table.

5. A ball impinges on an equal ball at rest at an angle of 45° to the line of impact: prove that if both are perfectly elastic their velocities will be equal after impact.

6. Two balls of given masses and moving in given directions with given velocities impinge on one another: find the resultant velocity of each ball and its direction,

167. When two bodies impinge, the **Energy of Impact** is broken into two parts, one being taken up in producing changes of form, heat, light, sound, etc., and the other the resultant motion of the bodies. With our usual notation we have for direct impact,

$$\text{energy before impact} = (mu^2 + m_1 u_1^2)/2,$$

$$\text{energy after impact} = (mv^2 + m_1 v_1^2)/2,$$

and the change during impact is therefore the difference between these two expressions. From Equations 1, 2, Art. 165, we find by a simple reduction

$$\tfrac{1}{2}(mu^2 + m_1 u_1^2) - \tfrac{1}{2}(mv^2 + m_1 v_1^2) = \tfrac{1}{2}(1-e^2)\frac{mm_1}{m+m_1}(u-u_1)^2,$$

which gives the change of kinetic energy produced by the impact. The change is greatest when $e = 0$, or the bodies are inelastic. The expression being a positive quantity (since $e^2 < 1$) would seem to indicate a loss of energy during impact. Whether the change is to be so regarded or not, depends on the end to be attained. If that is the propulsion of a missile or the driving of a pile, then change of form, heat, etc., are prejudicial, and the energy used in producing them is lost. If, on the other hand, change of form is the main thing, as in moulding metal under a hammer or in riveting, this so-called loss becomes the useful energy, and the energy of motion useful in the former case becomes prejudicial in this.

Ex. Two trains of equal weight, moving with velocities of 30 miles an hour each and in opposite directions, collide: show that the loss of energy produced by the impact is the same as in the case of a train moving at 60 miles an hour striking another at rest.

In the latter case find the velocity with which the débris will be moved along the track.

Also, show that before impact the total energy in the one case is double that in the other.

168. The case of impact that occurs most frequently in practice is when the bodies are inelastic, and one is at rest before impact. Placing $e = 0$, $u_1 = 0$, and substituting for v, v_1 their values from (3) Art. 165, we have for the collective energy of the two bodies before impact $mu^2/2$, and after impact $m^2u^2/2(m + m_1)$, making the change during impact $mm_1u^2/2(m + m_1)$.

Fig. 172

Take for illustration the **Pile Driver.*** The principle is the same as in driving a nail with a hammer, except that the motion is always vertical, gravity being the force acting.

When the ram of mass m in falling through a height h impinges on a pile of mass m_1 with velocity u, the pile is driven downward a certain distance s. Let F denote the resisting force offered by the ground. The work done on the resistance is Fs foot-poundals. The energy of impact is $m^2u^2/2(m + m_1)$ foot-poundals. The work done after impact by the force of gravity on ram and pile is $(m + m_1)gs$ foot-poundals. Hence

$$m^2u^2/2(m + m_1) + (m + m_1)gs = Fs,$$

and F is found.

In gravitation units, if $W =$ wt. of ram in pounds, $w =$ weight of pile in pounds, and $P =$ the resistance in

---

* The figure represents a piledriver made by the Vulcan Iron Works, Chicago.

pounds (or the ultimate load the pile will carry), then (remembering that $u^2 = 2gh$) the above equation reduces to

$$W^2h/(W+w) + (W+w)s = Ps,$$

the standard form.

At the last blow, the value of s being small, the second term may be disregarded in comparison with the first, and we have

$$W^2h/(W+w) = Ps.$$

Still more approximately, by neglecting the weight of the pile in comparison with that of the ram,

$$Wh = Ps.$$

For example, to find the ultimate load a pile weighing 500 lbs. could carry if the last blow from a height of 25 ft. of a one-ton ram sinks the pile one inch. The three formulas give 482,500; 480,000; 500,000 pounds, respectively.

The **Safe Load** to be carried by the pile is some fractional part of this, which experience has determined. Thus with the second of the above formulas Col. Mason, U.S.A., in a series of experiments at Fort Montgomery, N. Y., found the fraction to be $\frac{1}{4}$, so that he proposed

$$\text{safe load} = W^2h/4(W+w)s;$$

and Major Sanders, U.S.A., in an "extensive series of experiments made in establishing the foundations of Fort Delaware," concluded that the third formula was to be depended on in the form

$$\text{safe load} = Wh/8s.$$

The fact is, so much depends on local circumstances, particularly on the condition of the head of the pile at the last blow, that pile-driving formulas must remain essentially empirical.

It is useful to notice that the energy of the ram before impact being Wh, the loss of energy will be less the more nearly $W/(W+w)$ is equal to unity, that is, the greater W is in comparison with w. Hence the ram should be large in weight compared with the pile.

With the riveting hammer, steam hammer, etc., in which change of form is the end to be attained, the useful work done by the hammer depends on $Wwh/(W+w)$, which is the more nearly equal to Wh the greater w is in comparison with W, that is, the heavier the anvil is in comparison with the hammer.

Ex. 1. Find the safe load for a pile weighing 500 lbs. to carry if the pile sinks 0.1 ft. at the last blow under the 5-ft. fall of a 500-lb. ram. *Ans.* 3125 lbs.

2. A steam hammer weighing 500 lbs. has a stroke of 3 ft. If the piston pressure is 1000 pounds and the blow is vertical, find the work delivered in 6 blows.
Ans. 270,000 foot-pounds.

3. A pile is driven s ft. vertically into the ground by n blows of a steam hammer fastened to the head of the pile. Given p the mean pressure of the steam in pounds per sq. in., d the diameter of the piston in inches, l the length of the stroke in ft., w the weight in lbs. of the moving parts of the hammer, and w_1 the weight in lbs. of the pile and fixed parts of the hammer attached to it, and R the mean resistance of the ground in pounds, prove

$$nw(w + \pi pd^2/4)l = Rs(w + w_1).$$

4. In firing from a rifle of weight w lbs. a bullet of weight w_1 lbs. with velocity v ft. per sec., show that the energy of recoil is $gw_1^2v^2/2w$.

169. In the preceding sections the impact considered has been measured by the momentum developed. In most cases the time of impact is so small that it is impossible to measure it. If it can be measured or estimated, the acting force F is at once found from the relation (Art. 34)

$$Ft = mv.$$

Thus suppose a hammer weighing 4 lbs. to strike a blow with a velocity of 16 ft. per sec., and that the time elapsing from the first contact to the destruction of the motion is 1/1000 second, the average force F acting for this time would be given by

$$F = 4 \times 16 \times 1000 \div 32 = 2000 \text{ pounds.}$$

The effect produced results from the enormous force developed in the short time. If the time be increased the force is diminished in the same proportion. From this circumstance many familiar phenomena may be easily accounted for.

Ex. 1. Why do we receive a severe jar from a step downward when one expects to step on the level?

2. Account for the different effects of a cannon-ball in striking a granite wall and an earth wall.

3. The ram of a pile-driver of 250 lbs. falls through 10 ft. and is stopped in $\frac{1}{10}$ second: find the average force exerted.

4. The head of a steam hammer weighs 3 tons. If steam is admitted on the under side only for lifting, and the head has a drop of 4 ft., find the average compressive force exerted during a blow if its duration is $\frac{1}{10}$ second.

Ans. 15 tons.

CHAPTER IX.

STATICS OF FLUIDS (HYDROSTATICS).

170. ACCORDING to the general scheme outlined in Art. 4, we now pass on to discuss the action of force on bodies in the fluid state. Our ideas of a fluid are derived from common experience. Such substances as water, oil, air, steam, we call fluids. The one characteristic property by which they are distinguished from solids is the more or less ease with which the particles move among themselves; or in other words, fluids have less elasticity of form than solids. Some fluids offer more resistance to separation of the particles from one another, or to flow, than do others—thus molasses more than water, and water more than ether. This resistance to flow is known as **Viscosity**. We may, however, *conceive* of a fluid of such a kind as would offer no resistance whatever in any direction, the elasticity of form being altogether wanting. A fluid possessing this property has no existence in nature. It is an abstraction, just as a perfectly rigid solid or a perfectly elastic solid is, and our only reason for introducing the idea is that it leads to simplicity of treatment. The more any fluid in nature differs from the hypothetical fluid, the greater the modifications necessary in the results derived from the hypothesis. As the basis of our reasoning, then, we lay down this definition:

A fluid is a substance the particles of which can be moved by any force however small, and which act on one another or on any surface without friction.

171. Two Kinds of Fluids.—It follows from the definition that a fluid offers no resistance to change of form. Hence the fluid must be confined in a solid vessel or envelope either rigid or elastic. Suppose a fluid completely confined, and a force P applied to a piston entering the vessel. With some fluids (as water) the change of volume resulting from the force P will be so small as to be practically *nil;* with others (as air) the change will be dependent on the force, and such that when the force is removed it returns to its former volume. A rough illustration is afforded by the action of a closed syringe and of a pop-gun. We therefore subdivide fluids into non-compressible or inelastic and compressible or elastic. The former are known as **Liquids**, the latter as **Gases**. We shall assume the absolute incompressibility of liquids and the perfect elasticity of gases, which assumptions though not strictly true are very nearly so, as repeated experiments have shown.

172. The results of the action of forces on fluids not equally applied over the whole surface of the fluid is change of form or flow. If the forces acting over the whole surface balance, the fluid is in equilibrium. We are thus led to distinguish the statics of fluids and the kinetics of fluids.

The term **Hydromechanics** is used to designate the mechanics of fluids. It is divided into **Hydrostatics**, which treats of fluids at rest; and **Hydrokinetics**, which treats of fluids in motion. The term **Pneumatics** includes the properties of gases as distinct from liquids.

By some writers the term **Hydraulics**, originally applied to the motion of water through pipes, is taken to mean the mechanics of fluids.

173. From the conception of perfect mobility among the particles of a fluid we infer that if a fluid is in equilibrium under the action of external forces—

(*a*) *Each particle must be equally pressed in every direction.* For if not, the particles would move in the direction of least pressure, which contradicts the hypothesis of equilibrium :—

(*b*) *The force exerted by the fluid on any surface with which it is in contact* (*or the pressure on the surface*) *is normal to the surface.* For if not, friction must enter, which contradicts the hypothesis of perfect mobility.

These are the two fundamental principles of the statics of fluids.

174. Measurement of Pressure.—Suppose that a fluid is in equilibrium under the action of a number of external forces, and let P denote the pressure exerted by the fluid on an area A of the surface of the vessel containing it or of a surface immersed in it. Then P/A would be the pressure exerted on a unit of surface if the pressure were uniform over the surface, and would be the average pressure per unit if it were not uniform. Pressures are expressed in poundals per sq. in., pounds per sq. in., dynes per sq. cm., etc.

By making the unit of surface indefinitely small, we have the pressure on an indefinitely small surface, and can therefore speak in this sense of the pressure *at* a point. The expression is a conventional one. The pressure *on* a point is of course *nil*.

175. Transmission of Pressure.—Since every particle of a fluid in equilibrium is pressed equally in all directions, any assigned particle must exert an equal pressure in all directions on its adjoining particles, each of these an equal pressure on those adjoining, and so on throughout the fluid. Hence a pressure applied at any point is transmitted unchanged to every other point of the fluid, and a pressure applied to a surface is transmitted unchanged to every other unit of surface in contact with the fluid. This is sometimes called the *principle of Pascal.*

Suppose a vessel full of water and furnished with two pistons fitting in two openings A and B. Let A contain A square inches of surface, and B contain B square inches. Suppose a force of P poundals applied at A balanced by a force of Q poundals applied at B. The pressure per sq. in. at A is P/A, and at B is Q/B. Hence

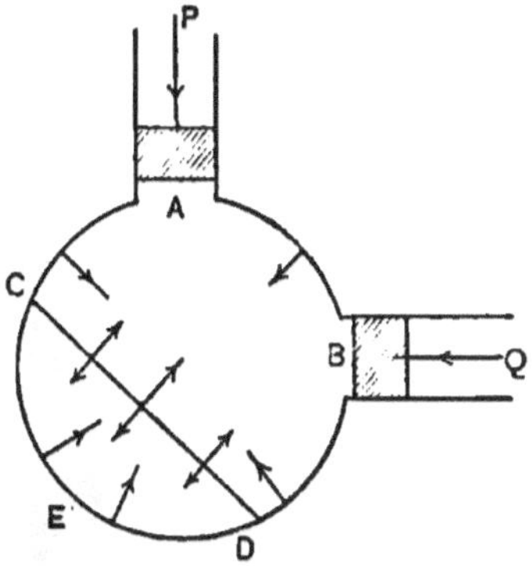

$$P/A = Q/B,$$

Fig. 173

from which relation, when any three of the quantities P, Q, A, B are given, the fourth can be found. Experiment confirms this result.

Again, suppose a plane CD to divide the fluid into two parts. The pressures on the two sides of this plane are equal, and are normal to the plane. There is equilibrium between the pressure on the surface CED and the pressure on one side of CD, also between the pressure on CAD and the pressure on the other side of CD. But CD is the projection of CED or of CAD, no matter what the form of these surfaces. Hence the pressure on a surface in a given direction is equal to the pressure on the projection of this surface on a plane normal to the given direction.

Ex. Show that the pressure on a pump plunger is the same whether the end of the plunger is rounded or flat.

Application: (1) The *safety-valve* of a water or steam engine.

The pressure on the valve will show the pressure in the boiler, and by suitably placing the weight on the lever, this pressure may be adjusted to any amount desired. When it exceeds this amount the valve will be lifted and the steam escape.

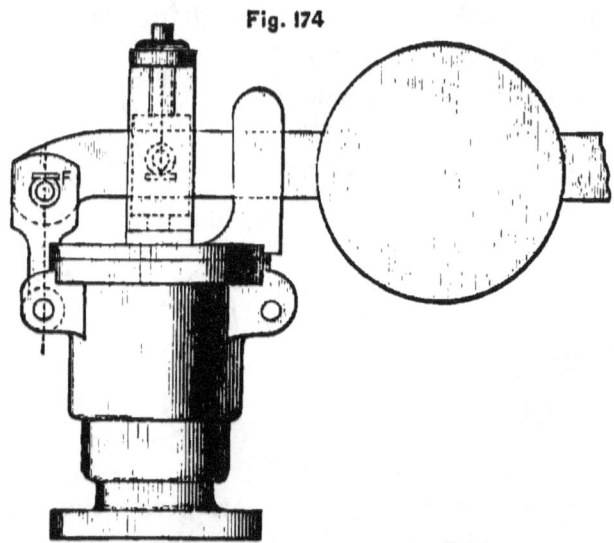

Fig. 174

Let W_1 = wt. of valve in lbs., A its area in sq. in., l_1 = distance of centre of valve from fulcrum F in inches;

W_2 = wt. of lever; l_2 = dist. of C. of G. of lever from fulcrum;

W'_3 = wt. on lever; l_3 = dist. of centre of weight from fulcrum;

p = pressure in pounds per sq. in. of blowing-off.

Take moments about the fulcrum, and

$$w_1 l_1 + w_2 l_2 + w_3 l_3 = p l_1 A,$$

the relation required.

Ex. 1. The valve weight is 3 lbs., diameter of valve 4 in., distance from fulcrum to centre of weight 36 in., distance from fulcrum to centre of valve 4 in., weight of lever 7 lbs., distance from fulcrum to centre of gravity of lever 15.5 in.: find the weight at the end of the lever to make the blowing-off pressure 80 pounds per sq. in.

Ans. 108.3 lbs.

2. With the same data find how far the weight must be

placed from the fulcrum to make the blowing-off pressure
75 pounds per sq. in. *Ans.* 33.7 in.

(2) *The Lifting-jack.*—The figure represents a section of
a Tangye jack. Water
is forced from the cistern by the force-pump
CG under the ram which
works in a water-tight
collar H. The weight
to be raised is placed on
the ram at W.

By unscrewing the
"lowering screw" the
water is returned to the
cistern. By means of
the "air-screw" air is
admitted when the jack
is in use.

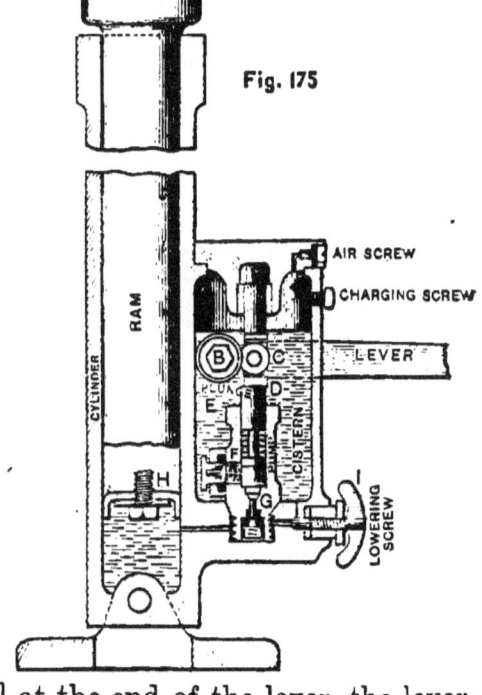

Fig. 175

Ex. 1. In a jack the
plunger is 1 in. diameter
and the ram 10 in. diameter. A weight of 10
tons is to be raised: what
pressure must be applied at the end of the lever, the leverage being as 10 to 1. *Ans.* 20 pounds.

2. In a jack the leverage is $a : b$, the pressure applied at
the end of the lever P pounds, and the weight on the ram
W lbs. Compare the diameters D, d of ram and plunger.
Ans. $D/d = \sqrt{Wb/Pa}$.

176. It is evident from the above apparatus that water
may be used to transmit force. Not only so, but it may
be used for the storing of energy. For suppose the ram
fixed, then the pressure by the action of the ram will
remain stored until the ram is freed, when it will rise to
the same height that it would have done if not interfered

with. A vessel for the storing of energy in water is known as a **Hydraulic Accumulator.**

The mode of action of an accumulator may be more evident from Fig. 176. *A* is a solid ram working water-tight in a vertical cylinder, and carrying a heavy weight *W*. This weight, which in an accumulator usually consists of cast-iron blocks, is carried by a platform *B*, which latter is supported by rods from a cross-piece *C*, fastened to the top of the ram *A*. *D* and *D* are vertical guides.

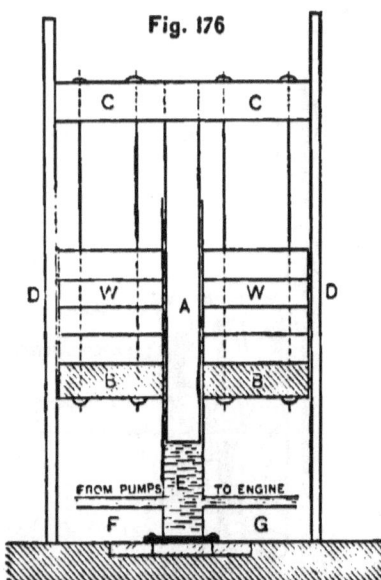

Fig. 176

Water is driven into the chamber *E* through the pipe *F* by means of a force-pump, thus raising the ram. The mechanism to be operated is connected with the pipe *G*, through which the energy stored is communicated. In this way hydraulic cranes, elevators, etc., may be worked from a central source by means of water-pressure.

Ex. 1. The ram is 21 in. in diameter and the load 120 tons: show that the water-pressure per sq. in. in the accumulator is 700 pounds, nearly.

2. In the hydraulic machinery for opening and closing the lock-gates of the St. Mary's Falls Canal, at the entrance to Lake Superior, the ram of the accumulator has a diameter of 21 in., and carries a load of 20.76 tons. The water-engine driven by this accumulator makes one revolution per minute, the diameter of the piston is 15 in., and the length of stroke 96 in. Find the H. P. developed.

Ans. 5.1, nearly.

177. In the last two sections we have considered the transmission of pressure in vessels completely filled with fluid

PRESSURES AT DIFFERENT DEPTHS. 219

and acted on by external forces. We now proceed to consider the influence of the weight of the fluid on the surface pressed.

178. Surface of a Liquid at Rest.—Consider a liquid in a vessel with the upper surface free and acted on by gravity only. This free surface is a horizontal plane. For the force of gravity on each particle is vertical, and as friction is wanting, the surface must arrange itself at right angles to the pressures,—that is, horizontally,—otherwise the particles would glide over one another.

This is the characteristic property of liquids as distinguished from gases. The surface is an example of an equipotential surface (Art. 143).

179. Pressures at Different Depths.—Let O be a point in the liquid at a depth h below the surface. Suppose a small horizontal circle ab of area A described about O as centre, and conceive the liquid contained in the vertical cylinder described on ab as base and extending to the surface cd to become solid. The equilibrium existing will not be disturbed thereby.

Fig. 177

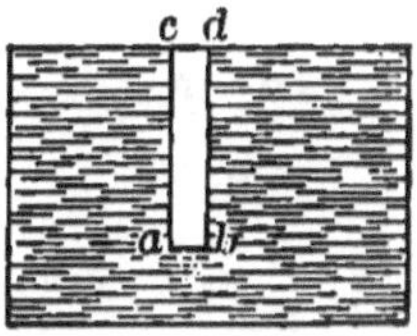

The pressures on the sides of the cylinder being normal to the curved surface, are horizontal. Resolving vertically, we have

press. on ab = wt. (grav. force) of cylr. ad.

Let p = press. per unit area of ab, δ = mass of cubic unit of the liquid or its *density*, and this becomes

$$p \times A = \delta A h g \text{ poundals,}$$
or
$$p = g \delta h \text{ poundals}$$
$$= \delta h \text{ pounds.}$$

Thus *the pressure varies directly as the depth below the surface of the liquid.*

If the base ab is not horizontal the pressure will vary from point to point of the base, and p becomes the *average* pressure per unit surface.

If we conceive the base to become smaller and smaller until it becomes indefinitely small, then p will represent the pressure *at* the point O. Hence *the pressure at any point within a liquid is proportional to the depth of the point below the free surface of the liquid.*

The weight (mass) of a cubic foot of water at the temperature 4° C. is 62.424 lbs., or 1000 oz., nearly. A cubic inch of mercury weighs 3429.5 grains, a cubic ft. 13,600 oz.

Ex. 1. Find the pressure at a depth of 100 ft. in Lake Superior. *Ans.* 43.3 pounds per sq. in.

2. A vessel is filled with mercury. At what depth is the pressure 20 pounds per sq. in.?

$$\text{Ans. } 20 = h \times 3429.5 \times 7000.$$

180. Total Pressure on a Surface immersed.—This follows from the preceding by adding the pressures on all the unit surfaces contained in the given surface. Thus, if $h_1, h_2 \ldots h_n$ are the depths of the unit surfaces, the total pressure

Fig. 178

$$= g\delta h_1 + g\delta h_2 + \ldots + g\delta h_n$$
$$= g\delta(h_1 + h_2 + \ldots + h_n).$$

Then, as in Art. 90, if A is the number of units of area in the surface and $\bar{h}$ the depth of its centre of gravity,

$$\bar{h} = (1 \times h_1 + 1 \times h_2 + \ldots + 1 \times h_n)/A,$$
or $\quad A\bar{h} = h_1 + h_2 + \ldots + h_n,$

and the total pressure on the surface $= g\delta A\bar{h}$.

That is, *the total pressure on a surface immersed is equal to the weight (= gravity force) of a column of liquid whose base is the area pressed, and height the depth of the centre of gravity below the liquid level.*

TOTAL PRESSURE ON A SURFACE IMMERSED. 221

Notice (*a*) that in this discussion nothing is said about the shape of the vessel. The result does not therefore depend on the shape. Also the surface pressed on may be placed anywhere in the vessel. It may therefore form its base. Hence *the pressure on the base of a vessel containing a liquid is independent of the shape of the vessel.* For example, the pressure against a dock would be the same if the dock were exposed to the Atlantic Ocean or were situated in a land-locked harbor, provided the depth of water at the dock were the same in both cases and the water at rest.

Ex. Explain the paradox, "Any quantity of liquid, however small, may be made to support any quantity, however large."

Notice (*b*) that a pressure P on a surface A may be considered as arising from a column of liquid whose base is the surface and whose height h is found from $P = g\delta Ah$. This height is called the **Head of Water**.

For a base of one sq. in. and head h ft. the pressure $= 62.424h/144 = 0.434\ h$ pounds; and conversely, a pressure of p pounds per sq. in. corresponds to a head of $2.304\ p$ feet.

Ex. 1. Prove that the water pressure on a surface 1 ft. wide, h ft. deep, is $31\frac{1}{4}\ h^2$ pounds.

2. Find the resultant pressure on a sluice gate, the water standing 10 ft. on one side and 6 ft. on the other.
Ans. 1 ton.

3. Compare the pressures on the upper and lower halves of a sluice gate. *Ans.* 1 to 3.

4. The slope of a reservoir wall is 1 in 8 and the height 25 ft. If the water reaches to the top of the sloping face find the horizontal pressure. *Ans.* 19,500 pounds.

5. If two liquids which do not mix are placed in a bent tube open at the ends, prove that their respective heights are inversely as their weights.

Hence, by attaching a graduated scale, show how to find

the relative weights of two liquids. Try water and mercury and see if the relation is 1 : 13.6.

6. A sphere is filled with liquid. Account for the total pressure of the liquid on the surface being greater than the weight of the liquid.

What is the relation between the pressure and the weight?

181. Centre of Pressure on a Plane Surface Immersed. — Suppose the plane surface of area A divided into areas of one unit each, and let $h_1, h_2, \ldots h_n$ denote their respective depths. The pressures on these areas are $g\delta h_1, g\delta h_2, \ldots g\delta h_n$, and being all normal to the surface, and therefore parallel, may be combined into a single resultant pressure equal to their sum. The point in which this resultant meets the surface is called the **Centre of Pressure**. To find its depth h_0 below the surface of the liquid proceed as in Art. 90, and

$$h_0 = (g\delta h_1 \times h_1 + g\delta h_2 \times h_2 + \ldots + g\delta h_n \times h_n)/(g\delta h_1 + g\delta h_2 + \ldots + g\delta h_n).$$

Let θ denote the inclination of the plane surface to the surface of the liquid, $r_1, r_2, \ldots r_n$ the distances of the unit areas from the line of intersection of the two surfaces, and $\bar{r}$ the distance of the centre of gravity from this line; then, since $h_1 = r_1 \sin \theta, \ldots$, we have

$$h_0 = (r_1^2 + r_2^2 + \ldots + r_n^2)/(r_1 + r_2 + \ldots + r_n)$$
$$= (r_1^2 + r_2^2 + \ldots + r_n^2)/A\bar{r} \quad \text{(from Art. 90),}$$
$$= \text{mom. inertia/area surf.} \times \text{dist. of C. of G.,}$$

a convenient formula.

A case of common occurrence is a canal lock-gate standing vertically. Suppose it to form a rectangle of breadth b, depth h, and with the upper edge in the liquid surface. Then

$$h_0 = \tfrac{1}{3}bh^3/bh \times \tfrac{1}{2}h = \tfrac{2}{3}h,$$

or the point of application of the resultant pressure is at $\tfrac{2}{3}$ of the depth of the rectangle.

CENTRE OF PRESSURE ON A PLANE SURFACE.

182. We can now discuss the **Stability of a Wall** subjected to water pressure on one of its faces,—as a reservoir wall, for example.

Suppose the cross-section of the wall rectangular or trapezoidal, $AB = a$, $DC = b$, the face exposed to the water vertical, the height h, and that the water reaches to the top of the wall.

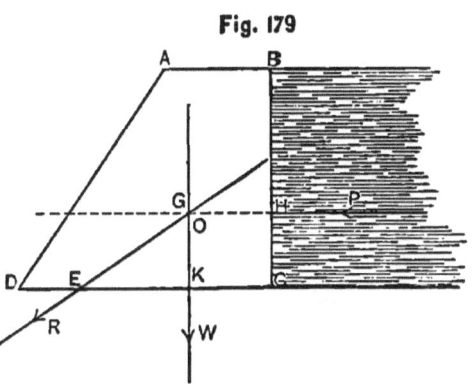

Fig. 179

The forces acting on the wall are the water pressure, the weight of the wall and the reaction of the ground support. The resultant water pressure P on one foot length of wall $= g\delta h \times h/3$, and acts horizontally through H when $HC = h/3$. The weight W of one foot length of wall $= \frac{1}{2}(a+b)hg\delta_1$, and acts vertically through G, the centre of gravity of the cross-section, δ_1 being the density of the wall. Let the directions of P and W intersect in O. Complete the parallelogram of forces to scale. The resultant R is equal and opposite to the reaction of the ground. Now, assuming that the wall is a single block, if the resultant R cuts the base between D and C the wall will stand; if not, it will be overturned. (Art. 96.)

The relation between the forces P and W for a certain assumed position of the resultant may be found by taking moments about the point in which its direction cuts CD. Thus if we assume R to pass through a point E we must have

$$P \times OK = W \times EK$$

as a condition to be satisfied.

The wall may also yield by *sliding* along its base. The frictional force f between the wall and foundation is the product of the weight of the wall by the coefficient of friction μ between wall and foundation (Art. 111), or

$$f = \tfrac{1}{2}(a + b)hg\delta_1\mu.$$

Hence, assuming the wall to be incapable of sliding along any joint other than the base, we have, if the base is horizontal, and therefore P and f parallel, the condition

$$P = \tfrac{1}{2}(a + b)hg\delta_1\mu$$

to be satisfied when the wall is just on the point of sliding.

Sometimes a wall is to be designed which shall have a certain **Factor of Safety**, the meaning being that the thrust necessary to overturn the wall or to cause it to slide shall be an arbitrary multiple of the theoretical thrust. This multiple is the factor of safety.

Ex. 1. Which is at the greater depth in a rectangular area immersed in water, the centre of pressure or the centre of gravity? *Ans.* The c. of p.

2. The cross-section of an embankment which weighs 125 lbs. per c. ft. is trapezoidal, with one face vertical. It is 5 ft. wide at the top, 11 ft. wide at the bottom, and 15 ft. high. The water is to press against the vertical side, reaching to its top. Will the embankment stand? *Ans.* Yes.

3. The depth of the c. of p. of a vertical right-angled triangular lamina whose base lies in the surface is $\tfrac{1}{2}$ the altitude: if the vertex is in the surface and base horizontal, it is $\tfrac{3}{4}$ of the altitude.

4. A reservoir wall, cross-section rectangular, height h, weight per cubic ft. w_1, water reaches to top of wall: find its thickness t that it may be on the point of being overturned by the water pressure about the outer edge C.

$$\textit{Ans. } \tfrac{1}{2}wh^2 \times \frac{h}{3} = w_1 ht \times \frac{t}{2}.$$

5. In (4) find the thickness of the wall that it may be just on the point of sliding on the base CD, the material weighing 125 lbs. per cubic ft., and $\mu = 2/3$.

Ans. $t = 0.38h$.

6. Show that whether a wall of rectangular cross-section is more likely to yield by rotation or by sliding depends on the coefficient of friction.

7. The height of water on one side of a canal lock is a ft., and on the other side b ft. Show that the resultant pressure acts at a height $(a^2 + ab + b^2)/3(a + b)$ ft.

8. The figure represents the cross-section of a dam 120 ft. high. The masonry is divided into three principal sections. It is required to find where the resultant pressures cut $CD(= 16$ ft.$)$, $EF(= 60$ ft.$)$, $GH(= 100$ ft.$)$. The dimensions are marked in the figure. The stone weighs 144 lbs. per cubic ft., and the water is on the left face.

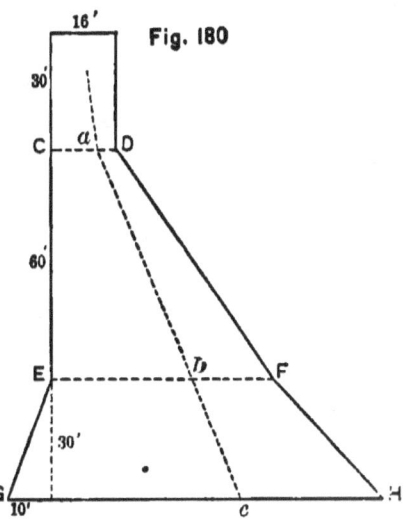

Fig. 180

Ans. $Da = 3.9$ ft., $Fb = 22.1$ ft., $Hc = 43.8$ ft.

183. Upward Pressure.—Conceive a portion ABC of a

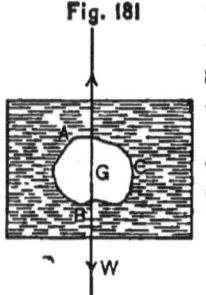

Fig. 181

fluid at rest to become solid. The equilibrium will remain undisturbed. The forces acting on the solid portion are its weight vertically downward through its centre of gravity, and the fluid pressures normal to the surface at every point. The resultant of these pressures balances the weight, and must therefore act vertically upward through the C. of G. of ABC.

Now if we place in the fluid a solid which displaces the same volume ABC, the upward pressure is the same as before, because the conditions of equilibrium are the same; that is, the upward pressure on a solid which displaces a portion of fluid is equal in magnitude to the weight of the fluid displaced, and its direction passes through the centre of gravity of the fluid displaced. This is known as the *principle of Archimedes.**

Ex. Infer from the principle of Archimedes that the loss of weight of a body immersed in a fluid is equal to the weight of the fluid displaced.

184. A solid placed in a fluid will either float partially immersed or float wholly immersed, or sink. Two applications of the principle of Archimedes to these cases are important.

(1) *Specific gravity* (= relative weight). Take a solid and let its weight in air be W. Suspend it by a fine wire from a hook attached to one scale-pan of a pair of scales, and find its weight W_1 when immersed in a liquid. The loss of weight $W - W_1$ is the upward pressure, and is equal to the weight of an equal volume of the liquid. The ratio of the weight W of the solid to the weight $W - W_1$ of the equal volume of liquid is called the *specific gravity* σ of the solid with reference to the liquid taken. Thus

$$\sigma = W/(W - W_1).$$

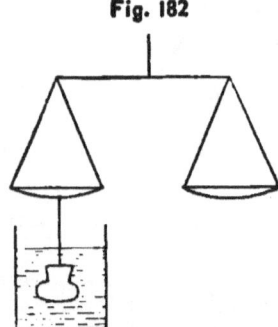

Fig. 182

* " Hiero, King of Syracuse, had a quantity of gold made into a crown, and suspecting that the workmen had abstracted some of the gold and used a portion of alloy of the same weight in its place, applied to Archimedes to solve the difficulty. Archimedes, while reflecting over this problem in his bath, observed the water running over the sides of the bath, and it occurred to him that he was displacing a quantity of water equal to his own bulk, and therefore that a quantity of pure gold equal in weight to the crown would displace less water than the crown, the volume of any weight of alloy being greater than that of an equal weight of gold. It is related that he immediately ran out into the streets, crying out, ' εὕρηκα, εὕρηκα ! ' "—*Besant.*

HYDROMETER. 227

As in what is called "weighing" we really compare masses (Art. 39), so in specific gravity the idea is a *relative* weighing or a comparison of masses. The term may, therefore, be defined—

The specific gravity of a body is the ratio of the mass of the body to the mass of an equal volume of some standard body; or since the density δ of a body is the mass of unit volume, it may be put in the equivalent form: *the specific gravity of a body is the ratio of its density to the density of some standard body.*

The standard taken is usually distilled water at its temperature of greatest density, 4° C. This standard is arbitrary, but is chosen on account of its convenience.

Note that specific gravity does not depend on volume, but on equality of volume. As we may assume any volume of the standard, take a cubic unit of water (cu. ft. or cu. cm.). Denote its density by δ. Then if σ be the sp. gr. of a body of density ρ_1, we have from the definition $\sigma = \delta_1/\delta$, and the mass M of a volume U of the body is given by

$$M = U\delta_1 = U\sigma\delta.$$

Since 1 cubic ft. of water at 4° C. weighs 62.4 lbs., then
Weight or mass M in pounds $= 62.4\,U\sigma$,
Weight or pressure W in pounds $= 62.4\,U\sigma$,
Weight or pressure W in poundals $= 62.4\,U\sigma g$,
when U is expressed in cubic feet.

Ex. 1. The true weight of a body is 25 grams. It weighs 15 grams when immersed in water: find its specific gravity.
Ans. 2.5.

2. If W_1, W_2, W_3 be the apparent weights of a body in three liquids the specific gravities of which are σ_1, σ_2, σ_3, prove that

$$W_1(\sigma_2 - \sigma_3) + W_2(\sigma_3 - \sigma_1) + W_3(\sigma_1 - \sigma_2) = 0.$$

3. A solid lighter than water, of weight W, has a sinker attached to it, and the two weigh W_1 when sunk in water.

The sinker alone weighs W_2 in water: find the sp. gr. of the solid. *Ans.* $W/(W + W_2 - W_1)$.

Take a piece of cork with iron or lead for sinker.

4. A man weighing 150 lbs., with a cork life-preserver of 5 lbs. attached, just floats in water. The sp. gr. of the cork being 0.25, find that of the man. *Ans.* 1.11.

5. The sp. gr. of an iceberg is 0.925: find the ratio of the volume submerged to the volume exposed, the sp. gr. of sea water being 1.025. *Ans.* 37 to 4.

6. A small stone of sp. gr. σ is dropped into a lake of depth h: find the time in which it will reach the bottom. *Ans.* $\sqrt{2h\sigma/g(\sigma - 1)}$ sec.

7. A gold ring contains by weight 22 parts gold and 2 parts copper: find the sp. gr. of the ring, that of gold being 19.3 and of copper 8.9. *Ans.* 17.6.

Various modifications and extensions of the preceding method are in use. Thus to find the specific gravity of a liquid take a vial of weight W, fill it with liquid, and let the total weight be W_1; next fill it with water, and let the total weight be W_2: then

$$\sigma = (W_1 - W)/(W_2 - W).$$

The same method may be used with a solid in fragments, or with soluble bodies, as sugar, salt, etc.

185. (2) Again, for a solid lighter than water, if we float it in water and find the ratio of the volume immersed to the total volume, we have the value of σ according to the definition. A convenient way of making the measurement is to use an upright cylinder of the solid graduated from bottom to top. Thus, if a cork cylinder 12 cm. high floats immersed to a depth of 3 cm., the sp. gr. of cork is $3/12 = 0.25$.

This same cylinder might be used to find the sp. gr. of a liquid in which it will float. The volumes displaced by the cylinder when placed in water and in the liquid are observed; then

$\sigma =$ vol. liq./vol. water $=$ depth imm. in liq./do. in water.

The common **Hydrometer**, invented by Boyle in 1675, is an instrument founded on this principle. It consists of a glass cylinder or rod arranged so as to float in a liquid in a vertical position. To effect this, two bulbs are added; one, D, filled with air, and the terminal one, E, loaded with mercury or shot. Suppose that when the instrument floats in water the point C on the rod is in the surface, and when it floats in a liquid of sp. gr. σ the point B is in the surface. Let W = the wt. of the instrument, U = its volume, and A the cross-section of the rod. Then

Fig. 183

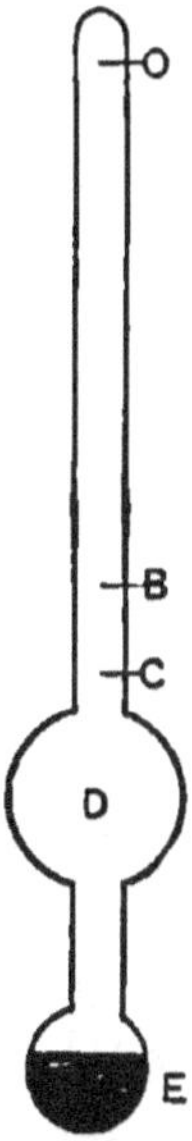

$$W = (U - A \times OC)g\delta,$$
$$W = (U - A \times OB)g\delta\sigma;$$

the weight of the instrument being equal to the weights of the liquids displaced. Hence

$$U - A \times OC = (U - A \times OB)\sigma,$$

and the sp. gr. of the liquid is found.

Hence we may graduate the rod so that when the instrument is placed in a liquid lighter than water the sp. gr. can be read off at sight. For by assigning different values to σ in the above equation the corresponding values of OB are found, and may be marked on the rod.

Ex. 1. How would you graduate the stem of a lactometer or milk hydrometer, so as to show various proportions of milk and water?

2. Explain the utility of a table of specific gravities.

186. *Floating Bodies.*—In order that a solid may float in a liquid, it is necessary that the weight of the solid do not exceed that of the liquid displaced. If the floating body be slightly displaced from its position of equilibrium and it tends to return to that position, the equilibrium is said to be **Stable**; if it tends to recede farther from that position, the equilibrium is **Unstable**. The determination of the stability of floating bodies is of great importance in ship-building. The general problem is quite complicated. (See treatises on *Naval Architecture*.)

Ex. 1. A segment of a solid sphere will float in stable equilibrium, the curved surface being down. Prove this.

2. A prismatic block height a, breadth b, length l, and specific gravity σ floats in water to a depth h: prove that equilibrium will be stable as long as b exceeds $1.225a$.

DYNAMICS OF GASES (PNEUMATICS).

187. A perfect fluid (liquid or gas) is distinguished by the perfect mobility of its particles, elasticity of form or figure being altogether wanting. Hence all of the properties regarding liquids, depending on this principle, which have been deduced in the preceding sections can be equally well applied to gases. The characteristic difference between liquids and gases relates to behavior under pressure. Liquids are fluids with small compressibility, and gases fluids with large compressibility. The perfect liquid is taken to be absolutely incompressible, and the perfect gas to possess infinite compressibility.

The gas with which we are most familiar and the one of most importance to us is atmospheric air. We live at the bottom of an ocean of air of whose existence we are conscious from daily experience. Just as in describing liquids we took water as a near approximation to the perfect liquid, so we shall take air as an approximation to the perfect gas.

188. Effect of Pressure.—Consider a portion of gas (air) enclosed in a cylinder and in equilibrium. On account of the perfect mobility among its particles, it will follow from the same reasoning as in Art. 175 that a pressure P applied as by a piston will be equally transmitted in all directions. The pressure at any point A within the cylinder is the same in every direction. An illustration of the applica-

BOYLE'S LAW. 231

tion of equality of pressure of a gas in all directions has been already given in describing the safety-valve.

If the pressure on the piston be increased the piston will descend in the cylinder, thus lessening the volume of the gas, but increasing its density. On removing the increased pressure the piston will return to its original position, showing that the gas possesses the power of expansion. Experiments with the ordinary gases go to show that with a perfect gas, if the pressure were doubled very slowly, the volume would be reduced to one half the original; trebled, to one third the original; and so on. In general, with a perfect gas *the pressure varies inversely as the space occupied by the gas, the temperature remaining constant.* This is known as **Boyle's Law**, and may be stated symbolically in either of the forms $PU = c$ or $P = c\delta$, where P is the pressure, U the volume, δ the density, and c a constant depending on the nature of the gas.

A familiar illustration of the effect of pressure on the volume of a gas is to take a tumbler and force its mouth down in a vessel of water. The farther down it is forced the greater the water pressure on the air inside and the less the volume becomes, as shown by the rise of water in the tumbler. The mass of air is the same, no matter what the pressure, but the volume varies.

189. Boyle's law may be represented graphically. Take OX, OY at right angles as axes of co-ordinates, and lay off OA to scale to represent U and AC to represent P: then (see any Analytical Geometry) the locus of a point C possessing the property $OA \times AC = $ a constant quantity, is a rectangular hyperbola, of which the axes OX, OY are asymptotes. Hence this curve is a geometrical representation of Boyle's law.

Fig. 184

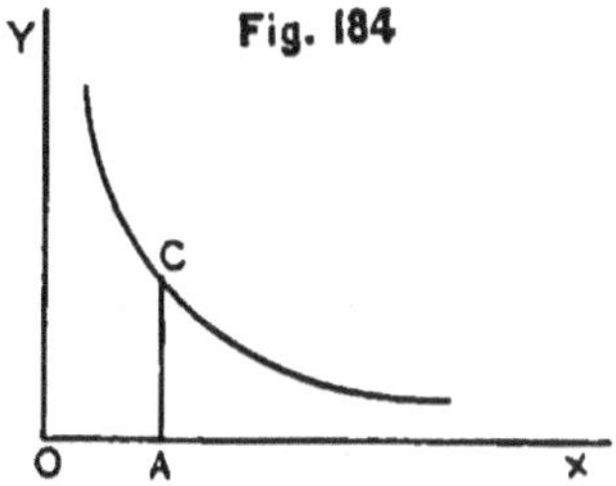

190. Extension to the Atmosphere.—We have so far confined ourselves to the properties of a gas when confined in a vessel. Boyle's law is founded on this limitation. So also are the principles of transmission of pressure, and of equality of pressure in all directions. In order to make use of these principles in the free atmosphere, we must *assume* that it is confined, and that the confining force is the force of gravity. The force of gravity keeps it encased in a huge envelope, as it were, surrounding the earth.

191. Pressure of the Atmosphere.—Air being a material substance and subject to the action of gravity, must exert pressure downward as other material substances do; that is, it must have weight.* Now the pressure of a fluid on any horizontal area is measured by the weight of a vertical column of the fluid whose base is the area. So the pressure of the atmosphere on any area would be measured by the weight of a column of air whose base is the area and height the height of the atmosphere. To measure this pressure take a bent tube of uniform bore (Fig. 185) and pour a quantity of mercury into it. The mercury will stand at the same height in both branches; or, in other words, the common surface AB will be a horizontal plane. The pressures P, Q of the columns of air whose cross-sections are the areas of the tubes are equal, and therefore do not affect the level of the mercury in A and B. Suppose,

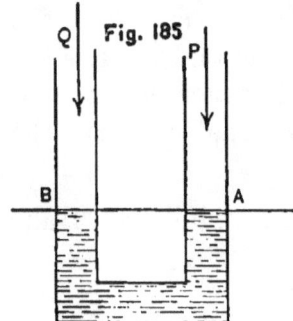

Fig. 185

---

*It is related that Aristotle (B.C. 384-322) "weighed a skin first empty and then inflated with air, and finding it to weigh the same in both cases, concluded that air was without weight." The experiment failed because the weight of the skin when inflated was diminished by that of the equal volume of air which it displaced. It was reserved for Galileo (1564-1642) to show that air was a heavy fluid,

now, by pulling up a tight-fitting piston that the air is removed from B or the pressure Q removed, the mercury in B will rise and in A will fall until a certain difference of level h is reached, when it will remain stationary. Hence the weight of the column of mercury whose height is h and base B must be equal to the atmospheric pressure on the same area; that is,

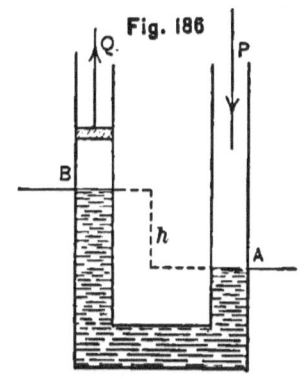

Fig. 186

$$P = g\delta_1 h,$$

when δ_1 is the density of mercury.

A simpler way of making this measurement is to take a

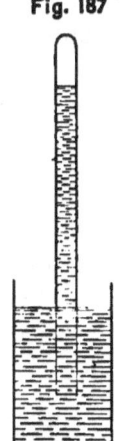

Fig. 187

long glass tube of uniform bore and closed at one end, fill it with mercury, close the other end with the finger, invert the tube, and plunge this end into a basin of mercury. On removing the finger the mercury in the tube will sink until the height h is reached. This was the method of Torricelli,* in 1643, the first to make the experiment.

The value of h is about 760 mm. or 30 in. Had the liquid used been water instead of mercury, the value of h would be 13.596 times greater, that is, 10,333 mm., or 33 feet.

The atmospheric pressure per sq. in., p, follows from considering that it is equivalent to the weight of a column of mercury of 1 sq. in. base and height 30 in.

Hence $\quad p = 32.2 \times \dfrac{13.6 \times 62.4}{1728} \times 30 = 473.3 \ \text{poundals}$

---

*A.D. 1608-1647. Pupil of Galileo.

per sq. in. = 14.7 pounds per sq. in. This is sometimes called the pressure of one atmosphere.

Ex. 1. The surface of an average man is about 6 sq. ft. Find the atmospheric pressure in tons. *Ans.* 6.4 tons.

2. Show that the atmospheric pressure = 1,013,663 dynes per sq. cm.

3. It is related that Otto von Guericke (A.D. 1602-1686), the inventor of the air-pump, in an exhibition before the Emperor Ferdinand III. placed side by side two hollow hemispheres of copper, and after exhausting the air showed that 30 horses, 15 back to back, were unable to pull them asunder. If d is the diameter of each hemisphere in inches and p the pull of each horse in pounds, show that p did not exceed $0.77d^2$.

192. The instruments shown in Figs. 185, 187 may be used for finding the pressure of gases. If, for example, in Fig. 185, the tube A were connected with a steam-boiler, the heights to which the mercury rises in B will show the excess of the steam-pressure over the atmospheric pressure. This forms a siphon **Manometer**.

The instrument shown in Fig. 187 forms a cistern **Barometer**, and will indicate atmospheric pressures according to the heights at which the mercury stands in the tube. For convenience of reading, a scale is usually attached to the tube. The term *water barometer* is applied to a barometer tube filled with water and of standard height, 33 ft.

Ex. 1. A cylindrical jar 2 ft. long is inverted and sunk in water until half-full : find the depth of its bottom below the surface of the water, the height of the water barometer being 33 ft. *Ans.* 32 ft.

2. Show that the tension of the chain with which a diving-bell is lowered increases as the bell descends.

3. A conical wine-glass is immersed mouth downwards in water: how far must it be depressed that the water within the glass may rise half-way up it? *Ans.* 231 ft.

4. A cylindrical diving-bell of height l is sunk until its top is a foot below the surface: show that the height x of the

PRESSURE OF THE ATMOSPHERE. 235

air-space within the bell is found from $x^2 + (a + h)x = hl$, where h is the height of the water barometer.

5. In Ex. 4 find how much air must be forced into the bell to completely drive out the water.

Ans. $(a + l)/h$ volume of bell.

193. *Measurement of Elevations.*—Since the pressure of the atmosphere at a place is equal to the weight of a column of air extending to the full height of the atmosphere at that place, it follows that the pressure will differ at different elevations, and that the height of the barometric column will give us a measure of this difference. We may therefore use the barometer as a measurer of differences of height. The first to propose this was Pascal in 1648.

The solution of this question, with the precautions necessary for making a measurement, is quite complicated and beyond our province.

194. *Upward Pressure of the Atmosphere.*—As in Art. 183, we may show that the upward pressure of the atmosphere on a body suspended in it is equal to the weight of the volume U of the air displaced, and that the direction of the pressure is vertical, and through the centre of gravity of the air volume. Hence if the weight of the body is less than that of the volume of air displaced, the body will float in the air. The balloon depends on this principle.

True and Apparent Weight.—Since a body is pressed upward by a force equal to the weight of the air displaced by it, it follows that the apparent weight of a body (weight in air) is always less than its true weight (weight in a vacuum). The more bulky a body is the greater the difference. If we balance a bulky body, as cork, against a dense body, as lead, under the receiver of an air-pump and then exhaust the air, we shall find the cork descend.

Ex. Show that the true weight of a ton of hay is more nearly found by weighing it in bales than in the loose form.

195. Illustrations of Atmospheric Pressure. — (1) The

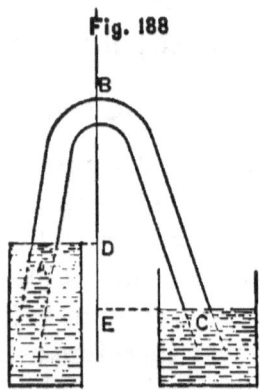

Fig. 188

siphon consists of a bent tube ABC open at both ends. It is filled with water and the ends inserted in two vessels of water as in the figure.

If h is the height of the water barometer and A the cross-section of the pipe, then the upward pressure at B
in tube $AB = g\delta hA - g\delta A \times BD$,
in tube $BC = g\delta hA - g\delta A \times BE$;
∴ resultant pressure at B

$$= g\delta A(BE - BD) = g\delta A \times DE,$$

and the water flows from A to C until $DE = 0$, or the surfaces of the water in the two vessels are at the same level.

An example of a siphon is seen in the common flush tank.

Ex. 1. If C discharges into the air, explain the action.

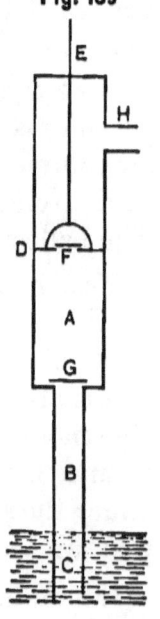

Fig. 189

2. If the height of B above D is greater than the height of the water barometer, what would happen when the end A is opened; when C is next opened?

3. The bore of a siphon is not uniform. Will the siphon work?

4. The apparatus in Fig. 188 is put under the receiver of an air-pump, and the air exhausted. What happens?

5. How would C need to be immersed to reverse the flow?

6. Explain how ventilation may be effected by means of a tall chimney.

(2) The common **Lifting** or **Suction Pump** consists of two tubes A, B, with the same axis, the lower terminating in the reservoir C; D is a movable piston operated by the rod E, and with a valve F in it opening upwards. Another valve G

opening upward is placed at the junction of the two cylinders.

Suppose the pump filled with air and the piston D to be at its lowest limit. By raising the piston the valve F will close and the air in A will be carried with it. The air in B will open the valve G and rush into A. Hence at the surface of the water C the pressure inside the barrel is less than the atmospheric pressure and water will be forced up the tube C until equilibrium is restored. When the piston descends the air in A is compressed, G closes and F opens. Continue, and the water will rise until it pass through G, next through F, and will thence be lifted by the piston to the spout H.

Ex. 1. Is it necessary to have two cylinders?

2. Suppose the tube B to be bent or irregular in figure, would the pump act?

3. If the height of the valve G above the water surface is greater than the height of the water barometer, what will happen?

4. In a common pump the suction pipe is 10 ft. long and the area of the barrel is 4 times that of the pipe. If the stroke is $2\frac{1}{2}$ ft., find how high the water will rise in the pipe at the first stroke. *Ans.* 7.5 ft., nearly.

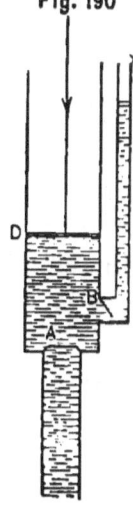

Fig. 190

196. The Force-Pump differs from the lifting-pump in that the piston or plunger D is without a valve. On lowering the piston the air in the barrel is forced before it, the valve B opens, A shuts, and the air passes through B. On raising the piston the air in the barrel is carried with it, B is shut by the atmospheric pressure, and A is opened, allowing the atmospheric pressure to force water into the barrel. The piston in descending now forces the water through B as it did the air.

The water will flow out in jerks, depending on the rapidity of the up and down strokes of the piston. By placing an air chamber on the exit pipe the expansive force of the confined air in the upper part of this chamber will cause the stream to flow with a continuous but varying flow.

The ordinary **Syringe** is an example of a force-pump. The driving force is applied by squeezing the rubber ball A. The heart of an animal works as a syringe, the force being the muscular action of the walls.

Fig. 191

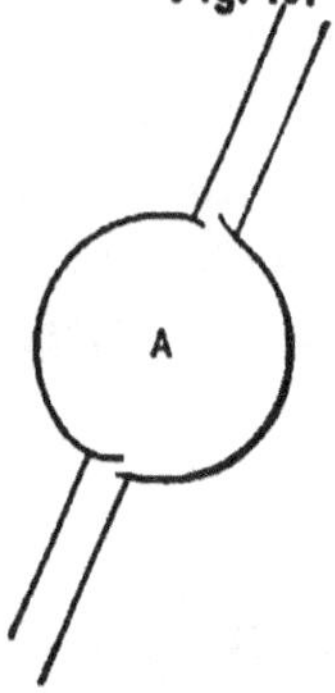

Ex. 1. The diameter of the plunger of a pump is $2\frac{1}{2}$ in., and it is driven by a crank 2 in. in length, making 30 revolutions per minute: find the number of gallons raised per hour. *Ans.* 153 gals.

2. In a steam-pump the diameter of the water cylinder is 7 in., the length of stroke 9 in., and the number of revolutions per minute 90: find the discharge per minute. *Ans.* 135 gals.

3. In a duplex pump the diameter of the water plunger is 7 in., the length of stroke 10 in., and the number of strokes of one plunger per minute is 100: find the number of gallons delivered by the plunger in 1 min.

Ans. 333.3 gals.

197. The **Air-Pump** is a pump for removing air from a vessel. The common lifting-pump and the force-pump already described are air-pumps, as their first function is to cause a partial exhaustion of air before lifting or forcing the water. The labor of working an air-pump constructed as in Fig. 189 would be very great on account of the difference of pressure on the two sides of the piston. To relieve the piston a third valve is introduced as in Fig. 192. It is evident that with this pump the exhaustion can never be perfect, as a certain amount of air must remain to lift the valves, which, even if made of oiled silk, as they commonly are, still possess some weight.

Fig. 192

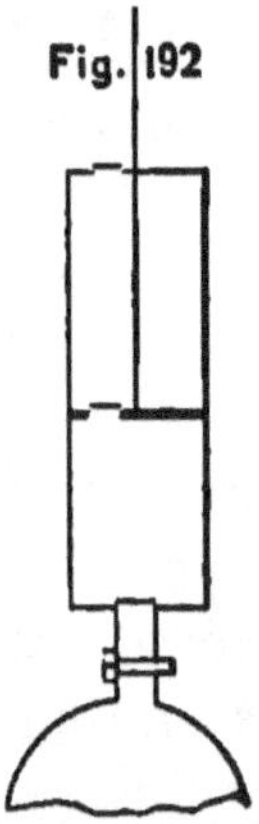

A modification of the air force-pump, in which the solid piston is replaced by drops of mercury, is known as the Sprengel air-pump. It is used largely in the arts, as, for example, in exhausting the globes of incandescent lamps.*

'A is the globe to be exhausted, B a basin of mercury, C a piece of tubing with a pinch-cock regulating the dropping of the mercury. A drop in falling acts as a solid piston, carrying with it the air in CD. The air in A expands and fills CD again. The next drop cuts this out, and so on, the air becoming rarer and rarer continuously. Almost perfect exhaustion can be had in this way.

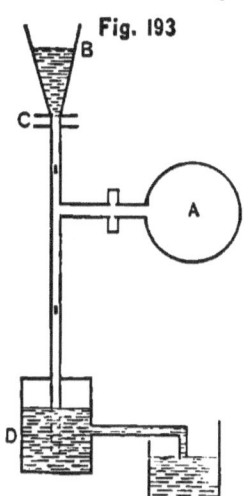

Fig. 193

Ex. 1. If U_1 is the volume of the vessel to be exhausted by an air-pump, and U_2 the volume of the barrel of the pump, show that after two strokes the density δ_2 of the air in the vessel is found from

$$\delta_2(U_1 + U_2)^2 = \delta U_1^2,$$

where δ is the density of the atmosphere.

2. If the volume of the vessel to be exhausted is twice that of the pump barrel, find what proportion of the air remains at the end of three strokes. *Ans.* 8/27.

3. If the volume of the vessel to be exhausted is twice that of the pump barrel, find after how many strokes the density of the air will be $\frac{1}{6}$ of its original density.

Ans. Between the fourth and fifth strokes.

---

* The Berrenberg pump, a recent invention (1890), makes it "possible to obtain rapidly and easily a vacuum comparable with that obtained with the best mercury pumps. The device is adopted of forming a vacuum jacket around the working cylinder so that whatever leaks in around the outer side of the box, which is closed with oil as in ordinary air-pumps, is pumped out by the subsidiary cylinders. The difference of pressure therefore tending to cause leaks in the joints and valves of the working cylinder can be reduced to a quantity almost negligible, and the leakage almost disappears."—*Electrical World, April,* 1890.

198. Condensers.—If the tube B of a force-pump opens into a closed vessel A, then air may be driven into this vessel, and the apparatus becomes a condenser or compressor.

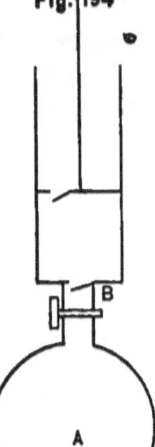
Fig. 194

The compressed air in the receiver may be called on to give up the energy stored in it by doing work, just as in the case of the water accumulator. Air and water are thus of great use in transmitting energy in cases where gearing and belts are out of the question.

In many cases air is more suitable than water for this purpose, as in the air-brake on locomotives, the pneumatic dispatch, the rock-drill, and more particularly in underground work, as mining, tunnelling, where the exhaust air is of use for ventilation.

199. The exact determination of the work done in compressing air is a complicated question in thermodynamics, but we may make a first approximation by neglecting the changes of temperature undergone during compression. Suppose a volume U_1 of air under a pressure P_1 has its volume changed to U_2 by changing the pressure to P_2. The relation between these quantities is given by Boyle's law to be

$$P_1 U_1 = P_2 U_2,$$

each product being equal to a constant quantity.

It was shown in Art. 189 that the geometrical representation of Boyle's law is an equilateral hyperbola, of which the axes OX, OY are asymptotes. The ordinates of this curve represent the pressures, and the abscissas the corresponding volumes.

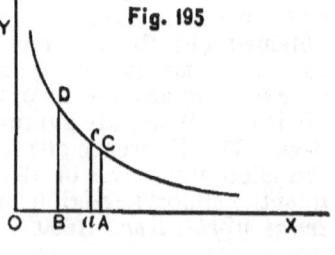
Fig. 195

Let $OA = U_1$, $AC = P_1$;
$OB = U_2$, $BD = P_2$.

Now for an indefinitely small distance Aa along AB, that is, for an indefinitely small change of volume dU, the pressure P may be considered constant. Hence the work done in changing the volume from U to $U + dU$ is represented by $P \times dU$, that is, by the element area $AaCc$. Summing up the element areas from A to B, we find the total work done in compressing the gas from volume U_1 to volume U_2 to be represented by the area $ABDC$. This area may be computed by Simpson's rule, or more simply by the aid of the polar planimeter, as in the case of the indicator diagram, Art. 136.

Or it may be computed directly by summing the expressions $P \times dU$ between the limits U_1 and U_2. We have

$$\text{work done} = \int_{U_2}^{U_1} P dU = \int_{U_2}^{U_1} PU dU/U$$

$$= P_1 U_1 \log_e U_1/U_2 = P_1 U_1 \log_e P_2/P_1;$$

or changing the logs to base 10,

$$\text{Work done} = 2.3\, P_1 U_1 \log_{10} P_2/P_1.$$

If P_1 is in dynes and U_1 in cubic cm., the work done is in ergs; if P_1 is in pounds and U_1 in cubic feet, the work done is in foot-pounds, etc.

Ex. 1. Find the work necessary to compress 1 cubic foot of air to half its volume.

Ans. $2.3 \times (14.7 \times 144) \times \log_{10} 2 = 1465.6$ foot-pounds.

2. Show that the work required to bring one cubic metre of air from atmospheric pressure to a pressure of 8 atmospheres is about 21,400 kilogrammetres.

3. Find the H. P. required for a blowing engine to drive 1000 cubic feet of air per minute from a pressure of 28 in. into a blast at a pressure of 30 in. *Ans.* 4 H. P., nearly.

4. How would you modify the apparatus in Fig. 187 to form a compressed-air manometer for measuring steam-pressures?

5. Show how, from knowing the height to which water rises in a diving-bell, we can compute the depth of the bell.

Hence show how a deep-sea-sounding apparatus might be made by sinking a tube closed at the upper end vertically into the s...

200. The Work done by the Expansion of a Gas, as steam, for example, is calculated in the same way.

Let P = the pressure of the steam on entering the cylinder of an engine. After it has moved the piston through a distance l, let it be cut off and allowed to expand to the end of the stroke L. At any distance x between l and L the pressure p is found by Boyle's law from

$$p : P = l : x \quad \text{or} \quad p = Pl/x.$$

Hence for the work K done during expansion

$$K = \int_l^L p\,dx = Pl \log_e L/l = 2.3\,Pl \log_{10} L/l$$

per unit area of the piston.

The work done by the steam up to the time of cut-off is $Pl \times A$ if A is the piston area. Hence

$$\text{Total work} = APl(1 + 2.3 \log_{10} L/l).$$

If A is expressed in sq. in., P in pounds per sq. in., the work done is in inch-pounds.

Ex. 1. An engine with cylinder of 28 in. diameter and 50 in. stroke carries 66 pounds of steam and is cut off at one-quarter stroke. Find the work done per stroke.
Ans. $616 \times 66 \times 12.5(1 + 2.3 \log 4) = 1{,}213{,}000$ inch-pounds.

2. At n strokes per minute find the H. P. developed.

CHAPTER X.

KINETICS OF FLUIDS (HYDROKINETICS).

201. THE doctrine of the motion of fluids is called **Hydrokinetics**. The subject is a very difficult one, and comparatively little progress has been made in it.

In order to discharge a fluid from a closed vessel containing it, an opening must be made in the vessel. If the opening is entirely submerged, it is called an **Orifice**; if not, a **Weir**. The fluid will flow through this opening with a certain velocity v, and in a certain time t a certain quantity D will be discharged. The velocity, time, and quantity depend on circumstances which will form our first inquiry.

If, in addition to a simple discharge, the fluid is to be conducted to another vessel as by pipes, the problem is complicated by our having to consider the mode of transit. This forms our second inquiry.

Lastly, in its passage from one vessel to another, as the fluid possesses mass and velocity, and therefore energy, it may be made to overcome resistance and do work. This is our third inquiry.

ORIFICES AND WEIRS.

202. Velocity of Efflux.—To find the velocity of efflux v through an orifice, the depth of the orifice being h.

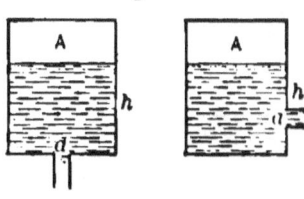

Fig. 196

As the liquid issues from the orifice with the velocity v the surface in the vessel must sink with a certain velocity. To avoid considering this, we shall *assume* the orifice to be very small in comparison with the cross-section of the vessel. The height h may then be considered constant. Also, for the present the friction of the orifice or any other resistance that may enter will be neglected. We shall therefore find only what is termed the *theoretical velocity of efflux*.

The pressure at the orifice is due to a column of the liquid of height h and cross-section A, and is equal to $g\delta hA$, which is therefore the effective force acting. The distance passed over by this column in a small time t is vt. Hence the work done during this passage by the column is $g\delta hA \times vt$.

Now the kinetic energy of the column issuing from the orifice with the velocity v is $\tfrac{1}{2}\delta Avt \times v^2$. Hence

$$g\delta hA \times vt = \tfrac{1}{2}\delta Avt \times v^2$$

and
$$v = \sqrt{2gh}$$
$$= 8.02\sqrt{h}, \text{ nearly,}—$$

the velocity sought. This velocity is the same as that acquired by a body falling freely through a height h. (Art. 57.)

If the discharge takes place from one vessel to another,

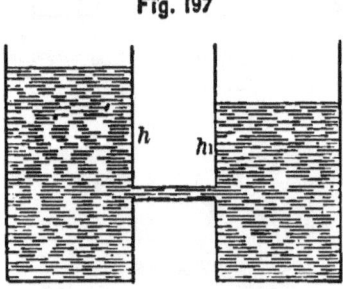
Fig. 197

the effective force would be the difference of pressure at the two ends of the connecting tube, and therefore equal to $g\delta A h_1 - g\delta A h_2$, or to $g\delta A h$ if $h = h_1 - h_2$, and A is the area of the cross-section of the tube. Hence, as before, $v^2 = 2gh$ when h is the effective head.

If the water surface is subjected to pressure, we reduce

VELOCITY OF EFFLUX. 245

to a free surface by adding a column of weight equivalent to this pressure. Thus a pressure by a piston could be written in the form $g\delta Ah_1$, that is, it could be replaced by a head of height h_1, so that the total head to which the velocity of efflux is due would be $h + h_1$, and

$$v = \sqrt{2g(h + h_1)}.$$

Again, if water flowed into a vessel with a velocity u, the head due to this velocity is $u^2/2g$, and the total head of efflux is $h + u^2/2g$. Hence

$$v^2 = 2g(h + u^2/2g) = 2gh + u^2.$$

Let A be the cross-section of the orifice, and A_1 that of the inflowing water: then if the inflow is equal to the outflow, or $uA_1 = vA$, we have

$$v = \sqrt{2gh(1 - A^2/A_1^2)},$$

and the velocity of outflow is determined.

Ex. 1. Show that the head to which a velocity v is due is found from $h = 0.016v^2$.

2. The piston of a force-pump is 9 in. in diameter, and it is driven down with a pressure of 2 tons: find the velocity of the issuing stream, neglecting all resistances.
Ans. 97 ft. per sec.

3. If the cross-section of the orifice is 0.1 that of the inflowing stream, show that the error in using the formula $v = \sqrt{2gh}$ to find the velocity of efflux is 0.5%.

4. If $A = A_1$, then $v = \infty$ and $u = \infty$. Explain.

5. The pressure in a boiler is 75 pounds per sq. in. Find the velocity of escape of the water into the air through a small orifice situated 1 ft. below the level of the water.

203. The values found for velocity of discharge are *theoretical*, or such as would result did no resistances enter.

On account of such resistances the *actual* value of the velocity is smaller than the theoretical, and the relation between the two must be found by experiment. Observation shows that water flowing through an orifice with a sharp edge approaches the orifice in contracting lines. The minimum cross-section is at a short distance outside the orifice, and this cross-section is about 0.64 that of the orifice. The velocity of the water at this section is about 0.97 of the theoretical velocity v. Hence, since theoretical discharge = cross-sec. $A \times$ vel. v, we have for the **Actual Discharge** D the expression

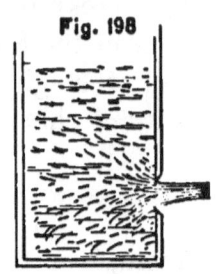

Fig. 198

$$D = 0.64A \times 0.97v$$
$$= 0.62Av.$$

The number 0.62 is called the **Coefficient of Discharge**. Putting for v its value in terms of the head h,

$$D = 0.62A \sqrt{2gh}$$
$$= 5A \sqrt{h},$$

which gives the actual discharge through a *small* orifice in a vessel.

The experimental values here given are average values. They are found to vary with the head of water and with the nature of the orifice. For the coefficient of discharge we shall use the letter c. By putting $c = 1$ in the formulas following the theoretic value is found, and by putting $c = 0.62$ the average actual value.

Ex. An orifice of 1 sq. in. cross-section was found in 10 min. to discharge 60 cu. ft. of water under a constant head of 9 ft. Compute the theoretic discharge, and find the coefficient of contraction.

204. If the orifice lies in a vertical plane and is *not* small, the value of the head h is not the same for all parts of the orifice, and we must sum up from element to element in order to find the velocity of discharge.

Fig. 199

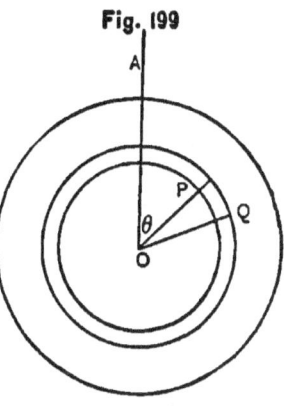

Suppose first the **Orifice Circular**. The summation is most readily effected by using polar coördinates. Take the origin at O, the centre of the orifice. Conceive the circle divided by concentric circles into rings of width dr, and let each ring be divided into elements PQ included between two radii inclined at an angle $d\theta$. Let r, θ be the coördinates of P. Then area of element $PQ = rdrd\theta$. Let $h =$ depth of O below the surface, then depth of element $PQ = h - r\cos\theta$. Hence

$$D = \int_0^r \int_0^{2\pi} c\, rdrd\theta \sqrt{2g(h - r\cos\theta)}$$

$$= c\,\pi r^2 \sqrt{2gh}(1 - r^2/32h^2),\text{ nearly,}$$

$$= 15.63 r^2 \sqrt{h}(1 - r^2/32h^2),\text{ approx.}$$

If the orifice reaches to the water surface, $h = r$, and

$$D = 0.964 c\pi r^2 \sqrt{2gh}$$

$$= 15.11 r^2 \sqrt{h},\text{ approximately.}$$

Ex. 1. Water is discharged through a circular orifice of diameter d in. under a head of h ft. Show that the discharge in gallons per minute is $12.2 d^2 \sqrt{h}$, nearly.

2. How many cubic feet per second would be discharged through an orifice 1 in. in diam. under a head of 25 ft.?
Ans. 0.135 c. ft. per sec.

3. Find the diameter of an orifice that would discharge 146 gals. per min. under a head of 9 ft.? *Ans.* 2 in.

4. Find the head necessary to discharge 110 gals. per min. through a 3-in. circular orifice?   *Ans.* 1 ft.

205. Suppose next the **Orifice Rectangular**, of breadth b,

Fig. 200

and the depth of its lower and upper edges below the water surface h_1, h_2. Consider a strip at a depth y below the surface, and of indefinitely small width dy. Along this strip $v = c\sqrt{2gy}$, and the discharge through this strip $= cb\sqrt{2gy}\,dy$. Hence

$$D = \int_{h_1}^{h_2} cb\sqrt{2gy}\,dy$$
$$= \tfrac{2}{3}cb\sqrt{2g}(h_2^{\frac{3}{2}} - h_1^{\frac{3}{2}})$$
$$= 3.33b(h_2^{\frac{3}{2}} - h_1^{\frac{3}{2}}),$$

and

average vel. of efflux $= D/b(h_2 - h_1)$,
$$= 3.33(h_2^{\frac{3}{2}} - h_1^{\frac{3}{2}})/(h_2 - h_1).$$

If $h_1 = 0$, or the upper edge is in the surface, the opening becomes a slot of breadth b and depth h, and is known as an overfall or **Weir**. Here

Fig. 201

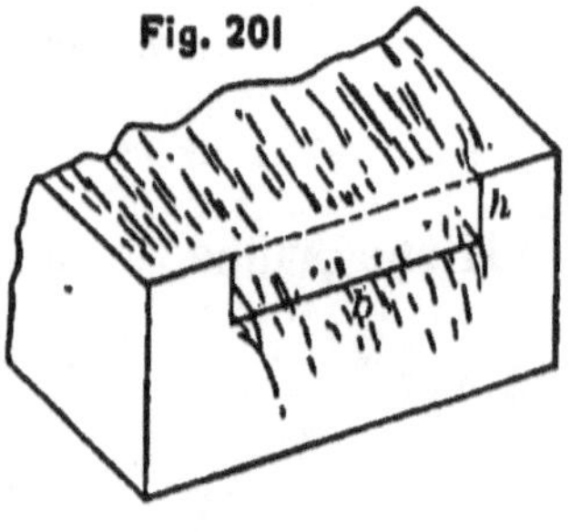

$$D = \tfrac{2}{3}cbh\sqrt{2gh}$$
$$= 3.33bh^{\frac{3}{2}} \text{ cu. ft. per sec.,}$$

and

aver. vel. $= 3.33h^{\frac{1}{2}}$ ft. per sec.

Ex. 1. The top of a rectangular orifice in the side of a vessel is 2 ft. and the bottom 3 ft. below the surface: find the discharge and the mean velocity of efflux, the orifice being 2 ft. wide.   *Ans.* 16 cub. ft. per sec.; 8 ft. per sec.

2. Show that the number of gals. per min. that will pass through a rectangular notch of breadth b and depth h, both expressed in inches, is $3bh^{\frac{3}{2}}$.

3. In a rectangular weir the head is 1 ft.: find the average velocity.   *Ans.* 3.33 ft. per sec.

TIME OF EFFLUX. 249

206. Of late a weir in the form of a **Triangle** has been introduced as possessing certain advantages, notably simplicity, over the rectangular form.

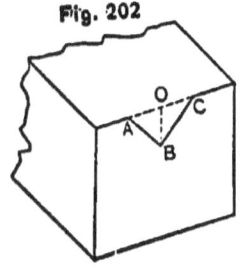

Fig. 202

Let the figure represent the weir, the angle $ABC = 90°$, and $AB = BC$. Take $h = OB$, the head of water, and let OC, OB be the axes of x and y. Then

$$D = 2c \int_0^h x\,dy\, \sqrt{2gy}$$

$$= 2c \int_0^h (h-y)\, \sqrt{2gy}\,dy$$

$$= 0.533 h^2 c\, \sqrt{2gh}$$

$$= 2.6 h^{\frac{5}{2}} \text{ cu. ft. per sec}$$

Ex. In a right-triangular weir the head is 6 in.: find the discharge.   *Ans.* 0.46 cu. ft. per sec.

207. In California, water supplied for irrigation and other purposes is usually expressed in **Miner's Inches**, meaning the average flow through each square inch of a rectangular orifice under a given head. The discharge per minute is the minute-inch, per hour the hour-inch, etc. The term is not a very definite one, but experiments made to determine it agree that a miner's inch will discharge 1.2 cubic ft. per min. under a 4-in. head. The miner's inch is thus equal to about 9 gals. per min.

208. To find the **Time of Efflux** through a small orifice O of cross-section A_1 in the bottom of a vessel of cross-section A.

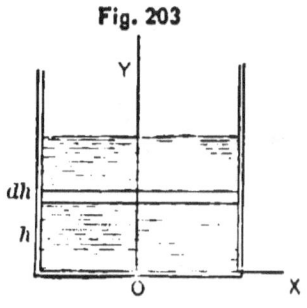

Fig. 203

In consequence of the efflux the surface A must sink with a certain velocity u. The volume of sinking must be equal to the volume of outflow; and therefore for the indefinitely small time dt, during which u and the velocity of efflux v may be considered constant, we have

$$Au = A_1 v.$$

Now during this same time h may be considered constant, and we may write

$$v = c\sqrt{2gh}.$$

Also dh is the distance sunk through in the time dt with the velocity u, so that $dh = udt$. Hence

$$A\,dh/dt = cA_1\sqrt{2gh},$$

and

$$t = \frac{A}{cA_1}\int_h^0 \frac{dh}{\sqrt{2gh}}$$

$$= 2A\sqrt{h}/cA_1\sqrt{2g}$$

$$= 2A\sqrt{h}/5A_1, \text{ approx.}$$

Ex. In what time would a bath-tub supposed of uniform cross-section, 8 ft. long, 2 ft. wide, empty through an inch hole in the bottom, if the water stood at a depth of 2 ft.
Ans. 2.75 min., nearly.

FLOW IN PIPES.

209. Short Pipes.—Consider the usual case of water entering a circular pipe with square edges at the entrance. If the pipe is *short*, or the length about two or three times the diameter, the velocity of outflow v_1 is found by experiment to be equal to $c_1 v$, when v is the theoretical velocity $\sqrt{2gh}$, and c_1 is a constant, depending on the head of water and on the size of the pipe. An average value of c_1 is 0.82.

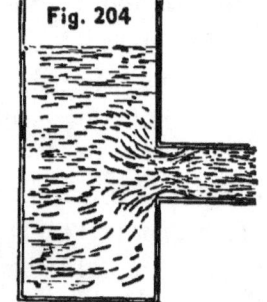
Fig. 204

We may therefore write

$$v_1 = c_1 v = c_1\sqrt{2gh} = 6.58\sqrt{h},$$

FLOW IN PIPES.

and the discharge D through a pipe of diameter d is

$$D = c_1 v \times \pi d^2/4 = 5.15 d^2 \sqrt{h}.$$

The resistance of the orifice at influx may be expressed as a "loss of head" h_2. The total head h may thus be regarded as consisting of two parts, h_1, h_2, of which h_1 generates the velocity of efflux v_1, and h_2 is spent in overcoming the resistance at entrance into the pipe. Now since

$$\sqrt{2gh_1} = v_1 = c_1 \sqrt{2gh},$$

we have $\qquad h_1 = c_1^2 h,$

and $\qquad h_2 = h_1 - h$

$\qquad\qquad = h_1(1 - 1/c_1^2)$

$\qquad\qquad = c_2 h_1,$ suppose.

Putting $\qquad c_1 = 0.82,$ this gives

$\qquad h_1 = 0.67 h,$

$\qquad h_2 = 0.50 h_1 = 0.34 h.$

The effective head is thus 2/3 of the total head, 1/3 being dissipated at entrance.

Ex. 1. Find the quantity discharged in one min. by a short tube 3 in. diam. under a head of 4 ft.

$\qquad\qquad\qquad\qquad\qquad$ *Ans.* 38.6 cu. ft.

2. Find the head under which 460 gals. per min. will be discharged by a short tube 5 in. diam. $\qquad$ *Ans.* 1.2 ft.

3. Show that the discharge through a short pipe = $15.7 d^2 \sqrt{h}$ gals. per min., when h is expressed in ft. and d in inches.

210. Long Pipes.—If the pipe is long, in addition to the loss of head h_2 arising from the resistance at entrance, there is an additional loss of head h_3 arising from the friction of the water in the pipe. The total loss of head is therefore $h_2 + h_3.$

The loss of head h_3 is found by experiment to be directly proportional to the length of the pipe l, and the velocity head of efflux h_1, but inversely proportional to the diameter of the pipe. We may therefore write

$$h_3 = c_3 l h_1 / d,$$

when c_3 is a constant. An *average* value of c_3 is 1/40.

Hence h, the total head of water which is considered as consumed in overcoming the resistance of entrance equal to a head of h_2, the resistance of friction equal to a head of h_3, and in producing a velocity v_1, equal to a head of h_1, may be written

$$h = h_1 + h_2 + h_3$$
$$= h_1 + 0.50 h_1 + 0.025 l h_1 / d;$$

and the velocity of efflux,

$$v_1 = \sqrt{2gh_1}$$
$$= \sqrt{2gh}/(1.50 + 0.025 l/d).$$

The values of v_1 for given lengths and diameters of pipe may be tabulated for convenience of computation.

Approximately, in a **very long pipe,** the length exceeding 1000 times the diameter, the head due to friction so much exceeds the others that it may be considered equal to the total head, so that

$$h = 0.025 l h_1 / d = 0.025 l v_1^2 / 2gd,$$

and the velocity of discharge

$$v_1 = 50 \sqrt{hd/l} \text{ ft. per sec.}$$

Also, $\quad D = v_1 \times \pi d^2 / 4$

$$= 40 \sqrt{hd^5/l} \text{ c. ft. per sec.;} —$$

convenient approximate rules.

FLOW IN PIPES. 253

This may be put in still more simple shape by calling A the area of the cross-section of the pipe, i the slope or fall in feet per mile, whence $h/l = i/5280$. And

$$v = \tfrac{2}{3} \sqrt{di}$$
$$D = \tfrac{2}{3} A \sqrt{di} \; ; -$$

rules sufficient for first approximations.

If a number of small vertical tubes of equal cross-section be inserted in a pipe through which water is flowing, the water columns will stand at different heights in these tubes,

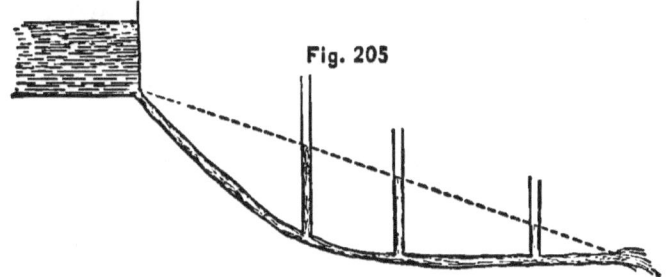

Fig. 205

showing the pressure heads at the points of insertion. The upper surfaces of these columns will lie in a straight line passing through the exit end of the pipe, and called the *hydraulic grade-line.* The tubes themselves are called *piezometers.*

If a pipe is laid so that part of it is above the hydraulic grade-line, it will act as a siphon.

Ex. 1. Find the discharge of a set of pipes 1000 ft. long and 6 in. diameter under a head of 5 ft.

Ans. 0.5 c. ft. per sec.

2. A set of pipes 1000 ft. long is required to discharge 2 cubic ft. per sec. under a head of 20 ft.: find their diameter.

Ans. 8 in.

3. With the same head and length, a 2-in. pipe will deliver nearly 6 times and a 3-in. pipe nearly 16 times as much as a 1-in. pipe.

4. A 6-in. pipe $2\frac{1}{2}$ miles long discharges 30 cubic ft. per minute : find the head.　　　　　　　　　　Ans. 66 ft.

5. Find the H. P. necessary to raise 1,000,000 gals. of water in 24 hours to a height of 100 ft. through a pipe 5000 ft. in length.

211. In an **Open Channel** as a canal or stream the flow is subject to laws similar to those governing the flow in pipes. The consideration of this subject will be found in special treatises.

ENERGY OF FLOW.

212. The kinetic energy of a body of water of mass m and moving with a velocity v is $\frac{1}{2}mv^2$. If D is the supply in cubic ft. per sec. and h the head in ft. corresponding to the velocity v in ft. per sec., then the kinetic energy per sec. $= \frac{1}{2} \times 62.4 \; Dv^2$ ft.-poundals $= 62.4 \; Dh$ ft.-pounds (since $v^2 = 2gh$), and the horse-power of the stream $= 62.4 \, Dh/550 = 0.1135 \, Dh$. This energy may be utilized in various ways in the driving of hydraulic machines.

It may also act destructively. For suppose water flowing through a pipe is suddenly checked by closing a valve, and the flow stopped. The energy of motion reacts on the valve and pipe, and imparts a shock known as the **Water Ram.** Thus in a pipe a mile long, 1 ft. in diameter, and in which water is flowing at $2\frac{1}{2}$ m. an hour, the energy $= \frac{\pi}{2} \, (\frac{1}{2})^2 \times 5280 \times 62.4 \times (1\frac{1}{3})^2$ ft.-poundals $= 54,380$ ft.-pounds. This very large number will show the need of a large factor of safety in designing pipes.

Ex. 1. Show that the energy of flow varies as the cube of the velocity, the cross-section being uniform.

2. Show that the H. P. of a stream supplying W lbs. per sec. under a head of h ft. is $0.0018 \, Wh$.

3. Show that it takes about 6.5 cubic ft. per second under a head of 8 ft. to give one H. P.

4. Find the H. P. of a waterfall 18 ft. high, if the stream at the fall passes through a notch 2 ft. × 3 ft. with a velocity of $2\frac{1}{2}$ m. an hour.　　　　Ans. 45 H. P.

ENERGY OF FLOW.

5. The cross-section of Niagara River is 40,000 sq. ft. and the current 7 m. an hour. Show that this current represents an energy of the water equivalent to a head of 1.6 ft.

6. In (5) show that if all of this head could be utilized, the energy available would be about 75,000 H. P.

7. If the energy taken out amounted to reducing the current velocity from 7 miles to 6 miles an hour, instead of to rest as in (6), to what H. P. is this equivalent?

8. If a tunnel 20 ft. diameter and 10 miles long were dug from the Niagara River to Buffalo, with a fall of 8 ft. per mile, and were running constantly full, show that the H. P. developed would be about 30,000.

INDEX.

Absolute units, 41.
Acceleration, 15, 17: unit of, 15: curve of, 17: angular, 181: central, 72: tangential, 181: of point moving in a circle, 72.
Accelerations, composition of, 22: resolution of, 23.
Accumulator, hydraulic, 218.
Air pump, 238.
Amplitude of S. H. M., 77.
Angular acceleration, 181.
Angular velocity, 179.
Arm of couple, 96.
Atmosphere, pressure of, 232.
Attraction, 127.
Atwood Machine, 59
Axis, instantaneous, 176.
Axle friction, 136.

Balance, 112.
Barometer, cistern, 234: water, 234.
Beam, 111, 115.
Bell crank lever, 100.
Belt friction, 139.
Belts, driving force of, 140.
Bending stress, 203.
Blackburn pendulum, 78.
Boyle's law, 231.

Capstan, 101.
Central forces, 66.
Centre, of parallel forces, 102: of gravity, 103: of oscillation, 192: instantaneous, 176.
Centrifugal force (so called), 73: effect of, on weight, 75: effect of, on belt tension, 141.
Centrifugal pendulum, 83.

Centripetal force, 72.
Centrode, 177.
Centroid, 104.
Circular motion, 72, 81.
Coefficient, of inertia, 33: of friction, 130: of restitution, 205.
Components, 20, 46.
Composition, of displacements, 19: velocities, 19: accelerations, 22: S. H. M.'s, 78: forces on a particle, 44, 45, 48, 51: forces on a body, 86: couples, 96.
Compression, 31, 203.
Condenser, 240.
Conservation of energy, 169.
Constrained motion, 57, 68.
Couple, arm of, 96.
Couples, composition of, 96.

Degrees of freedom, 57.
Density, 105: unit of, 105.
Differential pulley, 143: screw, 145.
Dimensions of units, 42.
Discharge through an orifice, 246–248.
Displacement, 9.
Dynamics, 30.
Dyne, 35.

Effective force, 182.
Efficiency, 161.
Efflux, velocity of, 243: time of, 249.
Elastic bodies, 201.
Energy, 164: principle of kinetic, 165: potential, 168: law of conservation of, 169.

INDEX.

Energy of rotation, 197: of impact, 207: of efflux, 254.
Equations of motion, of a particle, 36: of a body, 181.
Equilibrium, 53: of a particle, 55, 151: of a rigid body, 98, 153: of a system, 153.
Equipotential surface, 171.
Erg, 150.

Factor of safety, 224.
Falling bodies, 60.
Field of force, 170.
Floating bodies, 229.
Flow in pipes, 250.
Fluid, 212: pressure of, 214, 219, 225.
Fly wheel, 198.
Foot, 41.
Foot-pound, 150.
Foot-poundal, 150.
Force, 7, 33: units of, 35, 39: representation of, 45: elements of, 45: centripetal, 72: diagram, 48: moment of, 92.
Forces, composition of, 44, 48, 86, 90: resolution of, 50.
Free motion, 57.
Freedom, degrees of, 57.
Friction, 129: coefficient of, 130: angle of, 132: axle or journal, 136: belt, 139.

Governor, engine, 85.
Gram, 42.
Graphic statics, of simple trusses, 120: of a mechanism, 125.
Gravitation, law of, 127, 170: units of force, 39.
Gravity, force of, 38: centre of, 103: specific, 226.
Gyration, radius of, 190.

Harmonic motion (S.H.M), 76.
Head of water, 221.
Hodograph, 26.
Hoisting machine, 154.
Horse power, 159: of a steam engine, 163.

Hydraulic, accumulator, 218: grade line, 253: jack, 217.
Hydrokinetics, 243.
Hydrometer, 229.
Hydrostatics, 212.

Impact, 204: energy of, 207.
Impulse, 36: average force of, 211.
Inclined plane, motion on, 69: equilibrium on, 71.
Indicator diagram, 158.
Inertia, 32: law of, 33: coefficient of, 33: moment of, 184.
Instantaneous, axis, 176: centre, 176.

Jack, screw, 154: hydraulic, 217.
Jointed frames, 120.
Joule, 150.

Kilogram, 42.
Kinematics, 8.
Kinetic energy, 165: change of, on impact, 207.
Kinetics, 54.

Laws of motion, 32, 33, 36.
Length, units of, 41.
Level surface, 219.
Lever, 99, 153.
Long pipes, flow in, 251.
Longitudinal stress, 119.

Manometer, 234.
Mass, 34: unit of, 35.
Mass-acceleration, law of, 36.
Mechanics defined, 7.
Meter, 41.
Miner's inch, 249.
Moment, of a force, 92: unit of, 93: graphical representation of, 94: of inertia, 184.
Momentum, 36.
Motion, in a st. line, 10: in a curve, 24: in a circle, 72, 81: harmonic, 76: on a rough surface, 135: relative, 27.

INDEX. 259

Neutral equilibrium, 109.
Newton's laws of motion, 30.

Oblique impact, 206.
Orifices and weirs, 243.
Oscillation of a pendulum, 79, 192.

Parallel forces, 90.
Parallelogram of displacements, 19: accelerations, 19: velocities, 22: forces, 46.
Particle, 8.
Path, 10.
Pendulum, simple, 77: Blackburn, 78: centrifugal, 83: physical, 191.
Period of S. H. M., 77.
Permanent set, 203.
Phase of S. H. M., 77.
Pile driver, 208.
Planetary motion, 68.
Pneumatics, 230.
Pole of stress diagram, 88.
Polygon of forces, 55.
Position of a force, 88.
Potential, 169.
Potential energy, 108.
Pound, 35, 39, 42.
Poundal, 35.
Power, 158: units of, 159.
Projectiles, 62.
Prony brake, 160.
Pulley, 91: differential, 143: tackle, 142.
Pump, Lifting, 236. Force, 237: Air, 238.

Radius of gyration, 190.
Range of a projectile, 64.
Relative motion, 27.
Repose, angle of, 133.
Resolution, of accelerations, 23: of forces, 50.
Resultant, 45, 48, 51.
Rigid bodies, 174.
Rotation, 175: energy of, 197.

Safety valve, 215.
Screw, pitch of, 145: efficiency, 147: differential, 145: jack, 154.
Shear, 203.
Siphon, 236.
Smooth surface, 129.
Specific gravity, 226.
Speed, 11.
Sprengel air pump, 239.
Stability, 108: of a retaining wall, 110: of a reservoir wall, 223.
Standards of length, 41.
Statics, 53.
Steam engine, 13, 17, 125, 194.
Steam hammer, 210.
Steelyard, 114.
Strain, 203.
Stress, 31: law of, 32: longitudinal and transverse, 119: diagram of, 122: shearing, 203: in framework, 120: in steam engine, 125.
Strut, 122.
Syringe, 238.

Tension, 31, 203.
Thread of screw, 145.
Tie, 122.
Time, unit of, 41: of efflux, 249.
Toggle joint, 196.
Torque, 96.
Torsion stress, 203.
Translation, 19, 44.
Transmission of fluid pressure, 214.
Triangle of forces, 54.

Units, fundamental, 41: of work, 150: of power, 159: of angular velocity, 179: of angular acceleration, 181.

Velocities, composition of, 21: resolution of, 23.
Velocity, 10, 14: unit of, 11: curve of, 12: angular, 179.
Viscosity, 212.

Water ram, 254.
Watt, the, 159.
Weight, 40: effect of centrifugal force on, 75: true and apparent, 235.
Weirs, 248.
Winch, 102, 155.

Work done, 148: unit of, 150: dimensions of, 150: principle of, 152: against friction, 156: against a variable force, 157: in compressing air, 240: by expansion of a gas, 242.
Worm wheel, 155.

www.ingramcontent.com/pod-product-compliance
Lightning Source LLC
Chambersburg PA
CBHW021345230426
43666CB00006B/417